Economics

for the IB DIPLOMA

STUDY AND REVISION GUIDE

Economics

for the IB DIPLOMA

Paul Hoang

HODDER EDUCATION
AN HACHETTE UK COMPANY

Although every effort has been made to ensure that website addresses are correct at time of going to press, Hodder Education cannot be held responsible for the content of any website mentioned in this book. It is sometimes possible to find a relocated web page by typing in the address of the home page for a website in the URL window of your browser.

Hachette Livre UK's policy is to use papers that are natural, renewable and recyclable products and made from wood grown in sustainable forests. The logging and manufacturing processes are expected to conform to the environmental regulations of the country of origin.

Orders: please contact Bookpoint Ltd, 130 Milton Park, Abingdon, Oxon OX14 4SB. Telephone: (44) 01235 827827. Fax: (44) 01235 400401. Lines are open 9.00–5.00, Monday to Saturday, with a 24-hour message answering service.
Visit our website at www.hoddereducation.com.

© Paul Hoang 2014

First published in 2014 by

Hodder Education,

An Hachette UK Company

Carmelite House

50 Victoria Embankment

London EC4Y 0DZ

Impression number   5   4   3

Year   2017

Cover photo © jgroup/iStockphoto

Illustrations by Aptara, Inc.

Typeset in 10/12 Goudy Old Style by Aptara, Inc.

Printed in India

A catalogue record for this title is available from the British Library

ISBN: 978-14718-0718-3

Contents

Dedications

This book is dedicated to Mr Graham Hollamby, my economics teacher at Southwark College, London.

My heartfelt thanks and love to Kin, Jake and Luke for always putting up with me.

My sincere thanks to my publisher (and fellow Arsenal fan), So-Shan Au, for her help and guidance throughout this project.

Finally, my gratitude to Samson Wong, an outstanding student who provided invaluable feedback from the perspective of an IB learner.

Acknowledgements

The Publishers would like to thank the following for permission to reproduce copyright material:

Photos:

p. 86 © Tsvangirayi Mukwazhi/AP/Press Association Images.

Text:

p. 150: Figure 4.2, redrawn from http://en.wikipedia.org/wiki/List-of-countries-by-Human-Development-Index

How to use this study and revision guide

Welcome to the *Economics for the IB Diploma Study and* Revision Guide. This book will help you plan your revision and work through it in a methodological way. It follows the Economics syllabus topic by topic, with revision and exam practice questions to help you check your understanding.

Features to help you succeed

Expert tips

These tips give advice that will help you boost your final grade.

Common mistakes

These identify typical mistakes that students make and explain how you can avoid them.

Keyword definitions

Definitions are provided on the pages where the essential key terms appear. These keywords are those that you can be expected to define in exams. A **glossary** of other essential terms, highlighted throughout the text, is given at the end of the book.

Worked examples

Some parts of the course require you to carry out mathematical calculations, plot graphs, and so on. These examples show you how.

EXAM PRACTICE

Exam practice is given for the type of questions you might get. For the longer essay questions, sample sentences and paragraphs are given to show what examiners are looking for in your essay answers. For easy reference, the exam paper is indicated for each question. Use these questions to consolidate your revision and to practise your exam skills.

EXAM PRACTICE *(HL ONLY)*

Some parts of the Economics course require you to carry out mathematical calculations, plot graphs and so on. There are sample Paper 3 exam questions interspersed in the chapters, with suggested answers online.

You can keep track of your revision by ticking off each topic heading in the book. There is also a checklist at the end of the book. Use this checklist to record progress as you revise. Tick each box when you have:

- revised and understood a topic
- used the **Exam practice questions** and gone online to check your answers.

Use this book as the cornerstone of your revision. Don't hesitate to write in it and personalise your notes. Use a highlighter to identify areas that need further work. You may find it helpful to add your own notes as you work through each topic. Good luck!

Getting to know the exam

Exam paper	Duration	Format	Topics	Total marks
Paper 1	1.5 hours	Essay	1 and 2	50
Paper 2	1.5 hours	Data response	3 and 4	40
Paper 3 (HL only)	1 hour	Structured questions	All	50

At the end of your Economics course you will sit two papers – Paper 1 and Paper 2. Paper 1 is worth 30% of the final marks and Paper 2, 50% of the final marks. The other assessed part of the course (20%) is made up of the Internal Assessment, which is marked by your teacher.

HL students will sit an additional paper – Paper 3, worth 20%. For HL students, Paper 1 is worth 30% of the final marks, and Paper 2 also 30% of the final marks. The other assessed part of the course (20%) is the Internal Assessment (or IA) which is marked by your teacher.

Here is some general advice for the exams:

- Make sure you have learned the command terms (e.g. evaluate, explain, outline). There is a tendency to focus on the content in a question rather than the command term, but if you do not address what the command term is asking of you then you will not be awarded marks. (Command terms are covered on page x.)
- If you run out of room on the page, use continuation sheets and indicate clearly that you have done this on the cover sheet.
- The fact that the question continues on another sheet of paper needs to be clearly indicated in the text box provided.
- Plan your time carefully before the exams.

Paper 1

Paper 1 (1.5 hours) contains two sections: Section A is based on Microeconomics and Section B is based on Macroeconomics. You will need to answer one of the two questions from each section. Part a) of each essay is worth 10 marks and part b) is worth 15 marks. Hence, the total number of marks for this paper is 50.

- It is necessary to include definitions in the essays, so make sure you have learned the keyword definitions in this book.
- As the paper is only out of 50 marks, the questions cannot cover all aspects of Microeconomics and Macroeconomics. It is therefore essential that you thoroughly revise the whole of Topics 1 and 2 of the syllabus so that you can tackle any questions that come up.
- The 10-mark questions do not involve any evaluation, but do require a concluding statement that answers the question. The 15-mark questions do require an evaluation.
- Wherever appropriate, include fully labelled diagrams and the application of real-world examples to substantiate your answers.

Paper 2

Paper 2 (1.5 hours) contains two sections: Section A contains two data-response questions on International economics; you must answer one of these, which is worth a total of 20 marks. In Section B you must answer one of the two data-response questions on Development economics, again worth 20 marks. The total marks for the paper is therefore 40.

In Paper 2 you may be given a range of data in various forms (e.g. diagrams, graphs, charts and data tables) relating to a specific case study on International economics and Development economics. Questions will test your knowledge of Topic 3 and Topic 4 of the syllabus, and your ability to apply this to the given case studies.

- Do not spend too much time on one of the two sections.
- Plan your time carefully (do this *before* the exam!). You should spend no more than 45 minutes on each section.
- By practising past exam papers, you will be able to fine-tune your time management; this may vary from student to student.
- Choose your questions carefully. Look at all sections of the data-response questions before making your choices.
- You will be required to provide definitions (for the 2-mark questions) and to draw relevant diagrams (for the 4-mark questions). Practise drawing accurate and fully labelled diagrams.
- Some students write far too much for questions worth only 2 marks, and then run out of time later on for the 8-mark question. Look carefully at the number of marks available for each question and adjust the amount of time you spend on that question accordingly.
- There are several parts to each data-response question – make sure you answer all parts.
- Case studies help answer Paper 2 data-response questions – make sure you read the stimulus material and analyse the supplementary data as you will be expected to apply your knowledge.

Paper 3

Only HL students take the Paper 3 (quantitative) examination. It is a 1-hour paper, with students required to answer any two of the three questions.

- There are no evaluation-type questions in Paper 3.
- Paper 3 accounts for 20% of the overall weighting in the HL course.
- Each question is marked out of 25. Students must answer two questions, totalling up to 50 marks. This means there are 10 minutes remaining to check over your answers if you allocate about 1 minute per mark in the exam.
- Questions can test your knowledge from any of the four syllabus topics: Microeconomics, Macroeconomics, International economics and Development economics.

Assessment objectives and command terms

To successfully complete the course, you need to have achieved the following assessment objectives:

AO1	Demonstrate *knowledge* and *understanding* of specified content, including current economic issues and data
AO2	Demonstrate *application* and *analysis* of knowledge and understanding by: ■ applying economic concepts and theories to real-world situations ■ identifying and interpreting economic data ■ demonstrating the extent to which economic information is used effectively in particular contexts
AO3	Demonstrate *synthesis* and *evaluation* by: ■ examining economic concepts and theories ■ using economic concepts and examples to construct and present an argument ■ discussing and evaluating economic information and theories
AO4	Select, use and apply a variety of appropriate *skills* and *techniques* by: ■ producing well-structured written material, using appropriate economic terminology, within specified time limits ■ using correctly labelled diagrams to help explain economic concepts and theories ■ selecting, interpreting and analysing appropriate extracts from the news media ■ interpreting appropriate data sets

Source: *IB Economics Guide*, page 7

These assessment objectives are examined in the following way:

Assessment objective	Paper 1	Paper 2	Paper 3 (*HL only*)
AO1: Knowledge and understanding	30%	35%	30%
AO2: Application and analysis	30%	30%	30%
AO3: Synthesis and evaluation	20%	25%	–
AO4: Selection, use and application of a variety of skills and techniques	20%	10%	40%

Command terms indicate the depth of treatment required for a given assessment statement. Assessment objectives 1 and 2 address simpler skills, assessment objective 3 relates to higher-order skills, while assessment objective 4 refers to the skills of selecting, using and applying economic skills and techniques.

It is essential that you are familiar with these terms, so that you are able to recognise the type of response you are expected to provide as well as the required depth of your response.

The following table shows all of the command terms, with an indication of the depth required from your written answers.

Assessment objective	Command terms	Depth of answers
AO1: Knowledge and understanding	Define Describe List Outline State	These terms require you to learn and comprehend the meaning of information.
AO2: Application and analysis	Analyse Apply Comment Distinguish Explain Suggest	These terms require you to use your knowledge to explain actual situations, and to break down ideas into simpler parts and see how these parts relate.
AO3: Synthesis and evaluation	Compare Compare and contrast Contrast Discuss Evaluate Examine Justify To what extent	These terms require you to rearrange component ideas into a new whole and make judgements based on evidence or a set of criteria.
AO4: Selection, use and application of a variety of skills and techniques	Calculate Construct Derive Determine Draw Identify Label Measure Plot Show Show that Sketch Solve	These terms require you to demonstrate the selection and application of skills.

Source: *IB Economics Guide*, page 9

Countdown to the exams

4–8 WEEKS TO GO

- Start by looking at the syllabus and make sure you know exactly what you need to revise.
- Look carefully at the checklist in this book and use it to help organise your class notes and to make sure you have covered everything.
- Work out a realistic revision plan that breaks down the material you need to revise into manageable pieces. Each session should be around 25–40 minutes with breaks in between. The plan should include time for relaxation.
- Read through the relevant sections of this book and refer to the expert tips, common mistakes, keyword definitions, case studies and worked examples.
- Tick off the topics that you feel confident about, and highlight the ones that need further work.
- Look at past papers. They are one of the best ways to check knowledge and practise exam skills. They will also help you identify areas that need further work.
- Try different revision methods, for example summary notes, mind maps and flash cards.
- Test your understanding of each topic by working through the **Exam practice questions**.
- Make notes of any problem areas as you revise, and ask a teacher to go over them in class.

1 WEEK TO GO

- Aim to fit in at least one more timed practice of entire past papers, comparing your work closely with the mark scheme.
- Examine the checklist carefully to make sure you haven't missed any of the topics.
- Tackle any final problems by getting help from your teacher or talking them over with a friend.

THE DAY BEFORE THE EXAMINATION

- Look through this book one final time. Look carefully through the information about each exam paper to remind yourself what to expect, including timings and the number of questions to be answered.
- Check the time and place of the exams.
- Make sure you have all the equipment you need (e.g. extra pens, pencil and ruler for diagrams, a watch, tissues and water). If you are an HL student, make sure you have a GDC calculator for Paper 3.
- Allow some time to relax and have an early night so you are rested and ready for the exams. There is a huge opportunity cost if you are not refreshed!

MY EXAMS

PAPER 1

Date: ....

Time: ....

Location: ....

PAPER 2

Date: ....

Time: ....

Location: ....

PAPER 3 (*HL ONLY*)

Date: ....

Time: ....

Location: ....

Section 1 Microeconomics

1.1 Competitive markets: demand and supply

Revised ☐

Markets and demand

Revised ☐

- The **law of demand** states that the quantity demanded for a good or service falls as its price rises, *ceteris paribus*. Likewise, the quantity demanded rises at lower prices.
- The **demand curve** shows the inverse relationship between price and quantity demanded of a product (see Figure 1.1).

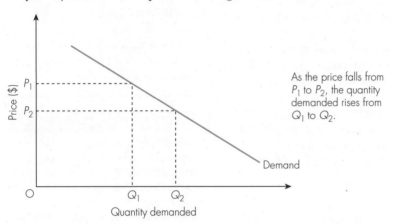

As the price falls from P_1 to P_2, the quantity demanded rises from Q_1 to Q_2.

Figure 1.1 The demand curve

> **Keyword definitions**
>
> A **market** is any place where transactions take place between buyers and sellers, for example shares are traded in a stock market and currencies are traded on the foreign exchange market. Scarcity must exist for a market to exist.
>
> **Demand** is the *willingness* and *ability* of customers to pay a certain price in a market to obtain a particular good or service. It is sometimes referred to as **effective demand** to distinguish it from a want or a desire to buy something.

There are three causes of the negative relationship between price and quantity demanded:

- The **income effect** – as price falls, the real income of customers rises, i.e. they are able to buy more products at lower prices.
- The **substitution effect** – as the price of a good or service falls, more customers are able to pay, so they are more likely to buy the product, i.e. substitute it for alternative products that they might have previously bought.
- **Diminishing marginal returns** – as people consume more of a particular good or service, the utility (return or satisfaction) gained from the marginal unit declines, so customers will only purchase more at a lower price.

> **Common mistake**
>
> Be careful when using the concepts of 'demand' and 'quantity demanded', as these are often confused by students in the exams. **Demand** refers to an entire demand curve, whereas **quantity demanded** refers to a point on the demand curve.

The **market demand curve** refers to the sum of all individual demand for a product. It is found by adding up all individual demand at each price level (see Figure 1.2). For example, if a cinema charges $10 for movie tickets and the demand is 500 from male customers and 400 from female customers, then the market demand is 900 cinema tickets per week.

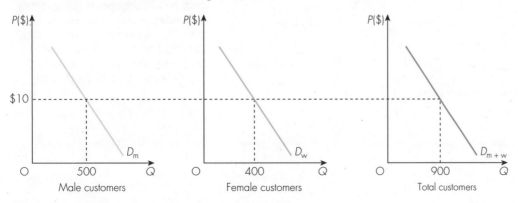

Figure 1.2 The market demand curve

Non-price determinants of demand

Price is not the only factor that affects the demand for a good or service. Factors that change the demand (or shift the demand curve) for a good or service can be recalled using the acronym **HIS AGE**:

- **H**abits, fashion and tastes – products that become fashionable (e.g. smartphones) cause an increase in demand, whereas unfashionable items (e.g. last season's clothes) reduce the level of demand.
- **I**ncome – higher levels of income mean that customers are able and willing to buy more goods and services. The average person in the USA, for example, will have a higher level of demand for products compared with the average person in Vietnam or Turkey.
- **S**ubstitutes and complements – if the price of a product falls, then it is likely that the demand for the substitute product will also fall. By contrast, if the price of a product increases, then the demand for its complementary good is likely to fall.
- **A**dvertising – marketing messages are used to inform, remind and persuade customers to buy a firm's products. Companies such as McDonald's and Samsung spend hundreds of millions of dollars each year on their advertising to increase the demand for their products.
- **G**overnment policies – rules and regulations such as the legal age on the purchase of tobacco and alcohol affect the demand for certain products. By contrast, government initiatives to educate people about energy-efficient cars could encourage more demand for environmentally friendly cars.
- **E**conomy – whether the country is in a recession or boom has a huge impact on the spending patterns of the population. For example, the global financial crisis of 2008 caused the demand for most goods and services around the world to decline.

Keyword definitions

Substitutes are products that can be used instead of each other, such as Coca-Cola or Pepsi and tea or coffee.

Complements are products that are jointly demanded, such as cinema movies and popcorn or pencils and erasers.

When the demand for a product increases with a rise in income, it is called a **normal good**. These include both necessities and luxury products.

An **inferior good** has a negative relationship between income and quantity demanded, i.e. customers switch to a superior (luxury) product as their income rises – for example, canned food products versus fresh food products.

Expert tip

Depending on the context of the good or service being considered, two other potentially important determinants of demand are the weather and demographics (e.g. age, gender, ethnicity or religious beliefs of customers).

Movements along, and shifts of, the demand curve

- A change in the price of a good or service causes a *movement* along the demand curve.
- A price rise will cause a *contraction* in the quantity demanded for the product
- A fall in price will cause an *expansion* in the quantity demanded (see Figure 1.3).

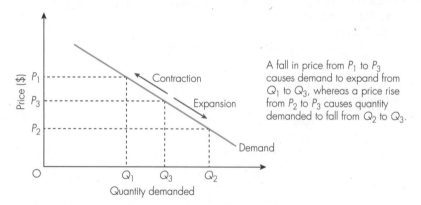

A fall in price from P_1 to P_3 causes demand to expand from Q_1 to Q_3, whereas a price rise from P_2 to P_3 causes quantity demanded to fall from Q_2 to Q_3.

Figure 1.3 Movements in the demand curve

Expert tip

It will be useful for you to know the difference between **changes in demand** and **changes in the quantity demanded**. A shift in demand is caused by changes in non-price factors that affect demand. A movement along a demand curve is caused by changes in the price of the product.

- A change in non-price factors that affect demand cause a *shift* in the demand curve.
- An increase in demand is shown by a rightwards shift in the demand curve from D_1 to D_3 (see Figure 1.4). At P_1, demand increases from Q_1 to Q_3.
- By contrast, a decrease in demand is shown by shifting the demand curve to the left, from D_1 to D_2, resulting in less quantity demanded at all price levels.

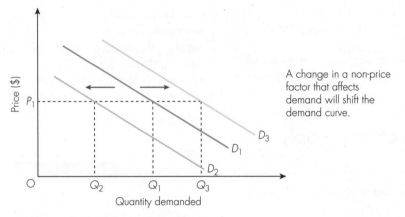

A change in a non-price factor that affects demand will shift the demand curve.

Figure 1.4 Shifts in the demand curve

Common mistake

Students often claim that the imposition of a **sales tax** on a product shifts its demand curve to the left. This is incorrect as the tax is imposed on firms, thereby raising their costs of production. The tax increases the price of the product, so therefore reduces the quantity demanded, i.e. it causes a movement along the demand curve.

Linear demand functions *(HL only)*

Revised

The demand curve is often graphed as a straight line for ease of illustration. The linear demand function is $Q_d = a - bP$, where:
- a = demand, irrespective of the price
- $-b$ = slope of the demand curve, i.e. how the price affects the quantity demanded.

Any change in a will cause a change in demand, i.e. shift the demand curve.

Any change in b will change the quantity demanded and the steepness of the demand curve.

EXAM PRACTICE *(HL ONLY)*

PAPER 3

1 Plot a demand curve from the given linear demand function $Q_d = 800 - 25P$.   [4]

2 From the diagram below, solve the linear function of the demand curve.   [2]

Expert tip

Make sure you know the difference between the cause of a shift and a movement in demand. A **shift** in the demand curve is caused by changes in non-price factors that affect demand, such as changes in income. A **movement** along a demand curve is caused by changes in the price of the product.

Supply

Revised ☐

The law of supply and the supply curve

Revised ☐

The law of supply states that there is a positive relationship between the quantity supplied of product and its price, *ceteris paribus*. This is shown diagrammatically by a supply curve. There are two reasons for the positive relationship between price and supply:

- Existing firms in the market can earn higher profit margins if they supply more.
- More firms enter the market as higher prices allow them to cover production costs.

> **Keyword definition**
> **Supply** is the *willingness* and *ability* of firms to provide a good or service at a given price level, per time period.

Movements along, and shifts of, the supply curve

Revised ☐

As with demand, the **market supply** curve is the sum of all individual producers' supply curves at each price level.

A *movement* along a supply curve occurs if the price changes, causing a change in the *quantity supplied* (see Figure 1.5).

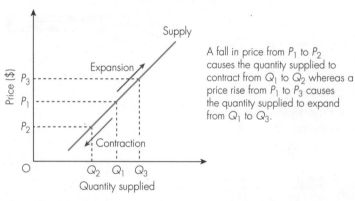

A fall in price from P_1 to P_2 causes the quantity supplied to contract from Q_1 to Q_2 whereas a price rise from P_1 to P_3 causes the quantity supplied to expand from Q_1 to Q_3.

Figure 1.5 Movements along the supply curve

A *shift* in the supply curve is caused by changes in non-price factors that affect supply, causing a *change in supply*. In Figure 1.6, a rightwards shift (from S_1 to S_2) shows an increase in supply, while a leftwards shift (from S_1 to S_3) shows a fall in supply.

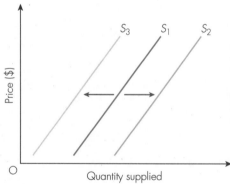

An increase in supply is shown by a rightward shift of the supply curve from S_1 to S_2. Similarly, a fall in supply is represented by a leftward shift of the supply curve from S_1 to S_3.

Figure 1.6 Shifts of the supply curve

> **Expert tip**
>
> A **shift** in supply is caused by changes in non-price factors that affect supply (such as taxes and adverse weather). A **movement** in supply is caused only by changes in price.

The non-price determinants of supply

Table 1.1 Factors that change supply or shift the supply curve

Non-price determinants of supply	How supply is changed by these determinants
Costs of production	Changes in any costs of production cause a shift in supply, for example changes in wages and rents.
Taxes	Indirect taxes are imposed on the supplier of a product, which basically adds to the costs of production. Hence, taxes tend to reduce market supply.
Subsidies	Financial assistance from the government to help encourage output by reducing costs of production for products that are beneficial to society as a whole, for example the provision of education, training and healthcare.
Technological progress	Advances in technology mean that there can be greater levels of output at every price level.
Expectations	Price acts as a signal to producers to move their resources to the provision of products with greater profitability. Thus, expectations of price movements affect supply.
Competitive supply	The output of a product (such as apples) takes place as an alternative to other products (such as oranges), based on the relative profitability of these products.
Joint supply	The output of one product (such as cows) routinely leads to the supply of another (such as milk).
Barriers to entry	The number of firms in the market, determined by the nature of barriers to entry to the industry, can affect the level of supply.
Time	Supply tends to be lower in the short run but can increase over time – for example, it is difficult for farmers to increase their supply of crops within a short period of time.
Weather	The output of some products depends on the weather – for example, agricultural output.

Expert tip

A useful way to remember some of the key non-price determinants of supply is to use the acronym **SWITCH**, i.e.

- **S**ubsidies
- **W**eather
- **I**CT (technology)
- **T**axes
- **C**ompetitive supply and
- **H**urdles (barriers to entry).

Linear supply functions *(HL only)*

The supply curve is often graphed as a straight line for ease of illustration. The linear supply function is $Q_s = c + dP$, where:

- c = supply, irrespective of the price (so this is also the intercept on the y-axis)
- $+d$ = slope (or steepness) of the supply curve.

Any change in c will shift the supply curve.
Any change in d will affect the price elasticity of the supply curve.

EXAM PRACTICE *(HL ONLY)*

PAPER 3

3 Plot a supply curve that has the linear supply function $Q_s = -100 + 10P$.   **[4]**

Expert tip

A supply function normally has a negative intercept, such as $S = -800 + 20P$, as firms need to cover their production costs. Here, if $P = \$40$, then zero units of output is supplied. Any price above \$40 will create an ability and willingness for firms to supply their products. A positive intercept means that even when the price is zero, the existence of government subsidies ensures that a minimum level of output is supplied.

Market equilibrium

Equilibrium and changes to equilibrium

Equilibrium exists when the quantity demanded for a product is equal to the quantity supplied (see Figure 1.7). Recall that changes in any of the non-price determinants of supply or demand will cause a change in the market equilibrium price. For example:

- A successful advertising campaign that promotes the consumption of fresh fish shifts its demand curve to the right, thereby raising the price and quantity traded.
- A severe drought would shift the supply curve of agricultural products to the left, leading to an increase in the price and a fall in the quantity traded.

> **Keyword definition**
> **Market equilibrium** occurs when the quantity demanded for a product is equal to the quantity supplied of the product, i.e. there are no shortages or surpluses.

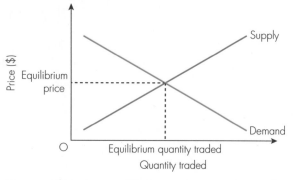

Figure 1.7 Market equilibrium

Excess supply occurs when the price is set above the equilibrium, i.e. a surplus exists, as shown by the green area in Figure 1.8.

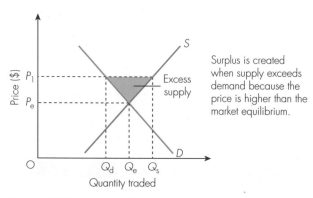

Surplus is created when supply exceeds demand because the price is higher than the market equilibrium.

Figure 1.8 Excess supply (surplus)

Excess demand occurs when the price is set below the equilibrium, i.e. a shortage exists, as shown by the green area in Figure 1.9.

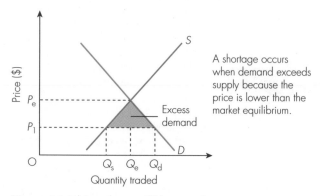

A shortage occurs when demand exceeds supply because the price is lower than the market equilibrium.

Figure 1.9 Excess demand (shortage)

If there is excess supply, there is a tendency for price to fall to remove the surplus. If there is a shortage in the market, the price will tend to rise to remove the excess demand.

Calculating and illustrating equilibrium using linear equations *(HL only)*

Equilibrium exists when the demand and supply functions are equal, i.e.:

$$a - bP = c + dP$$

EXAM PRACTICE *(HL ONLY)*

PAPER 3

4 Calculate the equilibrium price and quantity if the demand function is given as $Q_d = 600 - 3P$ and the supply function is $Q_s = -100 + 2P$.   **[3]**

The role of the price mechanism

Resource allocation

Resources are finite in supply whilst wants (desires, or goods and services that we would like to have) are infinite. This creates a situation of scarcity, which subsequently imposes production choices about *what to produce*.

Due to limited resources, including money, economic agents have to make choices. This results in an opportunity cost – for example, choosing to buy a smartphone may come at the opportunity cost of buying a games console or going on a holiday.

In a market economy, price has both a **signalling** function and an **incentive** function (see Figure 1.10). These functions result in the reallocation of resources if price changes due to changes that affect the demand for or supply of a product.

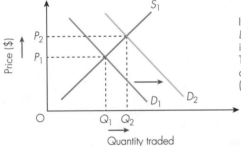

If demand for a product increases, from D_1 to D_2, the equilibrium price will increase from P_1 to P_2, *ceteris paribus*. This *signals* to firms to raise their supply as there is an *incentive* for them to do so (greater levels of profits).

Figure 1.10 Signalling and incentive functions of price

Market efficiency

Consumer surplus, producer surplus and allocative efficiency

Keyword definitions

Consumer surplus refers to the benefits to buyers who are able to purchase a product for less than they are willing to do so. By contrast, **producer surplus** is the difference between the price that firms actually receive and the price they were willing and able to supply at.

Allocative efficiency happens when resources are distributed so that consumers and producers get the maximum possible benefit, which means no one can be made better off without making someone else worse off (see Figure 1.11).

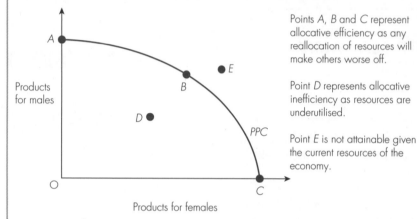

Points *A*, *B* and *C* represent allocative efficiency as any reallocation of resources will make others worse off.

Point *D* represents allocative inefficiency as resources are underutilised.

Point *E* is not attainable given the current resources of the economy.

Figure 1.11 Allocative efficiency and the production possibility curve (PPC)

Consumer surplus is shown by the difference between what consumers are willing to pay for a product and the amount they actually pay (see Figure 1.12). Hence, the consumers' marginal utility of consumption is greater than the market price.

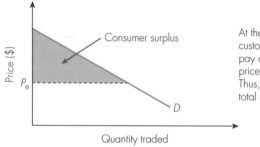

At the equilibrium price of P_e, there are customers who are willing and able to pay a higher price, as shown by all prices above the equilibrium price. Thus, the shaded area represents the total consumer surplus.

Figure 1.12 Consumer surplus

Producer surplus occurs when firms are able to charge a higher price than they are willing and able to (see Figure 1.13). Thus, they are able to earn abnormal profits.

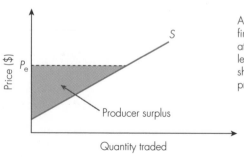

At the equilibrium price of P_e, there are firms that are willing and able to supply at a lower price, as shown by all prices less than the equilibrium price. Thus, the shaded area represents the total producer surplus.

Figure 1.13 Producer surplus

Social surplus (or community surplus) is the sum of producer surplus and consumer surplus (see Figure 1.14).

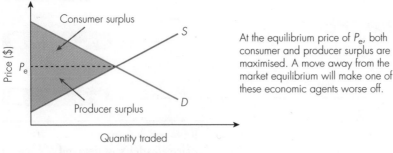

At the equilibrium price of P_e, both consumer and producer surplus are maximised. A move away from the market equilibrium will make one of these economic agents worse off.

Figure 1.14 Allocative efficiency and social surplus

In a competitive market economy, allocative efficiency occurs at the market equilibrium because both consumer and producer surplus are maximised at this point.

EXAM PRACTICE *(HL ONLY)*

PAPER 3

5 a Suppose the demand function for a product is given as $Q_d = 80 - 2P$ whilst its supply is given expressed as $Q_s = 2P$. Plot the demand and supply curves and identify the equilibrium price and equilibrium quantity. **[4]**

b Using your diagram from part a, calculate the quantity of excess demand at a price of $10 per unit and the excess supply at a price of $40 per unit. **[4]**

6

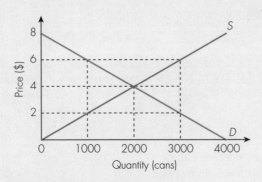

From the diagram above calculate the value of:

a consumer surplus **[2]**

b producer surplus **[2]**

c excess demand or supply at $6 **[2]**

d excess demand or supply at $2 **[2]**

1.2 Elasticity

Price elasticity of demand (PED)

Price elasticity of demand

Price elasticity of demand is calculated using the formula:

$$\frac{\text{percentage change in quantity demanded}}{\text{percentage change in price}}$$

The mathematical value of PED is usually negative due to the law of demand – for example, a rise in price tends to cause a fall in the quantity demanded.

The value of PED for a product depends on the degree of customers' ability and willingness to pay – for example, a rise in the price of a necessity will have a minimal impact, if any, on its level of demand.

Demand is **price inelastic** if a price change causes a relatively small change in the quantity demanded, i.e. buyers are not highly responsive to changes in price (see Figure 1.15).

> **Keyword definition**
> **Price elasticity of demand** (PED) measures the degree of responsiveness of quantity demanded for a product following a change in its price, along a given demand curve.

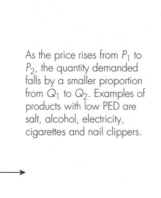

As the price rises from P_1 to P_2, the quantity demanded falls by a smaller proportion from Q_1 to Q_2. Examples of products with low PED are salt, alcohol, electricity, cigarettes and nail clippers.

Figure 1.15 The price inelastic demand curve

By contrast, demand is said to be **price elastic** if there is a relatively large change in the quantity demanded for a product following a change in its price (see Figure 1.16).

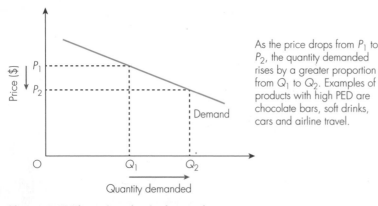

As the price drops from P_1 to P_2, the quantity demanded rises by a greater proportion from Q_1 to Q_2. Examples of products with high PED are chocolate bars, soft drinks, cars and airline travel.

Figure 1.16 The price elastic demand curve

Perfectly price inelastic demand exists when a change in price has no impact on the quantity demanded, i.e. the PED value = 0. This suggests that there are no substitutes for the product (see Figure 1.17).

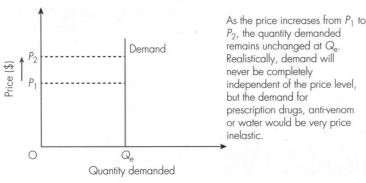

As the price increases from P_1 to P_2, the quantity demanded remains unchanged at Q_e. Realistically, demand will never be completely independent of the price level, but the demand for prescription drugs, anti-venom or water would be very price inelastic.

Figure 1.17 The perfectly price inelastic demand curve

Perfectly price elastic demand exists when a change in price leads to no demand, i.e. the PED value = infinity. This means that customers switch to buying other substitutes if firms increase their price (see Figure 1.18).

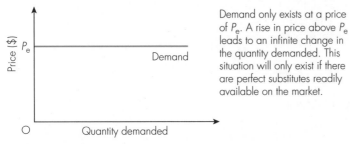

Demand only exists at a price of P_e. A rise in price above P_e leads to an infinite change in the quantity demanded. This situation will only exist if there are perfect substitutes readily available on the market.

Figure 1.18 The perfectly price elastic demand curve

Unit elastic demand occurs when a given price change leads to the same percentage change in the quantity demanded, i.e. the PED value = 1.0 (see Figure 1.19).

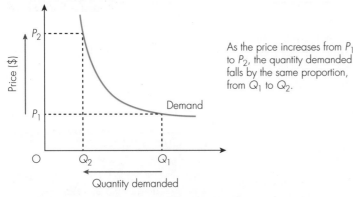

As the price increases from P_1 to P_2, the quantity demanded falls by the same proportion, from Q_1 to Q_2.

Figure 1.19 The unit price elastic demand curve

On a normal downwards sloping linear demand curve, the value of PED increases as the price level rises (and vice versa). This occurs because customers will be more responsive to changes in prices at higher levels (price now accounts for a greater proportion of consumers' income).

Despite the gradient of the linear demand curve being the same, the percentage change in demand is greater at higher price levels (see Figure 1.20).

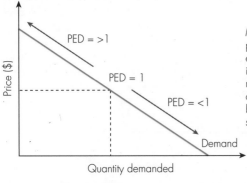

Mathematically, the PED value at the mid-point along a linear demand curve is equal to 1. At prices above this point, PED is greater than 1 as customers become more sensitive to changes in price. By contrast, at lower prices the PED value will be less than 1 as customers are far less sensitive to fluctuating price.

Figure 1.20 PED along a linear demand curve

> **Expert tip**
>
> Whether the demand for a product is price elastic or price inelastic really depends on the breadth of definition of the product. A broadly defined good or service (such as food rather than fruit, meat, apples or salmon) will be more price inelastic. There is clearly no real substitute to food! However, it is perhaps more useful to measure the PED for specific brands or products, such as carbonated soft drinks or Canadian beef.

EXAM PRACTICE *(HL ONLY)*

PAPER 3

7 Explain why the price elasticity of demand for many primary commodities (such as crude oil and iron ore) has a relatively low value, whilst the demand for manufactured products has a relatively high PED value. **[4]**

8 A jeweller reduces the price of her platinum earrings from $400 to $350 per unit, resulting in an increase in demand from 25 units to 30 units per month. Calculate the value of the price elasticity of demand for the earrings and comment on the result. **[4]**

9 Assume the demand for football match tickets at $50 is 50,000 per week. If the football club raises its price to $60 per ticket and demand subsequently falls to 45,000 per week, calculate the value of the price elasticity of demand and interpret the result. **[4]**

Determinants of price elasticity of demand

Revised ▢

- **Substitution** – The greater the number, availability and price of close substitutes there are for a good or service, the higher the value of its PED will tend to be. By contrast, products with few substitutes (such as private education and prescribed medicines) have price inelastic demand.
- **Income** – The greater the proportion of consumers' income spent on a good or service, the more price elastic demand will be, *ceteris paribus*.
- **Necessity** – Products that are regarded as essential (such as food, fuel and housing) tend to be price inelastic as households will continue to purchase these even if prices rise. By contrast, the demand for luxuries is relatively price elastic.
- **Habits, addictions, fashion and tastes** – If a product is habit-forming (such as tobacco) or highly fashionable (such as smartphones), its PED tends to be relatively price inelastic.
- **Advertising and brand loyalty** – Effective advertising for certain products not only helps to shift the demand curve outwards to the right, but can also reduce the PED for the product.
- **Time** – People need time to change their habits and preferences. Over time, they can adjust their demand based on more permanent price changes by switching to alternative products.
- **Durability** – The more durable a product is, such as home furniture or motor vehicles, the more price elastic its demand tends to be as there is no urgency to replace these if prices are high.
- **The costs of switching** – If there are high costs involved for customers to switch between brands or products, then demand tends to be price inelastic. For example, mobile phone subscribers are bound by lengthy contracts, thus switching between rival services is made less easy.

Applications of price elasticity of demand

- A firm that faces price inelastic demand can increase its prices to earn more total revenue (see Table 1.2). Similarly, a firm that has price elastic demand for its products can reduce its prices to earn more revenue (see Figure 1.21).
- Assuming that the PED for a firm's exports is price elastic, it will generally benefit from lower exchange rates (as export prices fall, so the firm becomes more price-competitive).
- Firms with different PED values for their products can use price discrimination to charge different customers different prices for essentially the same product. For example, theme parks charge adults higher prices and offer discounts for children and families to increase their revenues.
- Firms can pass on most of the incidence of indirect taxes on products that are highly price inelastic – for example, products such as alcohol, tobacco and petrol.
- Governments use PED to determine taxation policies – for example, imposing heavy taxes on demerit goods such as cigarettes knowing that the demand for such products is price inelastic (see Figure 1.15).

Table 1.2 The relationship between PED and total revenue

Price change	Inelastic	Unitary	Elastic
Increased price	Total revenue increases	No change in revenue	Total revenue falls
Reduced price	Total revenue falls	No change in revenue	Total revenue increases

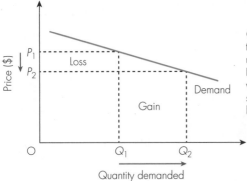

Ceteris paribus, a cut in price from P_1 to P_2 will lead to a net gain in sales revenue when demand is price elastic. If price was to increase, customers would simply switch to other substitutes, thereby generating a net loss in total revenue.

Figure 1.21 Price elastic demand and total revenue

> **Common mistake**
>
> Typically, students will write in the exam that 'price elastic' means that as the price of a good or service increases, its demand falls. This describes the law of demand, i.e. as price goes up, demand will fall irrespective of whether demand is price elastic or price inelastic. Instead, if demand is price elastic, the percentage fall in demand is greater than the percentage increase in price.

Cross price elasticity of demand (XED)

Cross price elasticity of demand and its determinants

Cross price elasticity of demand (XED) is calculated using the formula:

$$\frac{\text{percentage change in quantity demanded of product A}}{\text{percentage change in price of product B}}$$

Complements have a negative XED value because a fall in the price of one product, such as smartphones, leads to an increase in the demand for the complementary product, such as downloaded applications (see Figure 1.22).

Substitutes have a positive XED value because an increase in the price of one product, such as Pepsi Cola, leads to a rise in the demand for the alternative product, such as Coca-Cola (see Figure 1.23).

Unrelated products, such as helicopters and wedding rings, have a XED value of zero because the change in the price of one product does not directly affect the demand for the other.

The stronger the relationship, the higher the coefficient of the XED. Close substitutes have a high positive XED value, whilst strong complements have a high negative XED value.

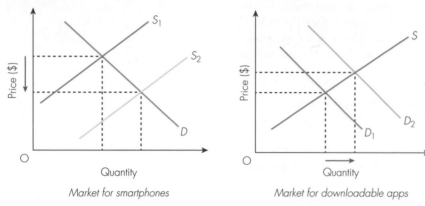

Figure 1.22 Negative XED for complements

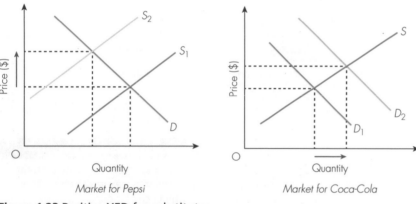

Figure 1.23 Positive XED for substitutes

Keyword definitions

Cross price elasticity of demand (XED) measures the degree of responsiveness of demand for one product following a change in the price of another product.

Complements are products that are jointly demanded – for example, cars and petrol, or a wedding dress and wedding rings.

Substitutes are products that can be used as alternatives – for example, Apple iPhones or Samsung Galaxy smartphones, and private jets or helicopters.

EXAM PRACTICE *(HL ONLY)*

PAPER 3

10 The price of monthly disposable contact lenses increases from $24.50 to $26.95 per pack and it is observed that the quantity demanded for contact lens solution falls from 225 boxes to 200 boxes per month. Calculate the XED and comment on your findings. [2]

11 Explain whether the value of the cross price elasticity of demand between private and public transport is likely to be a high or low/positive or negative value. [2]

Applications of cross price elasticity of demand

Revised ▢

- Knowledge of XED can be useful for firms because it can help to predict the effect on the quantity demanded if the price of a complementary good changes.
- It can affect a firm's pricing strategy depending on whether the XED value is very high or otherwise. For example, popcorn and carbonated soft drinks in cinemas are often expensive due to high XED with cinema tickets.
- It allows firms to predict the effect on the quantity demanded for their product (and hence total revenue) if a rival firm changes its price.
- It also lets firms know the extent to which customers will switch between competing brands, thus informing their pricing and marketing strategies to remain competitive.

12 Calculate the value of cross price elasticity of demand if the demand for Pepsi drops by 10% following a fall in the price of Coca-Cola by 8%, and comment on your finding. **[2]**

Income elasticity of demand (YED)

Income elasticity of demand and its determinants

Income price elasticity of demand (YED) is calculated using the formula:

$$\frac{\text{percentage change in quantity demanded}}{\text{percentage change in income}}$$

Normal goods (necessities and luxuries) have a positive YED value because people will tend to buy more of these products as income levels increase, *ceteris paribus* (see Figure 1.24).

Figure 1.24 Normal goods

Necessities have a YED value of between 0 and 1, i.e. demand is income inelastic as customers will continue to buy such essential needs even if prices begin to rise.

Luxuries have a YED value that is greater than 1, i.e. demand is income elastic because customers are relatively responsive to changes in income when buying superior products.

Inferior goods have a negative YED value, i.e. as income levels rise, customers will seek alternative superior-quality products (see Figure 1.25), for example fresh meats instead of frozen meats.

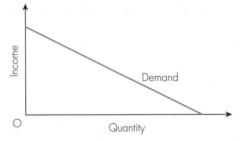

Figure 1.25 Inferior goods

If demand is income inelastic, then a change in income causes a proportionally smaller change in the demand for a product.

13 Assume the income elasticity of demand for sausages is –0.25 and that there has been a 3% increase in consumer incomes. Calculate the percentage change in the demand for sausages, assuming all other things remain equal. **[2]**

Keyword definitions

Income elasticity of demand (YED) measures the degree of responsiveness of demand following a change in income.

Normal goods are products that customers tend to buy more of as their income level increases. They comprise necessities (such as food) and luxuries (such as cars).

Inferior goods are products with a negative income elasticity of demand, i.e. the demand for such products falls when consumer income levels rise.

Luxury goods are superior goods and services as their demand is highly income elastic, i.e. an increase in income leads to a proportionally greater increase in the demand for luxuries.

Expert tip

Examples of inferior goods can vary from one country to another. For example, in some countries a bicycle might not be regarded as an inferior good, but could be classified as a normal good. It is therefore important for students to justify their reasoning.

Common mistake

Some students confuse YED with PED in the examinations, stating that demand is income elastic if customers buy more when the price falls. Although there is an income effect if price falls, YED measures how demand changes following a change in income, rather than changes in price.

Applications of income elasticity of demand

- Firms and governments can estimate the impact on different markets following changes in national income (GDP) – for example, supermarkets promote more inferior products during a recession.
- By contrast, luxury goods and services are the most affected products during an economic downturn when national income declines. Hence, firms may wish to diversify their output.
- Primary sector products such as oil and agricultural output have a relatively low YED value. This has potentially beneficial implications for producers and the economy as demand is stable despite fluctuations in the business cycle.
- Secondary sector output (manufactured goods) has a higher YED value. This means demand is more sensitive to changes in income levels than for primary sector output.
- Tertiary sector output (services) has a relatively high YED value, so producers and the economy suffer during an economic recession as customers are highly responsive to the fall in their income.

> **Expert tip**
>
> Whilst it is not necessary to use the negative coefficient for PED (due to the law of demand), it is vital that students use the negative coefficient of YED when referring to an inferior good (less is bought as real income levels rise) and the positive YED value when referring to normal goods.

> **Expert tip**
>
> It can be difficult to classify certain products as inferior or normal goods. For example, economy-class air travel may be considered as a luxury good as it tends to account for a large percentage of a consumer's income. However, this is relatively cheap (or inferior) compared with business-class or first-class air travel (luxury products). The key is good reasoning and critical thinking.

> **Common mistake**
>
> It is incorrect to assume that inferior goods are those that are of poor quality standards as this is not the meaning of inferior goods. For example, a Honda car is unlikely to be of poor quality but is inferior to brands such as Audi, BMW or Mercedes Benz.

Price elasticity of supply (PES)

Price elasticity of supply

Price elasticity of supply is calculated using the formula:

$$\frac{\text{percentage change in quantity supplied}}{\text{percentage change in price}}$$

Supply is price elastic if firms can quite easily increase supply without a time delay if there is an increase in the price of the product, for example mass-produced goods such as soft drinks. Such firms can gain a competitive advantage as they are able to respond to changes in price.

By contrast, supply is price inelastic if firms find it difficult to change production in a given time period following a change in the market price.

- If PES > 1 then supply is price elastic, i.e. responsive to changes in price (see Figure 1.26).
- If PES < 1 supply is price inelastic, i.e. unresponsive to changes in price (see Figure 1.27).
- If PES = 0 supply is perfectly price inelastic, i.e. a change in price has no impact on the quantity supplied, as there is absolutely no spare capacity to raise output (see Figure 1.28).
- If PES = ∞ (infinity) supply is perfectly price elastic, i.e. supply can change without any corresponding change in price due to the spare capacity that exists at the current price level (see Figure 1.29).
- If PES = 1 supply has unitary price elasticity, i.e. the percentage change in the quantity supplied matches the proportional change in price (see Figure 1.30).

> **Keyword definition**
> **Price elasticity of supply** (PES) measures the degree of responsiveness of quantity supplied of a product following a change in its price along a given supply curve.

EXAM PRACTICE *(HL ONLY)*

PAPER 3

14 Calculate the value of PES if the market price of beans increases from $2 per kilo to $2.20 per kilo and causes the quantity supplied to rise from 10,000 kilos to 10,500 kilos. **[2]**

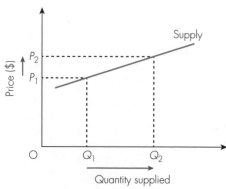

In this case, when price rises from P_1 to P_2, there is plenty of spare capacity for the firm, so the quantity supplied can increase by a greater proportion from Q_1 to Q_2, i.e. supply is price elastic. Examples of products with price elastic supply are mass-produced goods such as carbonated soft drinks and toothpaste.

Figure 1.26 The price elastic supply curve

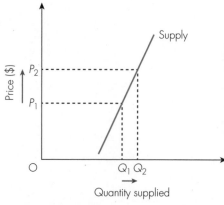

In this case, when price rises from P_1 to P_2, there is very little spare capacity for the firm, so the quantity supplied can only rise by a smaller proportion from Q_1 to Q_2. Examples are fresh fruit and vegetables that take time to grow (so supply is relatively unresponsive to changes in price).

Figure 1.27 The price inelastic supply curve

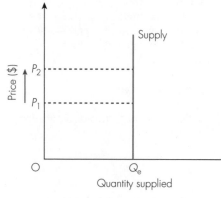

Here, supply is perfectly price inelastic at Q_e. Irrespective of price changes, the firm can only supply a maximum of Q_e, so changes in price have no impact on the quantity supplied, i.e. PES = 0. An example is a football stadium or a concert hall that cannot accommodate more than the seating capacity.

Figure 1.28 The perfectly price inelastic supply curve

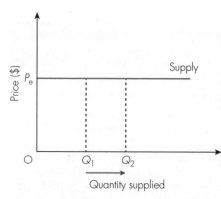

Here, supply is perfectly price elastic at a price of P_e. For example, Duracell might have a huge stock of batteries, so any increase in demand will simply result in more Duracell batteries being sold, without the price being raised. Hence, as quantity supplied can increase from Q_1 to Q_2 irrespective of a price change, the PES = ∞.

Figure 1.29 The perfectly price elastic supply curve

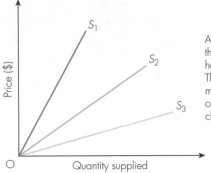

Any supply curve that starts at the origin (such as S_1, S_2 or S_3) has a PES value equal to 1. This theoretical outcome means that a change in price causes the same proportional change in quantity supplied.

Figure 1.30 The unitary price elasticity supply curve

Mathematically, supply curves have a different PES value at different points. Supply is more price elastic at lower prices and more inelastic at higher prices.

EXAM PRACTICE *(HL ONLY)*

PAPER 3

15 *Angry Birds* is a highly popular video game created by Finnish company *Rovio*, with over 12 million customers having paid $0.99 each to download the game from Apple's App Store. With the use of an appropriate diagram, explain why the high level of demand for *Angry Birds* games has no effect on the selling price. **[4]**

Determinants of price elasticity of supply

Revised

- **The time period** – Supply tends to be price inelastic in the short run, for example the supply of fresh vegetables is dependent on the time it takes to harvest the products. In the long run, firms can adjust their levels of production according to price changes in the market.
- **The level of stocks** – Firms with high inventories (stocks of unused raw materials, work-in-progress and finished goods) tend to have relatively price elastic supply as they are more able to respond quickly to a change in market prices.
- **The degree of spare productive capacity** – A firm with plenty of spare capacity can increase supply with relative ease (without increasing its costs of production), so supply is relatively price elastic. The opposite applies for the long run.
- **The ease and cost of factor substitution** – The easier it is to substitute factors of production (such as labour and capital), the more price elastic supply tends to be. Similarly, the more mobile factors of production are, the greater the PES will be, *ceteris paribus*.

> **Expert tip**
>
> The determinants of supply elasticity can be remembered by the acronym **TICS**:
> **T**ime
> **I**nventory (stocks)
> **C**apacity
> **S**ubstitution (of factors of production)

Applications of price elasticity of supply

Revised

- Firms that have a high PES are highly responsive to changes in price and other market conditions, so this makes them more competitive.
- The PES for primary products is relatively low due to the comparatively long time it takes to increase primary sector output, such as oil, iron, coal and agricultural harvests.
- By contrast, the PES for manufactured products is generally higher because many of these can be mass-produced in shorter time periods, for example toothpicks, nails and LEGO toys.

> **Expert tip**
>
> There are several ways firms can improve the value of their PES:
>
> - Create spare capacity.
> - Keep large volumes of stocks (inventories).
> - Improved storage systems to prolong the shelf-life of products.
> - Adopting or upgrading to the latest technology.
> - Improving distribution systems (how the products get to the customers).
> - Developing and training employees to improve labour occupational mobility (to perform a range of jobs).

EXAM PRACTICE *(HL ONLY)*

PAPER 3

16 A 10% increase in the price of computer keyboards leads to an increase in output of 20%. Calculate the price elasticity of supply of computer keyboards following this change in price. **[2]**

Expert tip

A key determinant of PES is the nature of barriers to entry. The existence of copyrights and patents, for example, reduces the number of potential firms in the industry and therefore lowers the value of PES, *ceteris paribus*.

1.3 Government intervention

Revised ☐

Indirect taxes

Revised ☐

Specific taxes and *ad valorem* taxes and their impact on markets

Revised ☐

Taxes are levies (or charges) imposed by the government, thereby limiting the output of certain goods and services and/or raising the price of goods and services paid by consumers.

Indirect taxes raise the costs of production. Specific taxes cause a parallel shift in the supply curve to the left (see Figure 1.31), whilst *ad valorem* taxes pivot the supply curve (see Figure 1.32).

The government will often intervene if the price mechanism fails to establish the socially optimal equilibrium – for example, taxing demerit goods such as alcohol and tobacco to reduce their consumption.

Indirect taxes are a major source of government revenue. They can be used to correct market failures, such as imposing fuel taxes on motorists. On a macroeconomic scale, indirect taxes can be used to affect the level of aggregate demand, by changing the rate of sales taxes, for example. They are used to protect domestic firms from overseas rivals by imposing tariffs on imports.

The imposition of indirect taxes means that consumers tend to lose out as they have to pay higher prices, especially if the demand is price inelastic. Producers also lose out as their costs of production increase. However, if PED is low then they are able to pass most of the tax onto customers without largely affecting the level of demand.

The tax also creates a **deadweight loss** (the combined loss of consumer and producer surplus), as shown by the shaded area in Figure 1.31.

Keyword definitions

An **indirect tax** is a government levy on the sale of certain goods and services. Examples include specific taxes and *ad valorem* taxes.

A **specific tax**, also known as a **per unit tax**, imposes a fixed amount of tax on each product. Examples include taxes on cigarettes, air passenger tax and electronic road pricing and road tolls.

An *ad valorem* tax imposes a percentage tax on the value of a good or service. Examples include property taxes, tariffs (taxes on imports) and sales taxes.

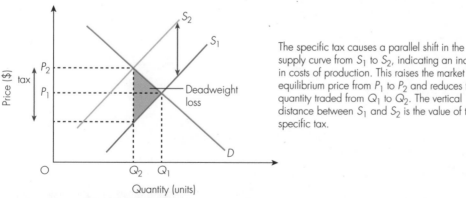

The specific tax causes a parallel shift in the supply curve from S_1 to S_2, indicating an increase in costs of production. This raises the market equilibrium price from P_1 to P_2 and reduces the quantity traded from Q_1 to Q_2. The vertical distance between S_1 and S_2 is the value of the specific tax.

Figure 1.31 Imposition of a specific tax

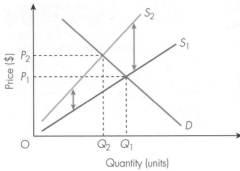

Figure 1.32 Imposition of an *ad valorem* tax

The *ad valorem* (percentage) tax causes a pivotal shift in the supply curve from S_1 to S_2 because the absolute amount of the tax is greater as the market price increases (as indicated by the two red arrows). The higher price reduces the equilibrium quantity traded from Q_1 to Q_2.

Tax incidence, and price elasticity of demand and supply (HL only)

A greater proportion of the incidence of tax falls on consumers if the PED is low, i.e. there is a lack of substitutes. This means that firms can pass on most of the higher costs to consumers (see Figure 1.33).

The opposite is true when demand is price elastic, i.e. producers are unable to pass on most of the indirect tax to the consumer because customers are highly responsive to an increase in price (see Figure 1.34).

If the PES is high, consumers pay a greater proportion of the incidence of tax. This is because firms are less able and willing to supply if production costs increase, so buyers end up paying a greater burden of the tax (see Figure 1.35).

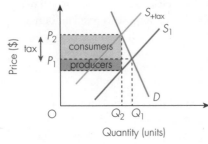

Figure 1.33 Tax incidence and price inelastic demand

The imposition of a specific indirect tax shifts the supply curve from S_1 to S_{+tax}, thus raising the equilibrium price from P_1 to P_2. With the relatively price inelastic demand curve, most of the incidence of the tax is paid by consumers (shown by the area in orange). The rest of the tax is paid by the producer (shown by the area in red).

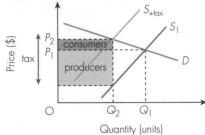

Figure 1.34 Tax incidence and price elastic demand

Here, the relatively price elastic demand means there are plenty of other substitutes, so the firm cannot simply pass on the tax to consumers in the form of higher prices. The high PED means consumers will be very responsive to an increase in price. Thus, the producer pays the larger proportion of the tax incidence.

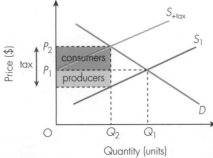

Figure 1.35 Tax incidence and price elastic supply

Here, the relatively price elastic supply curve means firms are highly responsive to changes in price, so must pass on the tax to consumers in order for them to be able to supply. Thus, the consumer pays the larger proportion of the tax incidence.

Expert tip

The incidence of tax falls mainly upon the stakeholder group (consumers or producers) that is less responsive to changes in price, i.e. the group that has the most price inelastic function.

EXAM PRACTICE (HL ONLY)

PAPER 3

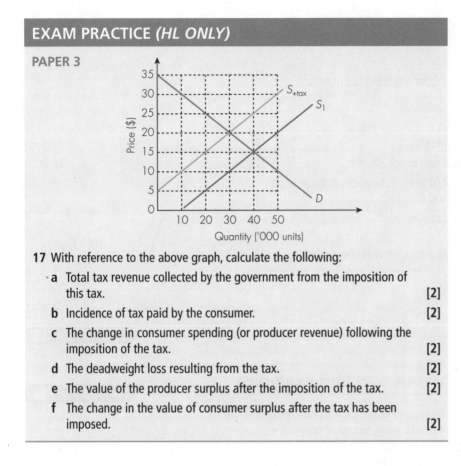

17 With reference to the above graph, calculate the following:

- **a** Total tax revenue collected by the government from the imposition of this tax. [2]

- **b** Incidence of tax paid by the consumer. [2]

- **c** The change in consumer spending (or producer revenue) following the imposition of the tax. [2]

- **d** The deadweight loss resulting from the tax. [2]

- **e** The value of the producer surplus after the imposition of the tax. [2]

- **f** The change in the value of consumer surplus after the tax has been imposed. [2]

Subsidies

Revised ▢

Impact on markets

Revised ▢

Subsidies reduce the costs of production for firms, thus shifting the supply curve outwards to the right (see Figure 1.36). Subsidies are given to producers for several reasons:

- To encourage the output of merit goods such as education, training and healthcare services.
- To limit negative externalities such as pollution by subsidising 'green' technologies.
- To protect certain industries and to prevent a subsequent decline in employment.

Consumers generally benefit from subsidies as the market price is lowered, thus more people are able and willing to buy the good or service.

Producers also benefit from the subsidy as their production costs are reduced. This helps to improve their competitiveness and profitability.

Whilst the government spends money on financing the subsidy, and there is an opportunity cost in doing so, the net benefits to society may outweigh the costs (in theory, at least). However, subsidies distort market forces and may subsequently protect inefficient firms.

> **Keyword definition**
> A **subsidy** is financial assistance from the government to encourage output (such as the sale of exports), to reduce the price of certain merit goods (such as education, training and healthcare), or to keep down the cost of living (such as food prices).

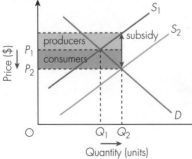

The subsidy enables firms to produce more output and each and every level of output, thus shifting the supply curve from S_1 to S_2. This reduces the market price from P_1 to P_2, with quantity traded increasing from Q_1 to Q_2, *ceteris paribus*. Hence, producers pass on the green section of the subsidy to consumers and retain the red section for lowering production costs.

Figure 1.36 Subsidies and market outcomes

EXAM PRACTICE *(HL ONLY)*

PAPER 3

18 Suppose the demand and supply functions for a product are given as:

$Q_d = 100 - 5P$

$Q_s = 20 + 3P$

    a Calculate the equilibrium price and quantity.   **[3]**

    b Calculate the price required for producers to sell 80 units.   **[2]**

    c Suppose the government grants a $2.67 per unit subsidy on the product. Calculate the new equilibrium price and quantity.   **[3]**

    d Using your answers from parts a and c, calculate the difference in consumer spending on the product.   **[2]**

    e Calculate the total amount spent by the government on the subsidy.   **[2]**

Price controls

Price ceilings: rationale, consequences and examples

A price ceiling can be used to protect the interest of consumers from soaring prices, such as escalating rents or food prices. Following the imposition of a price ceiling, consumer surplus is increased but producer surplus is reduced.

    Consumers can benefit from the lower price after the imposition of the price ceiling (see Figure 1.37). However, price ceilings distort market forces and therefore can result in an inefficient allocation of scarce resources. This creates a deadweight loss (see Figure 1.38).

    The excess demand can cause non-price rationing mechanisms (systems to restrict the allotment of goods and services). Examples include **queuing** (using waiting time as a means of distributing products), **ration coupons** (tickets that entitle individuals to buy a certain amount of a product) and **most-favoured customers** (those who receive special, preferential treatment).

    Maximum prices can also cause underground parallel markets to appear due to the shortages in supply. In Figure 1.37, traders in parallel markets will charge the high price of P_{pm}.

> **Keyword definition**
> A **price ceiling** (also known as a **maximum price**) occurs when the government sets a price below the market equilibrium price to encourage output and consumption.

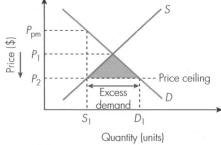

The maximum price, in this case imposed to control residential rents, results in more demand (D_1) than is supplied at the lower price (P_2). This results in excess demand, as shown by the area in orange. This shortage is made up by government supplying housing at a price of P_2 to stabilise rents in the economy.

Figure 1.37 Impacts of price ceilings

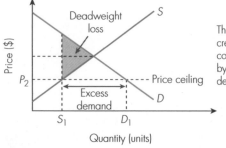

The maximum price reduces supply to S_1, creating a shortage. This reduces both consumer and producer surplus, as shown by the shaded area, i.e. there is a deadweight social welfare loss.

Figure 1.38 Welfare loss of price ceilings

EXAM PRACTICE (HL ONLY)

PAPER 3

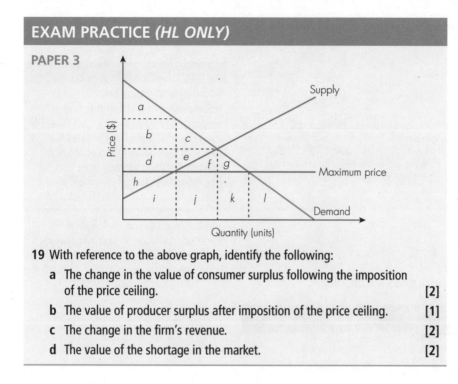

19 With reference to the above graph, identify the following:

a The change in the value of consumer surplus following the imposition of the price ceiling. [2]

b The value of producer surplus after imposition of the price ceiling. [1]

c The change in the firm's revenue. [2]

d The value of the shortage in the market. [2]

Price floors: rationale, consequences and examples

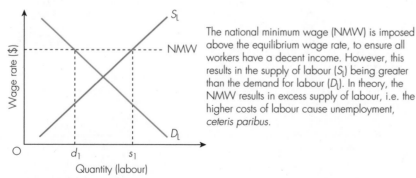

Revised ☐

Excess supply occurs when a price floor is imposed above the market equilibrium price, because supply outweighs demand when prices are so high (see Figure 1.39).

> **Keyword definition**
> A **price floor**, also known as a **minimum price**, is the imposition of a price guarantee set above the market price to encourage supply of a certain good or service.

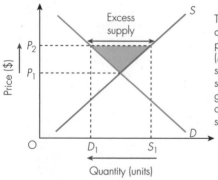

The minimum price, in this case offered to agricultural farmers, gives an incentive for producers to supply more (S_1) than is demanded (D_1) at the higher price (P_2). This results in excess supply, as shown by the area in orange. This surplus is bought at a price of P_2 by the government to support the farmers, and released onto the market during times of bad harvest to stabilise food prices.

Figure 1.39 Consequences of price floors

A price floor guarantees suppliers a higher price than before. This also applies in the labour market where more workers supply their labour services if there is a minimum wage (see Figure 1.40).

The national minimum wage (NMW) is imposed above the equilibrium wage rate, to ensure all workers have a decent income. However, this results in the supply of labour (S_l) being greater than the demand for labour (D_l). In theory, the NMW results in excess supply of labour, i.e. the higher costs of labour cause unemployment, *ceteris paribus*.

Figure 1.40 Consequences of a minimum wage

The inefficient allocation of resources results in a deadweight loss (see Figure 1.41).

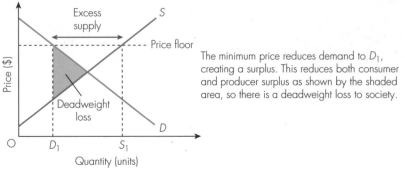

The minimum price reduces demand to D_1, creating a surplus. This reduces both consumer and producer surplus as shown by the shaded area, so there is a deadweight loss to society.

Figure 1.41 Welfare loss of price floors

Consumers tend to pay higher prices if price floors are imposed.

EXAM PRACTICE *(HL ONLY)*

PAPER 3

20 Refer to the diagram below and answer the questions that follow.

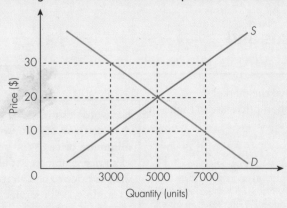

a Explain what situation arises if the government imposes a price floor of $30 for the product. **[2]**

b Calculate the change in consumer spending following the imposition of the price floor. **[2]**

c Calculate the change in producer revenue following the imposition of the price floor. **[3]**

d Suppose the government exports all the excess supply at $20 per unit. Calculate the amount of taxpayers' money needed to support this price control scheme. **[3]**

1.4 Market failure

Revised ☐

The meaning of market failure

Revised ☐

Market failure as a failure to allocate resources efficiently

Revised ☐

Examples of market failure include:

- under-provision of merit goods, such as education and healthcare, as these services would only be provided to those who were willing and able to pay
- under-provision of public goods, such as street lighting and public roads, because producers cannot exclude those who do not pay from benefiting from the provision of the service
- over-provision of demerit goods such as tobacco, alcohol and gambling (as there is a lack of government intervention in such markets)
- abuse of monopoly power – charging customers prices above market equilibrium – and hence the associated inefficiencies.

> **Keyword definition**
> **Market failure** exists when the price mechanism (the market forces of demand and supply) allocates scarce resources in an inefficient way, i.e. there is either over-provision or under-provision of certain goods and services.

Market failure occurs when the price mechanism cannot allocate resources efficiently but causes external costs or external benefits of production or consumption.

- **Private benefits** are the benefits of production and consumption enjoyed by a firm, individual or government.
- **Private costs** of production and consumption are the actual costs incurred by a firm, individual or government.
- **Social benefits** are the true (or full) benefits of consumption or production, i.e. the sum of private benefits and external benefits.
- **Social costs** are the true (or full) costs of consumption or production, i.e. the sum of private costs and external costs.

Types of market failure

Revised ☐

The meaning of externalities

Revised ☐

Marginal private benefit (MPB) is the additional value enjoyed by households and firms from the consumption or production (output) of an extra unit of a particular good or service.

Marginal private cost (MPC) is the additional cost of production for firms or the extra charge paid by customers for the output or consumption of an extra unit of a good or service.

External costs (also known as **negative externalities**) are costs incurred by a third party in an economic transaction for which no compensation is paid. Examples of external costs include:

- second-hand (passive) smoking
- air pollution caused by fumes from a factory
- noise pollution from a nightclub or nearby airport
- litter on public beaches
- child obesity from junk food and carbonated soft drinks
- climate change fuelled by continual demand for higher levels of consumption
- excessive advertising (known as advertising clutter) that causes visual blight.

> **Keyword definition**
> **Externalities** (or **spillover effects**) are the external costs or benefits of an economic transaction, causing the market to fail to achieve a social optimum level of output, where marginal social benefits equal marginal social costs (MSB = MSC).

External benefits (also known as **positive externalities**) are benefits enjoyed by a third party from an economic transaction. Examples of products with external benefits for which no money is paid directly by the beneficiary include:

- national defence
- law and order systems, for example police and emergency services

- flood defence systems
- sewage and waste disposal systems
- street lighting
- lighthouses
- public parks, libraries and museums
- public fireworks displays.

Marginal social benefit (MSB) is the added benefit to society from the production or consumption of an extra unit of output, i.e. the sum of MPC and marginal external costs.

Marginal social cost (MSC) is the extra cost of an economic transaction to society, i.e. the sum of MPB and marginal external benefits.

The production and consumption of public goods and merit goods exert positive externalities. The production and consumption of demerit goods exert negative externalities such as pollution.

Negative externalities of production and consumption

Revised ▢

Negative externalities arise from the production or consumption of goods or services that create negative spillover effects on a third party. These products are known as **demerit goods** (see Figures 1.42 and 1.43). Examples include: cigarettes, alcohol, hard drugs, recreational drugs, junk food, prostitution and gambling.

Although it is assumed that people are rational economic agents, it is often the case that they are not the best judge of their own welfare, so the government intervenes to discourage the production and consumption of demerit goods – for example, age limits for drinking, smoking and driving.

> **Keyword definition**
> **Demerit goods** are products that create negative spillover effects (or negative externalities) to society. Hence their production and consumption result in social costs being greater than private costs of production and consumption, i.e. MSC > MPC.

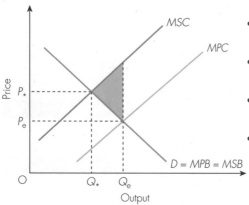

- In a free market without government intervention, output will be at Q_e where the *MPC* = *MPB* of production.
- However, the socially optimal level of output is at Q_* where *MSC* = *MSB*, with a higher price of P_* being charged.
- Hence, from society's point of view, there is overproduction of demerit goods.
- The shaded area shows the welfare gain from reducing output of the demerit good from Q_e to Q_*.

Figure 1.42 Negative externalities of production (of demerit goods)

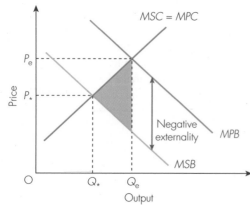

- In a free market, output is at Q_e, which exceeds the socially optimal level at Q_*, where the *MSC* = *MSB*, of consumption.
- The negative externality accounts for the difference between the *MSB* and *MPB*.
- Hence, there is overconsumption of demerit goods in the absence of government intervention.
- The shaded area shows the welfare loss of consumption (of products with negative externalities).

Figure 1.43 Negative externalities of consumption (of demerit goods)

> **Expert tip**
> When price is set equal to marginal cost ($P = MC$), economic welfare is maximised, i.e. consumer and producer surplus are maximised. This is because the price that consumers are willing and able to pay matches that of the producers.

Policy responses to negative externalities

Revised ☐

Governments try to solve market failure in two main ways:

- **market-based policies** – intervention in the price mechanism to make the market forces of demand and supply operate more effectively – for example, taxation and tradable permits
- **government regulations** such as environmental standards.

Taxation is used to 'internalise' negative externalities, i.e. the buyer and/or seller pay for the true costs of their actions without any burden being placed on third parties (see Figure 1.44) – for example, taxes on fuel, alcohol, tobacco and the use of plastic carrier bags.

In Figure 1.44, the tax imposed on cigarettes has caused the supply curve to shift from S_1 to S_{tax}, causing price to rise from P_1 to P_2 and the quantity demanded to fall from Q_1 to Q_2.

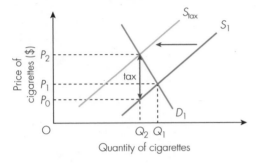

Figure 1.44 Indirect tax on cigarettes

> **Expert tip**
>
> Remember that a specific tax is shown by the vertical distance between the two supply curves. The consumer pays a higher price ($P_1 - P_2$) and the producer pays the remainder ($P_1 - P_0$). The more price inelastic the demand for the product, the greater the proportion of the tax paid by the consumer.

Table 1.3 The advantages and disadvantages of imposing a tax on the production or consumption of products with negative externalities

Advantages	Disadvantages
■ It increases the price and therefore should decrease the quantity demanded, for example Ireland's tax on plastic carrier bags aimed at reducing wastage and litter cut demand by 90% in the first 3 months of implementation. ■ It creates tax revenue for the government, which can be used on other goods and services. Scotland, for example, introduced a 5 pence tax per single-use bag in October 2013 following success in countries such as Ireland, Wales, Germany and Hong Kong.	■ The demand for many of these products (such as cigarettes, alcohol and petrol) tend to be price inelastic, i.e. the tax may have little impact on the level of consumption. ■ The tax on many of these products is regressive, so has a greater impact on low-income earners than on high-income earners. ■ It can encourage smuggling and unofficial market activity.

Another market-based policy is to use **tradable permits**. These are pollution rights issued to firms, thus capping the level of pollution from economic activity. The policy creates incentives not to pollute so that excess permits can be sold to other, less efficient, firms.

An increase in the demand for pollution permits would raise the price of pollution rights, just like in any other market, but without affecting the level of output and hence the level of pollution (see Figures 1.45 and 1.46). Hence, an increase in the price of tradable permits also increases the opportunity cost to firms that pollute.

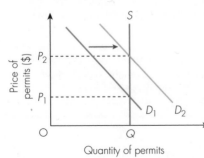

- Tradable permits can be highly effective in internalising negative externalities of production. An increase in demand for permits from D_1 to D_2 simply causes the price to rise from P_1 to P_2.
- The level of pollution is capped by the perfectly price inelastic supply curve of pollution permits.

Figure 1.45 Increased demand for tradable permits

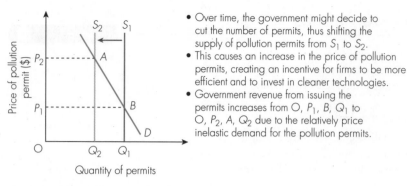

- Over time, the government might decide to cut the number of permits, thus shifting the supply of pollution permits from S_1 to S_2.
- This causes an increase in the price of pollution permits, creating an incentive for firms to be more efficient and to invest in cleaner technologies.
- Government revenue from issuing the permits increases from O, P_1, B, Q_1 to O, P_2, A, Q_2 due to the relatively price inelastic demand for the pollution permits.

Figure 1.46 Reduced supply of tradable permits

Apart from market-based policies, governments can also impose regulations to deal with negative externalities from production and consumption. Examples include:

- laws to regulate where people can drive, cycle and gamble
- laws to make it illegal for people to smoke, eat or to talk on a mobile phone while driving
- motorcyclists being made to wear a helmet and car passengers having to wear seat belts
- airport authorities regulating the number of night flights to limit noise pollution for nearby residents
- laws on the minimum age that a person must be before being legally allowed to purchase cigarettes or alcohol, thus helping to reduce the consumption of such demerit goods (see Figure 1.47). It is illegal to sell alcohol in Iran, Bangladesh, Brunei Darussalam and Saudi Arabia.
- regulations restricting where people can smoke. In many countries, smoking is banned in public places such as shopping malls, bars, restaurants, airports, railways stations and the beach.

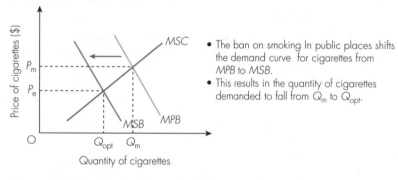

- The ban on smoking In public places shifts the demand curve for cigarettes from MPB to MSB.
- This results in the quantity of cigarettes demanded to fall from Q_m to Q_{opt}.

Figure 1.47 The impact of regulations on the demand for cigarettes

Table 1.4 The advantages and disadvantages of imposing rules and regulations to correct market failures

Advantages	Disadvantages
■ Consumption of the good or service may be reduced. ■ Awareness of the negative impacts of demerit goods (such as drinking and driving) may change the behaviour of people in the long term. ■ Awareness of the positive impacts of consumption of merit goods (such as education) is raised.	■ Restrictions cause underground (illegal) markets to develop where the good or service can be purchased, often at a very high price. ■ The government has no control over the quality of the goods produced in underground markets, which in some cases can be dangerous for consumption, such as illegally distilled vodka or contaminated baby milk powder. ■ People may still choose to break the rules – for example, underage smokers and drinkers of alcohol can bypass the law by obtaining false ID cards. ■ The fine or punishment for ignoring the ban must be enforced and set high enough to discourage consumption of the good or service.

EXAM PRACTICE

PAPER 1

21 With the aid of a market failure diagram, explain why a government might use congestion zone charging to reduce the use of motor vehicles in city centres such as London and Paris. **[10]**

Expert tip

Government regulation can be very effective in correcting market failures. Parents in the UK get fined if they do not send their children to school, and from 2015, full-time education in the UK will be compulsory for children up to the age of 18. The Hong Kong government imposes a fine of HK$1500 ($193) for each item of littering and for smoking in public areas.

Positive externalities of production and consumption

Revised ☐

Examples of merit goods include education, healthcare provision, training, research and development expenditure, and the provision of public sports and recreation facilities (such as public swimming pools, sports grounds, museums and public libraries).

Merit goods are deemed to be of value by society (due to the positive externalities of production and consumption), i.e. they improve the general standard of living in the economy.

Keyword definition

Merit goods are products that create positive externalities (spillover effects) when they are produced or consumed. Hence, the social benefits from the production and consumption of merits goods are greater than the private benefits.

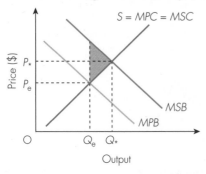

Figure 1.48 Positive externalities of consumption of a merit good

In Figure 1.48, positive externalities exist because $MSB > MPB$ of consumption at all levels of output. This is due to the existence of positive externalities of consumption. Hence, there is market failure at the free market equilibrium (Q_e and P_e), i.e. there is underconsumption of the merit good.

The socially desirable level of output is where $MSB = MSC$, i.e. at output level Q_*. The shaded area in Figure 1.49 represents welfare loss due to the underconsumption. With government intervention, resources are more efficiently allocated with a greater level of output at Q_*.

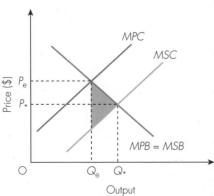

- The free market fails to supply goods with positive externalities at the socially optimum level of output, i.e. where $MSC = MSB$ (or at P_* and Q_*).
- There is underprovision of these goods and services as output is only Q_e, causing the price to be higher at P_e.
- The shaded area represents the welfare loss associated with the market failure since production is lower (than the socially optimum level) at Q_e and price at P_e.
- Government intervention means that output increases to the socially optimum level, i.e. at Q_* and a fall in price to P_*.

Figure 1.49 Positive externalities of production

Common mistake

Do not confuse the definition of public goods with that for merit goods. Both the state (public) and private sector of the economy provide merit goods, such as education and health services. Merit goods can also be rivalrous and excludable, for example selective grammar schools, single-gender schools, religion-based schools or private health clinics.

Government responses to positive externalities

A **subsidy** is a sum of money given to a producer to reduce the costs of production (to encourage higher levels of output) or to consumers to reduce the price of consumption. For example, governments often subsidise public transport to discourage people from using private cars (see Figure 1.50).

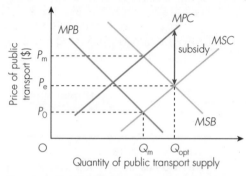

- If bus operators receive a subsidy, their production costs fall, thus shifting the supply from *MPC* to *MSC*.
- The subsidy provides an incentive for more people to consume the good, thus shifting demand from *MPB* to *MSB*.
- Price falls from P_m to P_e and the quantity demanded increases from Q_m to Q_{opt}.

Figure 1.50 The effects of a producer subsidy on public transport

In Figure 1.50, the specific subsidy is shown by the vertical distance between MPC and MSC. The producer passes some of this subsidy to consumers in the form of lower prices (from P_m to P_e) and keeps the remainder in the form of lower production costs.

An increase in the use of public transport, due to the subsidy, should lower congestion. Therefore the subsidy reduces the externality caused by driving private vehicles.

In another example, the government in China provides a subsidy of up to 60,000 yuan ($9800) to buyers of electric and hydrogen vehicles in a bid to combat rising air pollution.

Limitations of using subsidies to correct market failures include the following:

- Just as with taxation on negative production and consumption externalities, it is difficult to set a precise subsidy that ensures $MPC = MSC$ and $MPB = MSB$.
- The social return on the production and consumption of merit goods (such as education or the provision of libraries, sports facilities and museums) is difficult, if not subjective, to measure.
- If the price elasticity of demand for the good or service is inelastic, the lower price (due to the subsidy) has little impact on the quantity demanded.
- There is always an opportunity cost in the provision of subsidies as the money could have been used on other government projects.

Legislation is another government response to deal with the positive externalities of production and consumption. Laws are used to encourage greater consumption of goods and services with positive externalities, such as:

- compulsory education for children
- the requirement for school children to be vaccinated against certain diseases.

Advertising is a third approach to correcting market failures by influencing behaviour, i.e. informing and educating the public about the benefits of increased consumption. Examples include:

- the '5-a-Day' programme run in countries such as Germany, the UK and the USA in line with the World Health Organization's statement that people should eat at least 400 grams (or five portions) of fruits and vegetables each day (see Figure 1.51)
- schools educating students about safe sex and family planning
- advertising of health screening, for example to measure levels of cholesterol, blood pressure and risks of chronic illnesses such as diabetes, stroke and cancer
- advertising about the importance of environmental protections, for example conserving energy, waste minimisation and recycling.

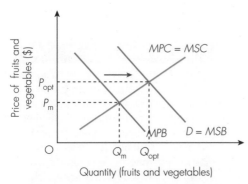

- Effective advertising shifts the demand for fresh fruits and vegetables from *MPB* to *MSB*.
- This boosts consumption from Q_m to Q_{opt}.
- Healthier people should mean less absences from work and school, with external benefits to society and the economy.

Figure 1.51 The impact of advertising on demand for fruits and vegetables

Table 1.5 The advantages and disadvantages of education and advertising to combat the problems of market failure

Advantages	Disadvantages
■ Behaviour and consumption patterns of individuals and firms change – there is a rise in the consumption of merit goods and a fall in the demand for demerit goods. For example, people learn about the dangers of smoking, so fewer people smoke. ■ Successful advertising may lead to a cultural change in behaviour, such as healthier diets, increased use of electric cars, recycling, waste reduction and the use of renewable energy.	■ Not all advertising is effective, i.e. advertising tactics may not necessarily work in changing people's behaviour. ■ It can take a long time to educate people and for the advertised message to be accepted and acted upon. ■ There is an opportunity cost of government expenditure on advertising, i.e. the money might have been spent on something else deemed to be more beneficial to society.

Direct provision of goods and services is a fourth government response to market failure, such as provision of public transportation services, education and healthcare.

The key advantage of direct government provision is that merit goods and public goods become accessible to everyone, regardless of their income or social status. However, government provision also has its limitations:

- Economic inefficiency – healthcare services (such as the UK's National Health Service) might encourage consumption beyond the socially optimum level. If people do not have to pay for healthcare, they are more likely to overuse it.
- There is an opportunity cost of government provision as the money could have been spent on something else, such as paying off government debt or possibly lowering tax rates.
- In the case of a shortage of supply due to excess demand, it can be difficult to decide who should be able to take advantage of the free government service. For example, the waiting list for a hip replacement operation in a government hospital may be very long.

Lack of public goods

Revised

The two main characteristics of public goods are:
- **Non-rivalrous** – A person's consumption of a public good does not limit the benefits available to other people. By contrast, a person's consumption of a private good reduces the amount available for other individuals.
- **Non-excludable** – Firms cannot exclude people from the benefits of consumption, even if they do not pay. Hence, private-sector firms are unlikely to supply public goods.

Examples of public goods include: national defence, the emergency services (police, fire and ambulance), streetlighting, lighthouses, weather warning systems, public firework displays, radio broadcasts, drainage systems and free downloadable apps for smartphones and tablet computers.

By contrast, private goods are rivalrous (e.g. cinema or theatre tickets), excludable (e.g. airlines, restaurants and hotels) and rejectable (e.g. rice, books or nail polish).

> Keyword definition
> **Public goods** are goods and services that exert positive externalities, with two key characteristics: non-rivalrous and non-excludable.

The lack of provision of public goods is another source of market failure. This is largely due to the **free rider problem** – where those who do not pay cannot be excluded from benefiting from the provision of public goods. Free riders are people who take advantage of the goods or services provided by the government but have not contributed to government revenue through taxation.

The existence of the free rider problem means that the market demand for a public good does not actually exist. In addition, its supply will be significantly below the social optimum level – if it exists at all.

Direct provision of public goods is generally seen favourably as these improve well-being in the economy (since the $MSB > MPB$ of production and consumption). For example, most public goods would simply not be available if it were not for government provision. However, there is always an opportunity cost involved in direct government provision. There is also potential government failure from intervening in markets, as governments do not necessarily know what is best for society.

Common mistake

Students often confuse merit goods with public goods. Whilst it is true that merit goods and public goods both have positive externalities, public goods (such as national defence and streetlighting) are highly unlikely to be provided by private-sector firms due to the free-rider problem. By contrast, merit goods are excludable (e.g. education, healthcare and staff training) so are often provided by private-sector firms.

Common mistake

Students often claim that public goods are those provided by the public sector. This is incorrect. Public goods have three key characteristics resulting in no incentives for any private-sector firm to provide such goods and services. Hence, the government must do so. However, this is a consequence, rather than a definition, of public goods.

Expert tip

Note that some goods and services are non-rivalrous and non-excludable only to some extent, for example public roads. There is rivalry to some extent (which is why we have traffic congestion) and there is some degree of excludability (as drivers need a licence). Such products are known as **quasi-public goods**.

EXAM PRACTICE

PAPER 1

22 Explain how merit goods and public goods are examples of market failure. **[10]**

Common access resources and the threat to sustainability

Revised

Common access resources are, by definition, not owned by any particular private individual so are vulnerable to overuse and abuse. Hence, they are often referred to as **open-access resources**. Examples of CARs include: forests, fishing grounds, rivers and the atmosphere.

The negative externalities linked to CARs include: deforestation, overfishing, congestion, pollution, soil erosion, destruction of natural habitats and climate change.

The lack of an effective pricing mechanism for CARs results in overuse (or abuse), depletion and degradation of the resources because consumers do not pay to use them. Clearly, this is inefficient and poses a threat to the sustainability of the common access resource.

The **tragedy of the commons** describes the consequences of the abuse and inefficient use of CARs, where the user's self-interest leads to the destruction of these resources in the long run.

CARs and the resulting tragedy of the commons present problems for economic sustainability as it becomes difficult to maintain or preserve the resources for future generations.

The use of fossil fuels (those formed by natural processes, such as coal, crude oil and natural gas) to satisfy economic activity can pose a threat to sustainability. Fossil fuels can take millions of years to generate, so economic activity depletes these scarce, non-renewable resources.

The existence of **poverty** in less economically developed countries (LEDCs) can create a threat to sustainability because the over-exploitation of land for agricultural use can lead to negative externalities, for example soil erosion.

Keyword definition

Common access resources (CARs), also known as a **common-pool resources** (CPRs), refer to communal or public property. They are rivalrous in nature, but are non-excludable. As these resources are used by the general public, they suffer from overuse and therefore lack of sustainability.

Expert tip

Common access resources differ from public goods because they are subtractable (over-used) rather than non-rivalrous (the use by an individual does not diminish the amount available for others).

Government responses to threats to sustainability

Legislation (laws and regulations) on the use of scarce resources include:
- laws to protect fish and marine life
- legislation to curb CO_2 emissions from cars and commercial vehicles.

A **carbon tax** is a per unit tax on greenhouse gas emissions. The purpose is to create incentives for firms (and households depending on the scope of the carbon tax) to reduce pollution in order to reduce their tax liability.
- Carbon taxes are set by assessing the pollution costs and the associated administrative costs of controlling the pollution.
- Establishing the correct tax level is key to the effectiveness of carbon taxes in responding to market failures. If the tax is too low firms will simply continue to pollute, whereas if the tax is too high the escalated costs negatively affect profits, employment and consumers.

Cap-and-trade schemes (CATS) are government-regulated emissions trading schemes using a market-based approach. The regulator sets a limit (the cap) on the total amount of emissions allowed in an industry and firms are issued emissions permits.
- Permits within a cap-and-trade scheme are freely traded (based on the price mechanism), allowing more efficient firms to sell their excess permits. This also creates an incentive for firms to develop clean technologies.
- Whilst CATS help to reduce carbon emissions, they can also raise a significant amount of revenue for the government.
- The European Union Emissions Trading Scheme (EUETS), set up in 2005, is one of the largest cap-and trade schemes. It aims to regulate economic activity to prevent dangerous climate change.
- Critics of CATS argue that they are anti-competitive (against smaller firms) and they can cause job losses (due to higher costs of production).

Funding for clean technologies is provided by governments to create incentives for firms to adopt a sustainable approach. It includes:
- subsidies for the adoption of renewable energy sources, such as wind, sun and biomass
- forest investment funding programmes to reduce emissions from deforestation and the negative impacts of forest degradation.

However, policy responses to the threat to sustainability are limited by:
- the global lack of ownership of common access resources
- the escalating global demand for scarce resources, including fossil fuels, due to higher levels of economic activity and globalisation
- the need for international cooperation to deal with these global issues threatening sustainability (such as deforestation, overfishing and climate change).

Asymmetric information

Asymmetric information exists when one economic agent (buyer or seller) in an economic transaction has more information than the other in a certain market – for example, life assurance policies, stock market products, pension fund schemes, second-hand cars and works of art.

The existence of asymmetric information between buyers and sellers in a market results in market failure and inefficiencies, i.e. consumer and producer surplus are not maximised.

Governments can deal with this type of market failure in a number of ways:
- legislation, for example health warnings on cigarette packets
- regulation, for example rules and regulations about advertising (e.g. the UK's Advertising Standards Authority, which requires adverts to be 'legal, decent, honest and truthful')
- provision of information, for example nutritional information on food packaging.

Abuse of monopoly power

The lack of competition means that profit-maximising monopolists are likely to supply less than the social optimum and charge higher prices, i.e. there is productive and allocative inefficiency. This results in a welfare loss for society, so the abuse of monopoly power (such as their ability to exploit consumer surplus by using price discrimination) is a type of market failure.

Examples of abuse of monopoly power include:

- monopolists charging excessively high prices
- collusion – the agreement between firms with market power to set higher prices
- predatory pricing – setting low prices, perhaps below the costs of production, to force rival firms out of the industry.

Possible government responses to the abuse of monopoly power (to prevent the market failing to reach an optimal allocation of resources) include the following:

- **Legislation** – It is illegal in most countries for monopolists to abuse their monopoly power, such as charging excessively high prices or cutting prices below production costs to force out rivals. In extreme cases, the government can break up a monopoly if it becomes too powerful.
- **Regulation** – Rules are set by governments to control the operation of firms with monopoly power. For example, European Competition Law prohibits anti-competitive acts and the abuse of monopoly power. Rail regulators check the safety record of rail operators.
- **Nationalisation** – This occurs when the government takes control of an industry previously in the private sector in order to run it in the best interest of the public. Government control of certain industries prevents the potential exploitation of monopoly power.
- **Trade liberalisation** – This refers to the reduction or removal of barriers to the exchange of goods and services between countries. This creates greater competition and thus reduces the potential for firms to exploit their monopoly power.

> **Expert tip**
>
> Do not assume that monopolists are 'bad' for the economy. Instead, consider the extent to which their behaviour is in the best interest of the general public. Abuse of monopoly power is a type of market failure, so governments intervene to protect the interest of society as a whole.

EXAM PRACTICE (HL ONLY)

PAPER 3

23 Calculate the total value of the positive externality of production from the information in the diagram. [2]

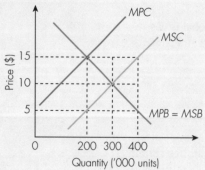

1.5 Theory of the firm and market structures *(HL only)*

Production and costs *(HL only)*

Production in the short run: the law of diminishing returns *(HL only)*

> **Keyword definitions**
>
> The **short run** is the period of time when at least one factor of production, such as land or capital, is fixed in the production process.
>
> The **long run** is the period of time when all factors of production are variable, so all costs of production are variable.
>
> **Diminishing returns** occur in the short run when a variable factor input (such as labour) is successively added to a fixed factor (such as capital), which eventually reduces the marginal and hence total output.

In the short run, capital is likely to be a fixed factor because factory buildings, machinery and capital equipment cannot be varied in the limited time period.

In the long run, the quantities of all factors of production are variable as there is sufficient time to change output based on changes in the level of demand.

- **Average product** refers to the output per unit of factor input – for example, the average product of labour calculates the value of output per worker.
- **Marginal product** measures the extra output due to a change in factor inputs. It is calculated by dividing the change in total output by the change in factor inputs.
- **Total product** is the sum of all physical output for a given amount of factor inputs, for example the total output of the country's labour force.

The relationship between *AP*, *MP* and *TP* is shown diagrammatically in Figure 1.52.

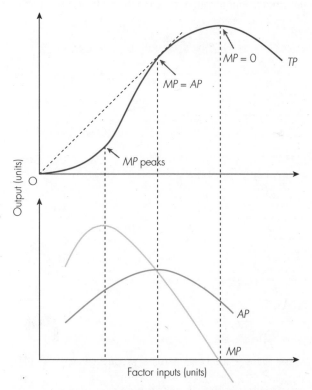

Figure 1.52 Relationship between marginal and average product costs

Average product is maximised at the output level where the average product (AP) is equal to the marginal product (MP). This is because:

- if $MP > AP$ the latter will rise
- if $MP < AP$ the latter will fall.

Hence, AP is maximised when $MP = AP$.

Total product (TP) is maximised when the marginal product is equal to zero because:

- if $MP > 0$ (i.e. positive) TP will rise
- If $MP < 0$ (i.e. negative) TP will fall.

Hence, TP must be maximised when MP = zero.

Expert tip

To understand the relationship between marginal and average product, consider the example of average and marginal homework grades. If your last (marginal) essay grade is greater than the average of all your previous essays, this would increase your overall average essay grade. However, if your last essay was below the average of your grades then the average essay grade would fall. Finally, if the marginal essay grade is the same as your average, then there is no change to your overall average essay grade.

EXAM PRACTICE *(HL ONLY)*

PAPER 3

24 Study the data below for two real estate firms selling residential property over a typical weekend. The number of units sold and the number of sales staff involved are also shown.

FIRM	TOTAL SALES ($)	UNITS SOLD	SALES STAFF
Sharma Realty	3,950,000	10	8
Mintjens Realty	3,800,000	14	10

Calculate the average product as measured by sales volume and sales value per worker for both Sharma Realty and Mintjens Realty. Comment on which firm is more productive. [4]

25 a Calculate the missing average, total and marginal product values from the information shown in the table below. [4]

LABOUR (NUMBER OF WORKERS)	AVERAGE PRODUCT	TOTAL PRODUCT	MARGINAL PRODUCT
0	–	0	
			8
1		8	
2	12		
3	15		
4		60	
5		70	
6	10		

b Using your calculations, plot a diagram on graph paper to show the average, total and marginal product curve. [4]

c Identify the units of labour that maximise total product. [1]

Cost of production: economic costs *(HL only)*

Revised ☐

Economic costs are the explicit and implicit costs of all resources used by a firm in the production process.

Explicit costs are the identifiable and therefore accountable costs related to the output of a product. Examples include wages, raw material costs, utility bills and rent.

Implicit costs are the opportunity costs of the output, i.e. the income from the best alternative that is foregone.

For example, a student might give up the opportunity to work in a job that pays $25,000 per year and choose to study at university, which costs her $15,000 a year. The economic cost to the student is therefore $15,000 + $25,000 = $40,000 per year.

Costs of production in the short run *(HL only)*

Revised ☐

The short run (when there is at least one factor input fixed in supply) will vary between industries – for example, the short run for aircraft manufacturers is longer than that for bakers.

Total fixed costs are production costs that do not change with the level of output, for example rent, management salaries and loan interest repayments.

Total variable costs are production costs incurred directly from the output of a particular good or service – for example, variable costs for Emirates Airlines include fuel and in-flight meals.

Total costs are the aggregate amount of production costs spent on the output of a given good or service. They are calculated using the formula:

$$TC = TFC + TVC$$

Average costs are the unit costs of production. These are is calculated by dividing the total costs of production (TC) by the output level (Q):

$$AC = \frac{TC}{Q}$$

Marginal costs are the costs of producing an extra unit of output. They are calculated by dividing the change in total costs by the change in the level of output:

$$MC = \frac{\Delta TC}{\Delta Q}$$

> **Keyword definition**
> **Fixed costs**, such as insurance premiums and advertising costs, do not change with the level of output. By contrast, **variable costs** (such as labour costs and raw material costs) continually rise with greater levels of output.

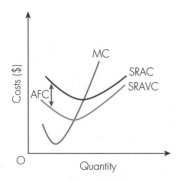

- The downward-sloping section of the *SRAC* curve is caused by *MC* being lower than *AC*.
- *AC* will reach its minimum point when *MC = AC*, i.e. at the minimum point on the *SRAC* curve.
- When *MC > AC*, the *SRAC* curve will begin to rise due to diminishing marginal returns.
- Notice that this relationship is the same for the average product and marginal product.

Figure 1.53 The relationship between *AC* and *MC*

In the short run, average fixed costs (AFC) will continually fall with increased levels of output because the fixed costs are spread over an increasingly larger level of output. For example:

- Assume fixed costs = $5000 and unit variable costs = $10
- At 1000 units of output, AFC = (5000/1000) + 10 = $15.0
- At 2000 units of output, AFC = (5000/2000) + 10 = $12.5

> **Common mistake**
> Students often state that fixed costs are those that do not change. This is incorrect, as fixed costs can and do change – for example, rents and salaries can change over time. The key is that fixed costs are the same, irrespective of the level of output.

This relationship is shown by the short run average variable cost (SRAVC) curve. The vertical distance between *SRAC* and *SRAVC* is the *AFC* at each output level. Notice that this is greater at a lower level of output than at larger levels of output.

EXAM PRACTICE *(HL ONLY)*

PAPER 3

26 Calculate the following costs from the data below:

a	fixed costs of production	[2]
b	average fixed costs at 10 units and 15 units of output	[3]
c	average variable costs at 10 units and 15 units of output	[3]
d	average costs at 10 units and 15 units of output	[3]
e	the marginal cost of production	[2]

OUTPUT	VARIABLE COST ($)	TOTAL COSTS ($)
10	2000	4545
15	2850	5395

The relationship between the product curves and the cost curves are shown in Figure 1.54.

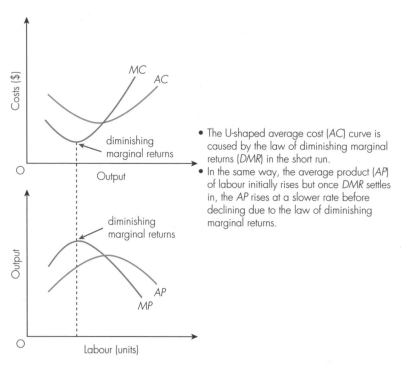

- The U-shaped average cost (*AC*) curve is caused by the law of diminishing marginal returns (*DMR*) in the short run.
- In the same way, the average product (*AP*) of labour initially rises but once *DMR* settles in, the *AP* rises at a slower rate before declining due to the law of diminishing marginal returns.

Figure 1.54 The relationship between marginal and average product and costs

Production in the long run: returns to scale (HL only)

Increasing returns to scale occur when factor inputs are increased by a certain amount, leading to output increasing by proportionately more. Thus, average costs of production fall.

Decreasing returns to scale occur when factor inputs are increased by a certain amount, leading to output increasing by proportionately less. Thus, average costs of production rise.

Constant returns to scale occur when factor inputs are increased by a certain amount, leading to output increasing by the same proportion. Thus, average costs remain constant.

Costs of production in the long run *(HL only)*

The long run average cost (LRAC) curve is 'U'-shaped due to economies and diseconomies of scale (see Figure 1.55). The **minimum efficient scale** occurs when all economies of scale have been exploited, shown by the bottom of the LRAC curve.

The LRAC curve encompasses all short run average cost (SRAC) curves.

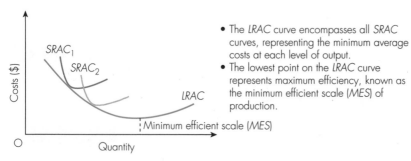

- The LRAC curve encompasses all SRAC curves, representing the minimum average costs at each level of output.
- The lowest point on the LRAC curve represents maximum efficiency, known as the minimum efficient scale (MES) of production.

Figure 1.55 The long run average cost (LRAC) curve

Internal economies of scale are generated and enjoyed within the firm that operates on a large scale. By contrast, external economies of scale occur within the industry, thus benefiting all firms. Factors that give rise to internal economies of scale include the following:

- Specialisation – Specialised labour (such as divorce or criminal lawyers, economics professors and aircraft pilots) is highly productive in the output of goods and services, thus helping to reduce the average costs of production.
- Efficiency – Specialised machinery, equipment and tools can be used to their full potential to raise output (such as in car manufacturing or the production of ball bearings), again helping to reduce the average costs of production.
- Marketing – Effective advertising and branding boosts sales, so firms are able to produce on a large scale. For example, Nike and McDonald's are able to market their brands to a global audience, thus reducing their marketing costs per unit of sales.
- Indivisibilities – Large plants can only work effectively if large volumes of output are generated, for example mass-produced cars, jam, soft drinks or bottled water. By contrast, product differentiation, such as bespoke wedding dresses, leads to higher unit costs.

External economies of scale arise from having specialised back-up services available in a particular region where firms are located. For example, Silicon Valley in California, USA is home to many of the best-known technology companies.

Diseconomies of scale occur when a firm becomes too large to manage effectively, causing its unit costs to increase – for example, a firm increases its factor inputs by 50% but the subsequent output only increases by 20%. Diseconomies occur at all output levels beyond the MES point.

Internal diseconomies of scale are caused by problems of coordination, control and communication within a firm. For example, as firms get larger, managers find it more difficult to coordinate, control and communicate with a larger workforce, resulting in higher unit costs.

Causes of **external diseconomies of scale** (those that affect all firms in an industry) include:

- traffic congestion causing costs to increase
- higher rent costs due to the high demand for firms locating in a certain area
- labour shortages in a particular area, thus leading to increased labour costs.

Common mistake

Students often state that costs of production will fall as a firm increases the scale of its operations. This is not quite correct – clearly it is cheaper to produce 1000 cans of Coca-Cola than it is to produce 500,000 cans. However, it is cheaper to produce *each* can on a larger scale, i.e. economies of scale reduce the *average* costs of production.

Expert tip

Whereas internal economies of scale involve a movement down the LRAC curve, external economies of scale will involve a downward shift of the whole LRAC curve. Likewise, internal diseconomies are shown by a movement up along the LRAC curve, whilst external diseconomies shift the whole LRAC curve upwards.

EXAM PRACTICE *(HL ONLY)*

PAPER 3

27 Crispian's Candies has monthly fixed costs of $4800 and average variable costs of $1.5. Demand for its candies is 4000 units each month. The average unit price is $4.

  a Calculate the average costs for Crispian's Candies each month. **[2]**

  b Calculate the units of output required for Crispian's Candies to break even. **[2]**

  c Calculate the profit made by Crispian's Candies each month. **[2]**

> **Expert tip**
>
> Students need to demonstrate that they clearly understand the distinction between internal economies of scale (which relate to a specific firm) and external economies of scale (which relate to the whole industry).

Revenues *(HL only)*

Revised ☐

Total revenue, average revenue and marginal revenue *(HL only)*

Revised ☐

Total revenue is the overall amount of money received by a firm from selling its entire output. For example, Nike and Adidas receive most of their revenues from the sale of sports apparel and sports equipment. It is calculated using the following formula, where P = price and Q = quantity sold:

$$TR = P \times Q$$

Average revenue refers to typical price received from the sale of a good or service. It is calculated using the formula:

$$AR = \frac{TR}{Q}$$

Average revenue (AR) is mathematically the same as the price per unit (P). This is because:

$$AR = \frac{TR}{Q}$$

and

$$TR = P \times Q$$

so

$$P = \frac{TR}{Q}$$

Hence

$$AR \equiv P$$

For example, if a cinema earns $60,000 from the sale of tickets to 7500 customers, the average revenue (or average price) would be $60,000/7500 = $8 per ticket.

Marginal revenue is the extra revenue received from the sale of an extra unit of output. It is calculated by dividing the change in total revenue by the change in the level of output:

$$MC = \frac{\Delta TR}{\Delta Q}$$

> **Keyword definition**
> **Revenue** is the money received from the sale of a firm's output.

Mathematically, the marginal revenue (MR) curve intersects the x-axis at the mid-point of a downward sloping demand (average revenue) curve, as in Figure 1.56.

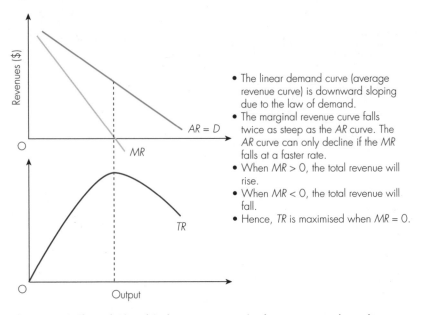

- The linear demand curve (average revenue curve) is downward sloping due to the law of demand.
- The marginal revenue curve falls twice as steep as the *AR* curve. The *AR* curve can only decline if the *MR* falls at a faster rate.
- When $MR > 0$, the total revenue will rise.
- When $MR < 0$, the total revenue will fall.
- Hence, *TR* is maximised when $MR = 0$.

Figure 1.56 The relationship between marginal, average and total revenue

EXAM PRACTICE *(HL ONLY)*

PAPER 3

28 a Use the diagram below to calculate the total revenue at $16. **[2]**

  b Identify the average revenue when 120 units are sold. **[1]**

  c Outline what the difference between area A and area B shows. **[2]**

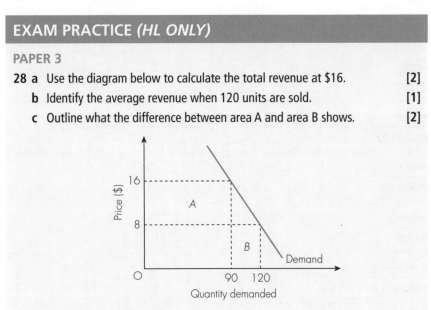

> **Common mistake**
>
> Students often incorrectly use the terms 'cost' and 'price' interchangeably. Remember, costs (of production) are paid for by firms in the production process, whereas price is paid by the customer to purchase a good or service.

Profit *(HL only)*

Revised ☐

Economic profit and normal profit *(HL only)*

Revised ☐

Normal profit is the minimum revenue needed to keep a firm in business. Hence, it is also referred to as **zero economic profit** and occurs at the point where a firm breaks even by covering both economic and implicit costs from its sales revenue.

Break even means a firm does not make a profit or a loss. This occurs when price is equal to average cost, or total revenue equals total costs, i.e.:

$$P = AC \text{ or } TC = TR$$

Economic profit occurs when total revenue exceeds total economic costs. It is profit that is over and above normal profit. A firm might choose to continue to operate even if it earns zero economic profit because total revenue covers all

> **Keyword definition**
> **Economic profit (abnormal profit)** exists when total revenue exceeds the economic costs of a transaction, thus creating incentives for firms to produce.

economic costs (both implicit plus explicit costs), so it still earns normal profit, i.e. the minimum amount required to keep factors of production in their current use.

Negative economic profit occurs when a firm makes a loss, i.e. its total cost of production exceeds its total revenue.

EXAM PRACTICE *(HL ONLY)*

PAPER 3

29 The table below refers to the costs and revenues of Tandy Toys Ltd when operating at 5000 units of output per month.

ITEM	COST/REVENUE ($)
Price	$20
Raw materials per unit	$8
Rent	$7000
Salaries	$8000

    a Calculate the total cost of producing 5000 units. [2]

    b Calculate the profit made by Tandy Toys Ltd if all its output is sold. [2]

Table 1.6 Costs and revenues formulae table

Type of cost or revenue	Formula	Annotation
Average cost	$\dfrac{\text{total costs}}{\text{quantity produced}}$	$AC = \dfrac{TC}{Q}$
Average fixed cost	$\dfrac{\text{total fixed cost}}{\text{quantity produced}}$	$AFC = \dfrac{TFC}{Q}$
Average variable cost	$\dfrac{\text{total variable cost}}{\text{quantity produced}}$	$AVC = \dfrac{TVC}{Q}$
Average revenue (or price)	$\dfrac{\text{total revenue}}{\text{quantity traded}}$	$AR = \dfrac{TR}{Q}$
Marginal cost	$\dfrac{\text{change in total costs}}{\text{change in output level}}$	$MC = \dfrac{\Delta TC}{\Delta Q}$
Marginal revenue	$\dfrac{\text{change in total revenue}}{\text{change in output level}}$	$MR = \dfrac{\Delta TR}{\Delta Q}$
Total cost	total fixed costs + total variable costs	$TC = TFC + TVC$
Total revenue	unit price × quantity traded	$TR = P \times Q$

Goals of firms *(HL only)*

Revised ▢

Profit maximisation *(HL only)*

Revised ▢

It is generally assumed that firms are profit maximisers, seeking to produce at the level of output that generates the highest level of profits. This occurs at the level of output where marginal cost equals marginal revenue (i.e. MC = MR):

■ If MR > MC, firms increase their output because profits will rise.

- If MC > MR, firms reduce their output as the marginal cost outweighs the marginal revenue.
- Hence, profits are maximised when MC = MR.

Alternative goals of firms *(HL only)*

Revised

Table 1.7 Alternative goals of firms

Revenue maximisation	Some firms might choose not to profit maximise (so earn less profits) but opt to sell more, thus raising the popularity of the product to keep out other firms from entering the industry.
Growth maximisation	Many firms seek to expand their operations. Firms such as Coca-Cola, Subway and McDonald's have expanded throughout the world.
Satisficing	This goal occurs when firms aim for a satisfactory or adequate level of profit, rather than the maximum profit. This is because profit maximisation might require significant expenditure of time, effort and financial resources.
Corporate social responsibility (CSR)	Firms are increasingly involved in CSR, i.e. they consider the impact of business activity on the environment and on social welfare. Examples include business ethics (such as avoiding unethical advertising), sustainable operations (such as avoiding excessive packaging) and measures to boost the welfare of workers (such as a pleasant working environment and decent wages for all staff).

Perfect competition *(HL only)*

Revised

Assumptions of the model *(HL only)*

Revised

Assumed characteristics of perfect competition include the following:
- A very large number of buyers and sellers exist in the market.
- All firms in the industry sell a **homogeneous product,** i.e. products are identical.
- Firms are **price takers** – no individual firm is large enough to have the market power to influence the equilibrium output or the price.
- Extremely low barriers to entry – there is freedom of entry into and exit from the perfectly competitive industry.
- Perfect information – buyers and sellers have **perfect knowledge** of prices.
- There is perfect factor mobility, i.e. there are no barriers to the use of land, labour, capital and enterprise, which are all adjusted according to changing market conditions.

Expert tip

Where appropriate, try to use real-world examples in your written answers. For perfect competition, a real-world example could be markets that sell fresh fruit and vegetables, where the demand is highly price elastic because firms sell homogeneous products (carrots or oranges from one vendor are no different from those sold by other firms in the market). No individual firm is large enough to influence market supply or market price, i.e. firms are price takers. It is also relatively easy for firms to enter or leave the market.

Revenue curves *(HL only)*

Revised

The demand curve for an individual firm in perfect competition is perfectly price elastic (see Figure 1.57). A price above the market price means no demand, due to perfect substitutes, yet there is no advantage in reducing price as firms can sell their entire output at the higher price.

As the MR curve for an individual firm in perfect competition is horizontal, the AR curve is also constant, i.e. it sells all output at the same market price. Mathematically, since $P \equiv AR$ and AR is constant, then:

$$MR = AR$$

under perfect competition.

The perfectly competitive firm's average revenue curve ($AR = MR = D$) is determined by the market forces of demand and supply (see Figure 1.57).

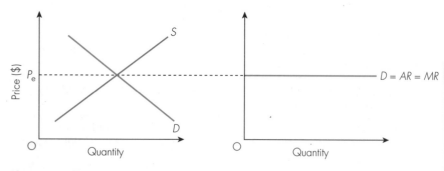

Figure 1.57 Revenue curves under perfect competition

Expert tip

As there is perfect knowledge, a firm trying to cut price would simply result in others following, so there is no benefit in doing so. Besides, firms are assumed to be price takers, so accept the market price.

Profit maximisation in the short run *(HL only)*

Revised

In the short run, it is possible for a perfectly competitive firm to make economic profit (see Figure 1.58), negative economic profit (see Figure 1.59) or normal profit (see Figure 1.60).

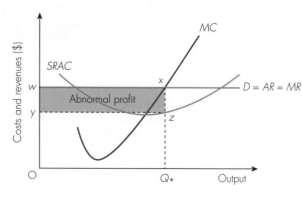

Figure 1.58 Short-run economic profit

The profit maximising firm produces Q_* output, where $MC = MR$ (point x). As price (w) is greater than the short run average cost (z), the firm makes abnormal profits as shown by the shaded area w, x, z, y.

Common mistake

When drawing diagrams for theory of the firm and market structures, make sure you do not label the *y-axis* as 'Price'. The diagrams contain both cost and revenue curves, so the correct label is 'Costs and revenues ($)' instead.

Expert tip

To gain top marks, you must show evidence of critical thinking. This means you should consider the advantages and disadvantages of operating in competitive markets – for example, healthy competition can ensure consumers get the right products at the right price in an efficient way. However, there are limitations to the model – few industries, if any, actually fit the model in the real world. Branding means that most products are heterogeneous in reality and it is not possible for consumers to have perfect information about all prices for all products.

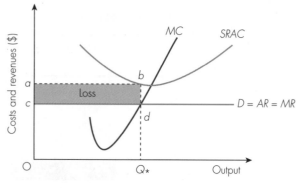

Figure 1.59 Short-run negative economic profit

The profit maximising firm produces where $MC = MR$, i.e. at Q_*. As price (c) is less than the average cost (b), the firm makes a loss in the short run, shown by the shaded area a, b, d, c.

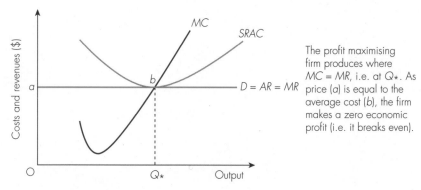

Figure 1.60 Short-run zero economic profit

Profit maximisation in the long run *(HL only)*

Revised ▢

In the long run, perfectly competitive firms can only earn normal profits (zero economic profit), as shown in Figure 1.60. Any losses in the industry (see Figure 1.59) lead to some firms exiting, so total supply falls, leading to a higher market price until the industry returns to normal profit.

Any abnormal profits in the industry will attract more firms to enter (see Figure 1.61) due to the absence of barriers to entry. This raises market supply (from S_1 to S_2) and reduces the price (from P_1 to P_2) until equilibrium is restored.

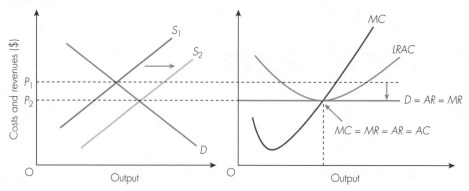

Figure 1.61 Long-run equilibrium competition

Hence, in the long run, perfectly competitive firms can only make normal profits, i.e. AR = AC. As these firms are also profit maximisers, they produce at the output level where MC = MR. This means the following long-run condition must hold in perfectly competitive markets:

$$MR = MC = AR = AC$$

Shut-down price and break-even price *(HL only)*

Revised ▢

An individual firm in perfect competition will not necessarily shut down if it makes a loss in the short run. However, it has fixed costs irrespective of its level of output. Therefore, by continuing to operate, even at a loss in the short run, any revenue it can earn over and above its variable costs contributes towards paying its fixed costs.

The shut-down price for profit-maximising firms in perfect competition occurs at the point where MC = MR = AVC. The perfectly competitive firm's short-run supply curve will therefore be the part of the MC curve above its AVC curve (shown by the red line in Figure 1.62).

In the long run, the perfectly competitive firm will not produce unless it can cover all its costs. Hence, its supply curve is the MC curve above the SRAC curve (the red line in Figure 1.63).

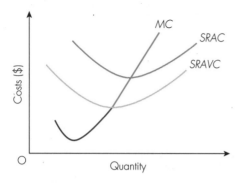

Figure 1.62 The short-run shut-down price

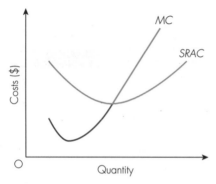

Figure 1.63 The long-run shut-down price

EXAM PRACTICE *(HL ONLY)*

PAPER 3

30 Use the information below to calculate:
   a the break-even price
   b the shut-down price. **[4]**

Monthly production costs for Adrian's Awning Company

COMPONENTS AND MATERIALS	$35,500
WAGES	$45,000
RENT	$30,000
OUTPUT (UNITS)	500

Perfect competition and efficiency *(HL only)*

Revised

Allocative efficiency occurs when firms produce at the optimal level of output from society's point of view, i.e. where the marginal social costs (MSC) of production equal the marginal social benefits (MSB) of consumption. It is achieved when firms charge a price equal to the marginal cost of production, i.e. $P = MC$ (or when $MSB = MSC$), i.e. no one can be made better off without making someone else worse off.

Productive efficiency occurs at the output level where average costs are minimised, i.e. where $MC = AC$. Hence, there is no wastage or unemployment of scarce resources. It requires **technical efficiency** – when the maximum output is produced with the minimum amount of factor inputs, i.e. the least-cost method of output.

On a macroeconomic scale, productive efficiency occurs when the economy operates on its production possibility curve, i.e. it is not possible to produce more goods and services for one stakeholder group without producing less for another stakeholder group.

A key advantage of perfect competition is **economic efficiency**, because firms are:

- allocatively efficient (charging a price that is equal to marginal cost) in both the short run and the long run
- productively efficient (they operate at the lowest point on the average cost curve) in the long run, although not necessarily in the short run (as they can temporarily earn abnormal profit).

> **Expert tip**
>
> An economy can be productively efficient but allocatively inefficient at the same time, because the latter is concerned with the optimal distribution of scarce resources. For example, an economy might devote a significant amount of resources to efficiently supply national defence (resulting in a socially undesirable allocation of resources) rather than to supply public education and healthcare services (which are more socially desirable).

Monopoly *(HL only)*

Revised ☐

Assumptions of the model *(HL only)*

Revised ☐

A pure monopoly exists if only one firm supplies the whole market. In the USA, this would include the United States Postal Service (the only service provider of first class postage) and the Federal Reserve (the sole supplier of banknotes and coins).

In reality, a monopoly exists in a market dominated by one firm with significant market power, e.g. Coca-Cola (carbonated soft drinks), YKK (zip fasteners), Tetra Pak (packaging) and Mabuchi (which makes 90% of the micro-motors used to adjust rear-view mirrors in cars).

The monopolist has significant market power as it controls enough of the market supply to be able charge higher prices. Hence, it is a **price maker** (or price setter). Yet due to the absence of competition, the monopolist can supply at a lower level of output. Therefore, monopoly is less efficient than perfect competition due to the combination of higher prices and lower output than would be the case under perfect competition.

A monopolist is able to protect its prestigious position as customers and rivals have **imperfect knowledge**. This includes the monopolist's ability to protect its trade secrets.

Monopolists can earn abnormal profit in the long run as there are extremely high **barriers to entry** that prevent other firms from setting up in the industry, i.e. there are no close substitutes.

> **Keyword definition**
>
> A **monopoly** is a market structure where there is a single supplier of a particular good or service, thus having the power to influence the market supply and price.

> **Expert tip**
>
> It is incorrect to claim that monopolists can charge 'whatever' price they want because they are the single supplier of a good or service. Whilst monopolists have the ability to control market supply, they cannot control the level of market demand. Customers will switch to, or seek, alternatives if prices rise too high. Hence, monopolists must lower prices if they want to sell more.

Barriers to entry *(HL only)*

Revised ☐

A monopolist can only remain so if in the long run there are extremely high barriers to entry. These are obstacles that prevent other firms from effectively entering the market. Hence, the nature and scale of barriers to entry permit the monopolist to earn economic profit (abnormal profit).

Barriers to entry can be classed as either artificial barriers or natural barriers. Artificial barriers are deliberately set up by monopolists to prevent competition, whereas natural barriers are obstacles that simply exist characteristically in the industry.

Examples of **artificial barriers to entry** include the following:

- Advertising and branding, if effective, can act as significant entry barriers due to the established brand loyalty of customers – for example, imagine trying to compete against Coca-Cola!
- The existence of intellectual property rights, such as trademarks, copyright and patents, helps to establish market power and market dominance.
- Large advertising budgets of existing firms can act as a deterrent to new entrants.
- Predatory pricing involves the lowering of prices to prevent new firms entering the market or to force weaker rivals out of the industry.

> **Keyword definition**
>
> **Barriers to entry** are the obstacles that prevent other firms from effectively entering a particular market, for example extremely high set-up costs or legal barriers.

- Loyalty schemes, such as those used by credit card companies (e.g. American Express and Visa), help to establish customer loyalty.
- Switching costs mean that customers find it uneconomical to change between brands or products. For example, Apple uses a different operating system and power chargers from its rivals.

Examples of **natural barriers to entry** include the following:
- High set-up costs discourage firms from entering some industries, for example airline manufacturing and pharmaceuticals.
- Sunk costs are those that cannot be recovered if a firm is unsuccessful and exits the industry, so high sunk costs act as an entry barrier.
- High research and development (R&D) costs in an industry act as a signal to potential entrants that they need large financial reserves to compete.
- Huge economies of scale earned by the existing monopolist can deter new entrants.
- Ownership and control of essential resources for a certain industry create a considerable barrier to entry – for example, favourable access to raw materials such as oil.
- Legal constraints exist in some industries to prevent wasteful competition – for example, postal services, railroad networks and electricity power generation.

Revenue curves and profit and revenue maximisation *(HL only)*

Revised

The AR curve for a monopolist is the market demand curve, as it is assumed there is a single supplier, i.e. the firm is the industry. Hence, the $AR = D$ curve is downward sloping because the monopolist must reduce price in order to sell more output.

The gradient of the linear MR curve is twice that of the linear AR curve, because for the AR to fall continually, the MR must fall at a faster rate.

The **revenue-maximising monopolist** will supply at the output level where $MR = 0$, at Q_{rm} and charge a price of P_{rm} (see Figure 1.64). The **profit-maximising monopolist** will supply at the output level where $MC = MR$, i.e. at Q_{pm} and charge a price of P_{pm}, whilst average costs are AC_1. The abnormal profit earned is therefore shown by the red shaded area.

In the short run, a monopolist might choose to deliberately operate at a loss, shown by the shaded green area (see Figure 1.65) in order to deter new entrants or to force out a rival firm from the industry. In reality, such actions are likely to be deemed illegal in most countries.

Mathematically, $MR = 0$ at the mid-point of the AR curve for the monopolist. To the left of the mid-point of the AR curve, demand is relatively price elastic. The monopolist will never choose to operate on the inelastic half of its AR curve because MR will be negative, i.e. both revenue and profit cannot be maximised if MR is negative.

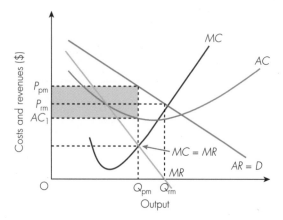

Figure 1.64 Monopoly (long-run abnormal profit position)

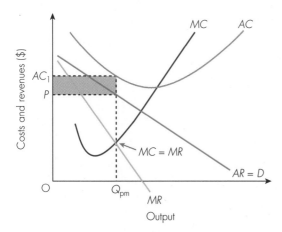

Figure 1.65 Monopoly (short-run loss-making position)

EXAM PRACTICE *(HL ONLY)*

PAPER 3

31 With reference to the diagram below, identify the following:

    a The price charged by the profit-maximising monopolist.   **[1]**

    b The total costs for the profit-maximising monopolist.   **[1]**

    c The amount of abnormal profit earned by the profit-maximising monopolist.   **[1]**

    d The output level of the revenue-maximising monopolist.   **[1]**

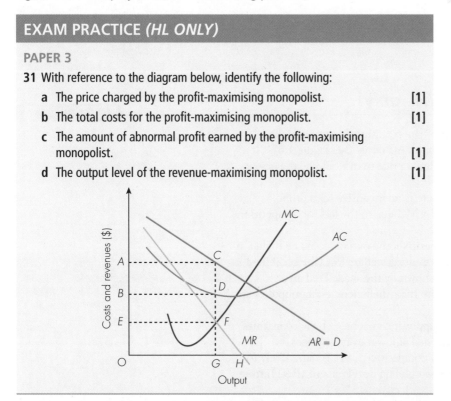

EXAM PRACTICE

PAPER 1

32 Explain why a monopolist is able to earn abnormal profits in the long run.   **[10]**

Natural monopoly *(HL only)*

Revised ☐

A **natural monopoly** exists when the industry can only sustain one supplier, to avoid wasteful competition and to maximise economies of scale by having a single provider. Natural monopolies exist in industries that have extremely high fixed costs and sunk costs required to ensure supply. Hence, these costs can deter entrants to the industry.

It is more economical to have a single supplier of postal services, gas pipes, telephone cables, electricity cables and railway tracks since a monopolist could provide these with substantial cost savings compared with many smaller firms in direct competition. Therefore, trying to increase competition in such industries actually creates a potential loss of efficiency as new entrants would mean a wasteful duplication of scarce resources.

However, as there is the potential for natural monopolists to exploit their power, governments tend to nationalise these industries or regulate them heavily to protect the general public.

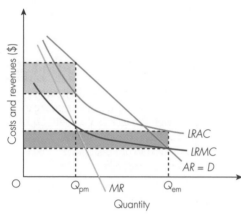

- The unregulated profit-maximising monopolist will supply at Q_{pm} where $MC = MR$, thus earning abnormal profit (shown by the red area).
- A single supplier can achieve huge cost savings by operating at a larger scale along its *LRAC* curve.
- The natural monopolist can supply more at Q_{em} where $P = MC$, but will make a loss (shown by the green area). This loss could be subsidised by the government.

Figure 1.66 Natural monopoly

Monopoly and efficiency (HL only)

Revised ☐

Productive inefficiency occurs when a profit-maximising monopoly lacks incentives to operate at the lowest point of its AC curve (see Figure 1.67). It can limit supply, enabling it to charge a higher price than would be the case in competitive markets.

Allocative inefficiency occurs when there is no incentive for a profit-maximising monopolist to supply where $P = MC$ due to the lack of competition. Instead, for the monopolist, $P > MC$.

Arguably, if the market was more competitive, the output would be higher at Q_{pc} and price would be lower at P_{pc}. The resulting welfare loss (the combined loss of consumer and producer surplus) is shown by the shaded red area. Nevertheless, there are reasons why, despite their inefficiencies, monopolies are desirable:

- As a monopolist controls the market supply, it can achieve huge economies of scale, i.e. it can sell larger quantities *and* at lower average prices.
- A monopolist, rather than small highly competitive firms, is more likely to have the financial ability to finance research and development (R&D) from its economic profits.
- R&D helps to create new innovations (ideas, products and processes), thus improving the productive capacity and international competitiveness of the economy.

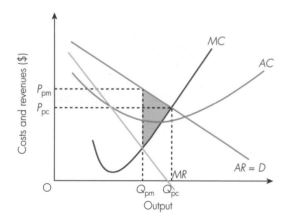

Figure 1.67 Monopoly and efficiency

Policies to regulate monopoly power *(HL only)*

Revised ▢

If monopolies exploit their market power and act against the public interest (perhaps by deliberately charging unreasonably high prices, restricting competition, or by engaging in price fixing) then the government can intervene to break up their monopoly powers. For instance, a merger between the two largest firms in an industry can be prohibited if it is believed that the resulting monopolist's market dominance will be against the public's interest.

In 2013, Visa and Mastercard were fined a record $7.25 billion for colluding to fix their fees to commercial customers (retailers who pay to process credit card payments).

Advantages and disadvantages of monopoly compared with perfect competition *(HL only)*

Revised ▢

Table 1.8 Advantages and disadvantages of monopolies

Advantages	Disadvantages
■ As monopolists control industry supply, they operate on a very large scale, thus benefiting from huge economies of scale, i.e. they can actually supply more output and at lower prices. ■ Monopolists have the financial resources to invest in innovation. R&D expenditure can help to generate new ideas, new products and production processes. ■ Therefore, monopoly power can be an important source of international competitiveness against foreign competitors. ■ Some monopolies can eliminate wasteful competition. For example, it makes more economic sense to have one supplier of postal services rather than allowing private-sector firms to compete to provide such services since profit-seeking firms could be reluctant to service remote areas.	■ Monopolies can be inefficient in terms of resource allocation. In pursuit of profit maximisation, they can restrict output and/or charge a higher price, thus creating a welfare loss. ■ High barriers to entry prevent new firms from entering the market. This limits the degree of competition and ensures that monopolists can continue to charge relatively high prices. ■ Imperfect knowledge about prices and products can make it difficult for consumers to make rational choices – for example, the confusing pricing policies used by mobile phone service providers mean that customers find it troublesome to switch between suppliers. ■ Monopolists may have less incentive to innovate than firms in competitive markets. The lack of competitive pressure can mean that monopolists become complacent.

Monopolistic competition *(HL only)*

Revised ▢

The assumed characteristics of monopolistic competition are:
■ a large number of relatively small firms, each with insignificant market power and supplying differentiated products
■ absence of barriers to entry and exit from the industry.

Examples include clothing firms (such as H&M, Zara and Uniqlo), hairdressers, florists and restaurants.

Product differentiation gives monopolistically competitive firms a small degree of market power, i.e. such firms face a negatively sloping demand curve for their product.

In the short run, these firms can earn abnormal profit. However, the lack of entry barriers will attract new firms to the industry, thus reducing the market price and profits. Equally, the firms can also make a loss (see Figure 1.68). At the profit-maximising (or the loss-minimising) level of output, $AC > AR$, so a loss is made, shown by the shaded area.

In the long run, abnormal profits attract new entrants, whereas losses cause lower market supply, due to the absence of barriers to exit. Hence, only normal profit is made in the long run (see Figure 1.69).

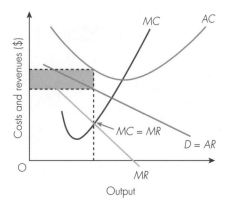

Figure 1.68 Monopolistic competition (short-run loss minimisation position)

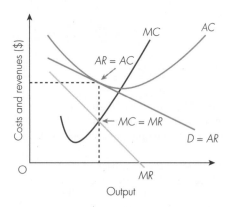

Figure 1.69 Monopolistic competition (long-run normal profit position)

EXAM PRACTICE

PAPER 1

33 Explain why product differentiation leads to a negatively sloped demand curve in monopolistically competitive markets. **[10]**

Non-price competition *(HL only)*

Revised ▢

Since monopolistically competitive firms produce differentiated products, non-price competition is a key feature in such industries. **Price competition** is the use of pricing strategies to compete. Examples include:

- going-rate pricing – the pricing decision is based on the average price charged by firms in the industry
- loss-leader pricing – setting the price of a product below its cost price to entice customers, who might also buy other, often related, products sold by the firm
- penetration pricing – used by new entrants that set a low introductory price to establish some market share
- promotional pricing – charging a low price to attract customers to raise brand awareness and to develop customer loyalty
- psychological pricing – for example, $9.99 can seem much cheaper than $10 to some customers.

Non-price competition refers to all other forms of competition. Examples include the following:

- Advertising is used extensively to differentiate between the products of firms. Branding is used in an attempt to gain customer loyalty.
- Packaging can be used to distinguish products from one another and to act as a distinctive selling point, for example fruit juices, potato chips (crisps) and specialised boxes for jewellery.

- Product development, such as special features and limited editions of a product, or new innovative products being released to the market.
- Quality of service (the level of customer service) at hairdressers, restaurants and other retailers can give firms a competitive advantage over their rivals.
- Similarly, after-sales care can also create competitive advantages for monopolistically competitive firms, for example guarantees (warranties), technical support and delivery service.

Monopolistic competition and efficiency *(HL only)*

Revised

Like monopolists, monopolistically competitive firms are neither allocatively efficient nor productively efficient in both the short run and long run. Inefficiencies can occur in monopolistically competitive markets due to the vast degree of choice that consumers have.

Monopolistically competitive firms do not operate at the lowest point on their AC curve (see Figure 1.69) because there are limited opportunities to exploit economies of scale.

Like a monopolist, the monopolistically competitive firm is a price maker (although to a lesser extent), so its price exceeds marginal cost ($P > MC$), as seen in Figure 1.69.

Monopolistic competition compared with perfect competition and monopoly *(HL only)*

Revised

Like perfect competition, there are many small producers in monopolistic competition.

Product differentiation exists under monopolistic competition but not necessarily under monopoly (despite being the only supplier, monopolists can supply undifferentiated products). Due to this product differentiation, variety (choice) is greater in monopolistic competition than in perfect competition where firms only supply homogeneous products.

Monopolistically competitive firms can enjoy some economies of scale although these are limited due to the size of the firm and the differentiated products they supply.

Firms in perfect competition are productively and allocatively efficient in the long run, whereas those in monopolistic competition are not. Both monopolistic competition and monopoly are inefficient market structures in both the short and long run, although monopolistically competitive firms have much less market power. Whilst competition is generally beneficial, natural monopolists eliminate wasteful competition.

Monopolistically competitive firms have a small degree of monopoly power. Therefore, the demand curve of a monopolistically competitive firm is less price elastic than that of a perfectly competitive firm.

There is an absence of barriers to entry and exit under both perfect competition and monopolistic competition. Only monopolists earn abnormal profits in the long run due to the nature of barriers of entry.

Oligopoly *(HL only)*

Revised

Assumptions of the model *(HL only)*

Revised

The assumed characteristics of an oligopoly are as follows:
- The industry is dominated by a small number of large firms – for example, Samsung and Apple dominate the smartphone industry.
- Mutual interdependence – firms in oligopolistic markets consider the actions and reactions of their competitors when determining their price and non-price strategies.

> **Keyword definition**
> An **oligopoly** is a market structure in which a few large suppliers, each with a high degree of market share, dominate the industry.

- Firms can produce differentiated products (e.g. breakfast cereal, book publishing and music entertainment) or homogeneous products (e.g. oil, steel and aluminium).
- Barriers to entry – there are considerable entry barriers to the industry, including huge set-up costs and sunk costs.

Examples of oligopolistic industries include carbonated soft drinks, aircraft manufacturers, petroleum, sportswear and laptop manufacturers.

Due to the market power that oligopolistic firms have, there is asymmetric information in the industry, for example trade secrets. Oligopolistic firms are often faced with the dilemma of whether to collude or to compete.

Concentration ratio

A three-firm concentration ratio measures the combined market share of the three largest firms in an industry – for example, the UK supermarket industry is dominated by Tesco, Sainsbury's and Morrisons with a three-firm concentration ratio of over 65%.

The higher the concentration ratio for an industry, the more concentrated (oligopolistic) the market tends to be.

> **Keyword definition**
> **Concentration ratio** measures the degree of market power in an industry by adding the combined market shares of the largest few firms.

> **Expert tip**
>
> A clearer measure of market concentration is the **Herfindahl Index**, which gives greater weighting to the market power of larger firms simply by squaring the value of each market share. Assume that the three-firm concentration ratios for Industry A and Industry B are both 65%:
>
> - Industry A: Firm 1 = 30%, Firm 2 = 20% and Firm C = 15% market share
> - Industry B: Firm 1 = 25%, Firm 2 = 20% and Firm C = 20% market share
>
> The Herfindahl Index for Industry A = $30^2 + 20^2 + 15^2 = 1525$
> The Herfindahl Index for Industry B = $25^2 + 20^2 + 20^2 = 1425$
> Industry A has the higher Herfindahl Index value, so is more oligopolistic than industry B, even though they have the same three-firm concentration ratio.

Game theory *(HL only)*

Revised ▢

In game theory, the outcome of a firm depends on the actions taken by other firms in the industry, with each firm having incomplete information about the competitor's intentions.

Game theory, or the prisoner's dilemma, shows that oligopolistic firms can increase their profits through collusion rather than competing independently. It also helps to explain why price fixing is unlikely to succeed due to the tendency for firms to 'cheat' (to outdo their rivals), as shown in Figure 1.70.

> **Keyword definition**
> **Game theory** is an economic model that attempts to explain the nature of strategic interdependence in oligopolistic markets by considering the actions of competitors when making a decision, based on probable outcomes.

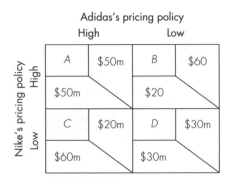

Figure 1.70 Game theory

- The dominant strategy for Adidas and Nike is to collude and raise prices together (decision A), yielding $50 million for each firm. Apart from collusion being illegal in most parts of the world, there is always the temptation for firms to cheat by opting for a low price strategy.

- However, if Adidas opts for a high-price strategy, Nike will earn $60 million by adopting a low-price strategy (decision C).
- Anticipating this, Adidas is likely to adopt a low-price strategy, in the hope that its rival charges a high price (decision B), thus allowing Adidas to earn $60 million.
- Therefore, independent decision making by Adidas and Nike is likely to lead to sub-optimal outcomes, with both failing to trust each other, and thus both adopting a low-price strategy (decision D).

Open/formal collusion *(HL only)*

Revised ▢

Collusive oligopoly exists when firms openly work together to limit the degree of competition, thereby acting as a collective monopolist, for example firms agreeing to simultaneously raise their prices. Collusion is more effective and easier to achieve if a very small number of dominant firms in an industry produce a homogeneous product.

The primary goal of a **cartel** is to restrict competition in order to maximise the profits for the colluding firms, which act as if they were a collective monopoly. For example, oligopolistic firms might use limit pricing – a pricing strategy used in a collusive oligopoly to set prices at a level that discourages new firms from entering the industry.

The most quoted example of a cartel is OPEC (Organization of Petroleum Exporting Countries), which limits the world supply of crude oil in order to keep prices high. However, cartels often break down in the long run because individual firms have a tendency to cheat (lower prices and increase output) to improve profitability at the expense of rival firms.

> **Keyword definition**
> **Collusion** is the agreement between two or more oligopolistic firms to limit competition by restrictive trade practices, for example price fixing or collectively limiting output.
>
> A **cartel** is formed when there is a formal agreement between oligopolistic firms to collude, for example in fixing prices or the level of output in the industry, thereby effectively acting as a monopolist.

Tacit/informal collusion *(HL only)*

Revised ▢

Price leadership, a common form of tacit collusion, occurs when a firm (usually the market leader) sets a price that is then accepted by other firms as the market price. Banks often adjust their savings and mortgage rates by following the pricing strategies of the largest firms in the industry. The same applies to petrol retailers.

As collusion is illegal in most countries, it is usually undisclosed, i.e. collusion takes place without any formal or written agreement. In 2013, the EU Commission fined electronics giants Samsung, Philips, Toshiba, Panasonic and LG a record €1.47 billion ($1.89bn) for conspiring to fix prices on some of their products between 1996 and 2006.

> **Keyword definition**
> **Tacit collusion** occurs when two or more oligopolistic firms implicitly (or informally) agree to use restrictive trade practices, for example price cutting or price leadership.

Non-collusive oligopoly *(HL only)*

Revised ▢

Price rigidity (stability) exists in non-collusive oligopolistic markets because competitors would simply retaliate by matching any price reduction from a rival firm. By contrast, firms in non-collusive oligopoly would not follow an increase in price in order to gain a competitive edge.

> **Keyword definition**
> **Non-collusive** oligopoly exists where firms in the industry act strategically by competing independently, taking into account the likely or possible actions of rival firms.

The **kinked demand curve** model is used to explain price rigidity (see Figure 1.71).

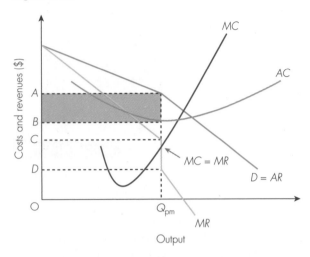

Figure 1.71 Price rigidity under non-collusive oligopoly

In Figure 1.71, it can be seen that the profit-maximising oligopolistic firm produces at the output level where MC = MR, thus supplying Q_{pm} at a price of OA. Since AC = OB whilst AR = OA, the oligopolistic firm earns abnormal profit, shown by the shaded area.

Due to the assumptions of mutual interdependence (a price hike is not matched by competitors whereas a price reduction is followed by rivals) and asymmetric information (game theory), there is a kink in the demand curve at the price OA.

The kink of the AR (demand) curve creates the vertical section of the MR curve due to the sudden change in the slope of the AR curve. Since profit maximisation occurs at MC = MR, there is price rigidity (P remains at OA) even if MC fluctuates between OC and OD.

In addition, the risk of **price wars** (when firms continually reduce prices to outstrip their rivals) can lead to huge losses for firms. Therefore, non-price competition is common in oligopoly.

Examples of non-price competition under oligopoly include:
- branding, for example Coca-Cola and Pepsi, Nike and Adidas, McDonald's and Burger King or Apple and Samsung
- added-value services, for example movies on-demand on certain airlines, extended opening hours at certain supermarkets, or customer loyalty schemes at certain retailers
- quality, for example Mercedes, BMW and Lexus, or Rolex and Omega.

Price discrimination *(HL only)*

Revised ☐

Necessary conditions for the practice of price discrimination *(HL only)*

Revised ☐

Firms with market power (oligopolists and monopolists) are able to use price discrimination. It occurs even if there are no differences in the cost of providing the service to different consumers groups. Examples of price discrimination used for students and adults include tickets for cinemas, airlines, swimming pools, public transport operators and theme parks.

The following three conditions must exist for effective price discrimination to take place:
- The firm must have some degree of market power, i.e. it must be a price-maker.

■ Different customer groups with different price elasticities of demand (PED) must exist – for example, adults and children have different willingness and ability to pay for certain products.

■ The firm must be able to separate the different consumer groups to prevent resale of the product from one group to another.

The three degrees of price discrimination are as follows:

■ **First-degree price discrimination** occurs when a firm can get each consumer to pay the highest price that s/he is able and willing to pay, thereby eliminating all consumer surplus, for example real estate agents and second-hand car salespeople.

■ **Second-degree price discrimination** occurs when discounted prices are used for customers buying in bulk – for example, theme parks use annual passes whilst supermarkets use 'multipack' offers.

■ **Third-degree price discrimination** occurs when a different price is charged to different customers based on their different degrees of price elasticity of demand – for example hotels, theme parks, cinemas, taxi firms and airlines often charge different prices during peak and off-peak times.

Figure 1.72 shows a train operator charging higher prices for adults than children due to the different degrees of PED. The firm produces where MC = MR. MC is horizontal as the extra cost of providing the service to an extra customer on the train is literally zero (assuming the train is not full). The firm can therefore gain revenue by using price discrimination to gain revenue from customers who might not be willing or able buy tickets at the higher price.

> **Expert tip**
>
> Do not assume that price 'discrimination' is necessarily a 'bad' act of monopolists. Price discrimination can lead to some consumer groups with relatively price elastic demand (such as students, pensioners and the unemployed) to consume more than if a single market price is charged to all consumer groups.

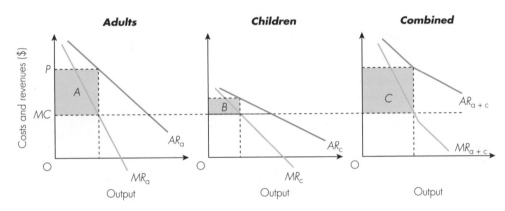

Figure 1.72 Third-degree price discrimination and profit maximisation

2.1 The level of overall economic activity

Economic activity

The circular flow of income model

In the circular flow model, **households** are individuals with effective demand for goods and services, whereas **firms** are businesses that produce (or supply) goods and services.

There are three types of **withdrawal**: savings (S), taxation (T) and import expenditure (M) as money leaves the circular flow to banks, government and the foreign sector respectively.

There are three types of **injection**: government spending (G), investment expenditure (I) and export earnings (X) as money enters the circular flow thereby stimulating economic activity.

For national income equilibrium, the following condition must hold:

$$S + T + M = G + I + X$$

The level of economic activity depends on the relative size of injections (J) and withdrawals (W). If $W > J$ then economic activity declines, and vice versa.

Income is the sum of the returns for use of the four factors of production:

- return (or income) for land = rent
- return for labour = wages (and salaries)
- return for capital = interest
- return for enterprise = profit

    Therefore,

    income = rent + wages + interest + profit

    Figure 2.1 shows the following:

- In a **closed economy** with only households and firms, households supply factors of production (land, labour, capital and enterprise) to firms to generate output of goods and services.
- In return, firms provide factor incomes to households, i.e. rent, wages, interest and profit.
- With the income, households spend their money on goods and services produced by firms, thus creating expenditure revenue for firms.
- Hence, the income flow is numerically the same value as the expenditure flow and the output flow.
- In an **open economy** in the circular flow of income model, there is a government sector, financial markets and foreign trade.
- In the financial sector, savings (S) represent a withdrawal whilst investments (I) are injections.
- With a government sector, taxes (T) represent a withdrawal, whereas government spending (G) is an injection.
- In an open economy, there is a foreign sector with international trade. Export revenue (X) represents an injection to the circular flow, whereas import expenditure (M) is a leakage.
- The circular flow of income and expenditure will change based on the relative size of all withdrawals ($W = S + T + M$) and all injections ($J = G + X + I$).

> **Keyword definition**
> The **circular flow of income model** is a macroeconomic tool used to explain how economic activity and national income are determined.

> **Common mistake**
>
> Students often describe income as the earnings that people gain from work. This is true for people only able to supply their labour services. Those with other factors of production (capital, land and enterprise) are able to gain other sources of income (interest, rent and profit).

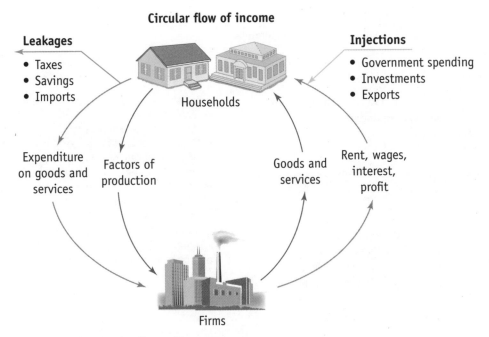

Figure 2.1 The circular flow of income

Measures of economic activity (GDP and GNP/GNI)

There are three ways to measure economic activity: the value of national output (O), national income (Y) and national expenditure (E).

- The output method of calculating economic activity adds up the final value of newly produced goods and services during the year.
- The expenditure method of calculating economic activity adds up the total spending on newly produced goods and services during the year.
- The income method of calculating economic activity adds up the total value of all factor incomes earned during the year.

All three methods give the same numerical result, i.e. O = Y = E, because the value of national output equals the value of what is spent on the output (national expenditure). This expenditure becomes the (national) income to households and firms that produced the output.

Using the expenditure method of calculating GDP, economists add the totals of consumption expenditure (C), investment expenditure (I), government expenditure (G) and export earnings (X) and then deduct the amount spent on imports (M) by using the formula:

$$GDP = C + I + G + (X - M)$$

Gross national product uses GDP but also accounts for net property income from abroad, i.e. the difference between what residents earn from overseas investments minus income earned by foreign residents within the domestic economy:

$$GNP = GDP + \text{net property income from abroad}$$

Net property income from abroad refers to the difference in value between incomes earned and incomes paid abroad.

Nominal GDP is measured using *current market prices*, i.e. the value of GDP at the time of measurement. **Real GDP** takes account of fluctuations in prices (inflation) over time.

Using real GDP (or real GNP) figures allows better comparisons of economic activity over time by using *constant market prices* (the values are adjusted for inflation over time). For example, if nominal GDP increases by 4% whilst the general price level rises by 3%, then the average person's income increases by only 1% in real terms. *(HL only)*

> **Revised** ☐

> **Keyword definitions**
> **Gross domestic product** (GDP) is the value of all final output of goods and services produced by firms within a country, per year.
>
> **Gross national product** (GNP) is the value of all final output of goods and services produced by a country's citizens, both domestically and abroad.

GDP per capita means expressing the GDP per head of the population, i.e. it averages out total GDP per person in the country. It is calculated using the formula:

$$\text{GDP per capita} = \frac{\text{total GDP}}{\text{population size}}$$

GNP per capita (or GNI per capita) is calculated in the same way – by dividing the total GNP or GNI by the country's population size.

A **price deflator** (or **GDP deflator**) is used to convert GDP at current prices to GDP at constant prices. (*HL only*)

Expert tip

The terms gross national product (GNP) and gross national income (GNI) can be used interchangeably for your IB examinations although in reality GNP differs slightly from GNI. The latter method deducts indirect business taxes, which differ between countries, to enable more meaningful international comparisons of national output and economic activity.

EXAM PRACTICE *(HL ONLY)*

PAPER 3

1 Calculate the value of gross domestic product (GDP) *and* gross national product (GNP) from the given information: Consumption = $150bn, Investment expenditure = $60bn, Government spending = $55bn, Export earnings = $31bn, Import expenditures = $28bn, Net income earned abroad = −$8bn. [3]

2 Calculate the real gross domestic product (GDP) in 2013 and in 2014 and explain your results. [4]

YEAR	NOMINAL GDP ($BN)	GDP DEFLATOR
2013	260.0	106.7
2014	262.4	108.5

The use of national income statistics

Revised

National income statistics give an indication of standards of living in a country, i.e. a higher real GDP per capita is associated with higher standards of living for the average person. This is because a person's standard of living is directly dependent upon the amount of goods and services that s/he is able to consume.

National income statistics reveal the level of economic activity in the country, which directly affects the average person's social and economic wellbeing. However, there are limitations in using national income statistics to measure standards of living in a country, including:

- the distribution of income and wealth in the country
- varying rates of direct and indirect taxes between countries – for example Andorra, Brunei Darussalam, Oman and Qatar have a zero rate of income tax
- differences in the cost of living, for example housing, education, healthcare and basic amenities
- the extent of social welfare benefits varying between countries
- exchange rate fluctuations making international comparisons of GDP over time less meaningful
- the composition of national output, for example North Korea's heavy expenditure on armaments and weapons compared with the huge spending on welfare benefits in Australia and the UK
- the extent to which national output generates negative externalities, thereby limiting the sustainability of economic activity and the quality of life in the country
- variations in the size of the unofficial economy (for goods and services that are not officially traded, such as home-grown fruits and vegetables and bartered services)
- consideration of alternative measures of GDP to measure of standards of living, for example the Human Development Index (HDI).

Another alternative to measuring nominal (or real) GDP is to use green GDP. This is calculated using the formula:

green GDP = nominal GDP − environmental production costs

Keyword definition
Green GDP is a measure of GDP that accounts for environmental destruction of economic activity by deducting the environmental costs associated with the output of goods and services.

The business cycle

Short-term fluctuations and long-term trends

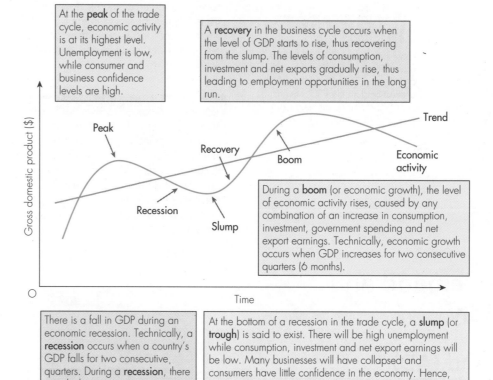

At the **peak** of the trade cycle, economic activity is at its highest level. Unemployment is low, while consumer and business confidence levels are high.

A **recovery** in the business cycle occurs when the level of GDP starts to rise, thus recovering from the slump. The levels of consumption, investment and net exports gradually rise, thus leading to employment opportunities in the long run.

During a **boom** (or economic growth), the level of economic activity rises, caused by any combination of an increase in consumption, investment, government spending and net export earnings. Technically, economic growth occurs when GDP increases for two consecutive quarters (6 months).

There is a fall in GDP during an economic recession. Technically, a **recession** occurs when a country's GDP falls for two consecutive quarters. During a **recession**, there is a decline in consumption, investment and net exports (due to falling export earnings).

At the bottom of a recession in the trade cycle, a **slump** (or **trough**) is said to exist. There will be high unemployment while consumption, investment and net export earnings will be low. Many businesses will have collapsed and consumers have little confidence in the economy. Hence, government spending may be needed to help the economy to recover from the recession.

Figure 2.2 The business cycle

The **boom** is the **peak** of the business cycle where economic activity is at its highest level. Unemployment is low whilst consumer and business confidence levels are very high.

During a **recession** the level of economic activity declines. Technically, this occurs when GDP falls for two consecutive quarters. Business failure is common and unemployment rises. Recessions create uncertainty for firms and damage consumer confidence levels. The **slump** (or **trough**) occurs at the bottom of a recession. There is mass unemployment as consumption, investment and net export earnings remain low.

A **recovery** occurs when GDP rises after the trough. Consumption, investment and net exports gradually rise, thus creating employment opportunities and increasing business confidence.

The potential national output (potential GDP) of an economy is shown by the long-term trend in the business cycle.

Exogenous shocks that affect the potential growth of an economy include global financial crises, the outbreak of infectious diseases and natural disasters such as earthquakes, tsunamis and severe flooding.

> Keyword definition
>
> The **business cycle** describes the fluctuations in economic activity in a country over time. These fluctuations create a long-term trend of growth in the economy.
>
> **Economic growth** is the increase in the level of economic activity, i.e. the annual percentage growth in national output.

Common mistake

Students should be aware of the difference between a *fall in GDP* and a *fall in GDP growth*. A fall in GDP (over two consecutive quarters) causes a recession, whereas a fall in GDP growth means that the economy is still growing, only at a slower rate than before.

Expert tip

Not all components of GDP necessarily fall during a recession – a boost in government spending may be needed to help the economy recover from the recession, such as the fiscal stimulus policies of many countries during the financial crisis of 2008.

Economic growth increases the long-term productive capacity of the economy, illustrated by an outwards shift of the production possibility curve. It suggests that the economy is more prosperous, so the average person earns more income (see Figure 2.3).

Expert tip

The best-performing students are able to show skills of evaluation and critical thinking. Not all businesses suffer during a recession. Counter-cyclical businesses are those that do well and survive during an economic downturn, for example suppliers of inferior goods (such as fast food restaurants and discount stores) and pawnbrokers.

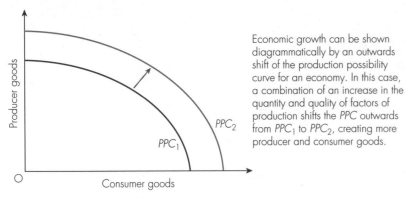

Economic growth can be shown diagrammatically by an outwards shift of the production possibility curve for an economy. In this case, a combination of an increase in the quantity and quality of factors of production shifts the *PPC* outwards from PPC_1 to PPC_2, creating more producer and consumer goods.

Figure 2.3 Economic growth

Expert tip

Make sure you know the difference between current and constant prices. National income statistics reported in current prices add the impact of inflation whilst those expressed as constant prices have the effects of inflation removed (allowing for better comparisons of GDP over time).

2.2 Aggregate demand and aggregate supply

Revised

Aggregate demand (AD)

Revised

The *AD* curve

Revised

In microeconomics, **demand** refers to the willingness and ability of consumers to pay for a particular product at each price level. In macroeconomics, **aggregate demand** (AD) refers to the value of total demand for all goods and services in the economy, per time period.

The *AD* curve shows the real national output that is purchased at each price level, per time period. It has a negative slope (i.e. it is downwards sloping) because when the general level of prices is high, the level of aggregate demand tends to be low (see Figure 2.4).

Keyword definition
Aggregate demand is the total value of all goods and services demanded in the economy, per time period.

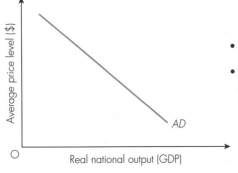

- The higher the price level, the lower the level of aggregate demand tends to be, *ceteris paribus*.
- Since *AD* has an inverse relationship with the general (average) price level, the *AD* curve is downwards sloping.

Figure 2.4 The aggregate demand curve

There are three reasons for the downwards-sloping *AD* curve:

- **The Pigou wealth effect** – English economist Arthur Pigou said that for any given nominal value of income, a lower price level allows households, firms and the government greater purchasing power, resulting in greater consumption, investment and government spending.
- **Keynes's interest-rate effect** – A fall in the general price level causes interest rates to drop, thus boosting the demand for money, *ceteris paribus*. This results in greater consumption, investment expenditure and government spending, i.e. higher aggregate demand.
- **Mundell-Fleming's exchange rate effect** – As the general price level falls, the interest rate also tends to fall, resulting in a depreciation of the exchange rate. This will tend to increase the demand for net exports because domestic products are cheaper, thus boosting *AD*.

The components of AD

The components of aggregate demand are consumption expenditure (C), investment expenditure (*I*), government spending (G), exports earnings (X) and import expenditure (M). Therefore:

$$AD = C + I + G + (X - M)$$

Consumption is the total spending on goods and services by households in the domestic economy, per time period. It is the largest component of aggregate demand.

Investment is the capital expenditure of firms in the economy, for example the purchase of fixed assets such as machinery, commercial vehicles and buildings. This results in a larger productive capacity in the long run.

Government spending is the total expenditure on goods and services by the government, including education, healthcare, national security and social welfare schemes.

Net exports, given by the formula $X - M$, measures the difference between the value of export earnings and import expenditure.

The determinants of AD or causes of shifts in the *AD* curve

The determinants of aggregate demand refer to the factors that cause shifts in the *AD* curve – for example, lower household and business indebtedness due to reduced interest rates will shift the *AD* curve to the right, *ceteris paribus* (see Figure 2.5).

Factors that cause a change in any component of aggregate demand $(AD = C + I + G + (X - M))$ will cause a shift in the *AD* curve, *ceteris paribus*.

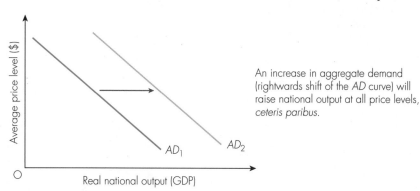

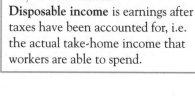

An increase in aggregate demand (rightwards shift of the *AD* curve) will raise national output at all price levels, *ceteris paribus*.

Figure 2.5 Shifts in the aggregate demand curve

Table 2.1 Factors that affect the level of consumption

Consumer confidence	The more confident consumers are about the economy, the greater the level of consumption will be. Consumer confidence is low during a recession and higher during a boom.
Interest rates	Higher interest rates tend to reduce consumption as households with loans and mortgages have lower income to use at their discretion.
Wealth	Changes in household wealth have a positive impact on the level of consumption, i.e. the wealthier households are, the more they tend to consume.
Personal income tax	If the level of disposable income falls due to higher income tax, consumption will also fall, *ceteris paribus*.
Household indebtedness	The more debts that households have (perhaps due to credit card and mortgage debts) the less income they have for consumption. Following the global financial crisis, US household debt reached $14 trillion in 2009 – the same value as its GDP!

Table 2.2 Factors that affect the level of investment

Interest rates	Higher interest rates tend to reduce investment because the cost of borrowing funds to invest will increase.
Business confidence	The greater the level of business confidence in the economy, the higher the level of investment will be. Business confidence is high when the economy is in a boom.
Technology	Technological progress and the associated productivity gains will tend to boost the level of investment expenditure.
Business taxes	The lower the rate of taxes in the economy, the more attractive investment becomes as firms are more able to make a return on their investment. Some countries such as the Bahamas and Estonia have a zero rate of corporation tax to attract foreign direct investment.
The level of corporate indebtedness	Like households, the more debts businesses have the less money they have available for investment expenditure. Indebtedness tends to increase during periods of rising interest rates or during an economic downturn when firms struggle to survive.

Factors that affect the level of **government spending** include the following:
- Political priorities – government spending will vary depending on the political priorities, for example increased national defence expenditure during a war, or more spending on education and healthcare prior to a general election (in order to win political votes).
- Economic priorities – the austerity measures following the global financial crisis of 2008 have meant that governments across Europe and many other parts of the world need to cut their spending in order to reduce their budget deficits.

Factors that affect the level of **net exports** include the following:
- The income of trading partners – due to globalisation and interdependence, when a country suffers from an economic downturn, there are negative impacts on its trading partners.
- Exchange rates – a higher exchange rate tends to reduce the demand for exports (as they become more expensive for foreign buyers), and vice versa.
- Changes in the level of protectionism – trade barriers such as tariffs and quotas raise the price of imports, thus tending to reduce the demand for foreign goods and services.

Aggregate supply (AS)

The meaning of aggregate supply

The short-run aggregate supply (SRAS) curve shows the total planned national output at different price levels, *ceteris paribus*.

The *SRAS* curve is upwards sloping as higher prices attract more firms to raise their output level (recall from microeconomics that the supply curve for a single firm is upwards sloping for the same reason).

In the short run, a change in non-price factors that affect AS will shift the *SRAS* curve (see Figure 2.6). These factors, which affect the cost of production, include:

- changes in resource prices – for example, the price of oil or other raw materials changes drastically
- changes in business taxes – for example, higher corporation taxes shift the *SRAS* curve to the left
- changes in subsidies – for example, an increase in subsidies in numerous industries will shift the *SRAS* curve to the right
- supply shocks – for example, a war, financial crisis, natural disasters, oil shortages or an outbreak of an epidemic (such as swine flu, malaria or dengue fever) will shift the *SRAS* curve to the left.

> **Keyword definition**
>
> **Aggregate supply** (AS) refers to the amount of real national output that firms are willing and able to produce at each price level. It is a measure of an economy's potential output.

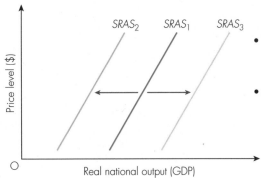

- Adverse changes in non-price factors that affect AS will shift the *SRAS* curve to the left, from $SRAS_1$ to $SRAS_2$.
- Favourable changes in non-price factors that affect AS will shift the *SRAS* curve to the right, from $SRAS_1$ to $SRAS_3$.

Figure 2.6 Shifts in the *SRAS* curve

> **Expert tip**
>
> The slope of the *SRAS* curve depends on the extent to which there is spare capacity in the economy. The flatter the *SRAS* curve, the greater that degree of spare capacity (underutilised resources). This means that the *SRAS* curve is relatively price elastic, and vice versa.

Alternative views of aggregate supply

Monetarists (or new classical economists) differ in their view of the long-run aggregate supply (LRAS) curve from that of Keynesian economists. Monetarists believe that the *LRAS* curve is vertical at the full employment level of output (see Figure 2.7). Hence, LRAS is independent of the price level, as this represents the maximum (potential) level of national output of the economy, per time period.

The quantity and quality of factors of production affect the LRAS, i.e. the quantity and quality of natural resources (land), labour, capital stock (e.g. buildings and infrastructure) and entrepreneurship.

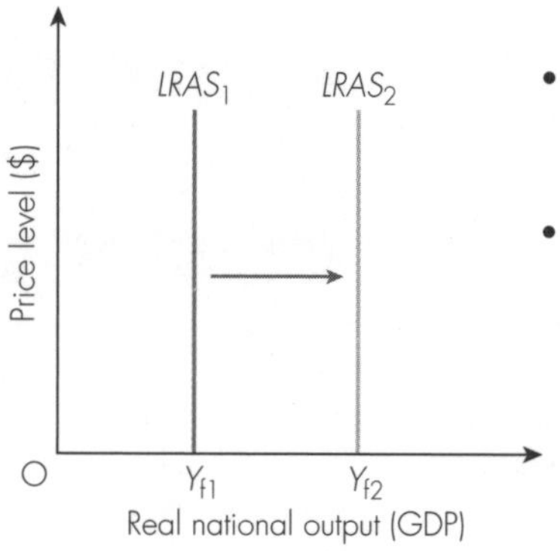

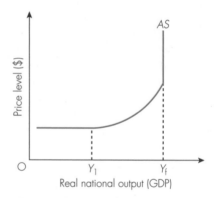

Figure 2.7 The monetarist LRAS curve

- According to the new classical model of *LRAS*, aggregate supply is independent of the price level in the long run, i.e, it is perfectly price inelastic at the full employment level of output (Y_f).
- A rightwards shift of the *LRAS* curve results from an increase in the productive capacity of the economy, e.g. an increase in the quantity and quality of factors of production, including technological progress.

By contrast, Keynesians believe that the AS curve has three sections (see Figure 2.8), mainly due to the varying degrees of spare capacity in the economy. Keynesians argue that wages are 'sticky downwards' (labour market inflexibility) for the following reasons:

- Firms may prefer to cut employment rather than wages because pay cuts can reduce worker morale and productivity.
- Existing employment contracts can also prevent wages from falling below the agreed level.
- Workers get used to a certain wage rate and are inflexible, through trade union action, in accepting pay cuts.
- It is not legally possible to cut wages below the national minimum wage, even during a major economic downturn.

Figure 2.8 The Keynesian *AS* curve

There is spare capacity in the economy up to the Y_1 level of national output, perhaps due to a recession, high unemployment and 'sticky' wages. Hence, the price level is stable even if national output changes.

The upwards-sloping section of the Keynesian AS curve shows increasing demand for resources and labour shortages, thereby causing the price level to rise as national output increases.

At the full employment level of national output (Y_f), firms compete for limited resources as the economy is at full capacity, thereby forcing up the general price level even though the economy cannot produce beyond its productive capacity.

Shifts in the aggregate supply curve

Revised

Changes in the quantity and/or quality of factors of production result in permanent shifts to the *LRAS* curve. Examples of such changes that shift the AS curve include:

- improvements in efficiency – higher productivity of resources will shift the AS curve to the right (see Figure 2.7)
- new technology – technological progress and innovations shift the *LRAS* curve rightwards

- reduction in unemployment – a fall in the number of unemployed people means that the productive capacity of the economy can increase, thus shifting the AS curve to the right
- institutional changes – better infrastructure, such as improved road, rail and air networks, enhance the economy's productive capacity, thus shifting the AS curve outwards.

The quantity of factors of production can also be increased by discovering new supplies (such as oil or other natural resources) or by a larger workforce (perhaps due to migration of workers).

The quality of labour resources can be increased by improved education, training and work practices.

Keynesians and monetarists differ in their view about the shape of the *LRAS* curve. Figure 2.7 shows a shift of the *LRAS* curve from the monetarist perspective, whilst Figure 2.9 shows the Keynesian view.

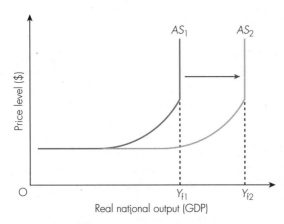

Figure 2.9 Shifts in the Keynesian *AS* curve

Equilibrium

Revised

Short-run equilibrium

Revised

Short-run macroeconomic equilibrium occurs when aggregate demand and aggregate supply intersect, thus determining the actual level of real national output and the average price level. Changes in any factor that affect AD or AS will change the equilibrium. For example, an increase in net exports or lower income tax will shift the *AD* curve rightwards, *ceteris paribus* (see Figure 2.10).

> **Keyword definition**
> **Equilibrium** in the economy exists when aggregate demand is equal to aggregate supply, i.e. $AD = AS$.

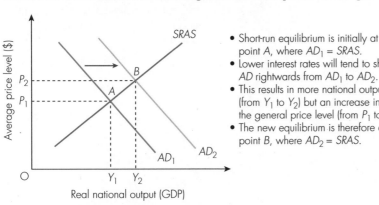

- Short-run equilibrium is initially at point A, where $AD_1 = SRAS$.
- Lower interest rates will tend to shift AD rightwards from AD_1 to AD_2.
- This results in more national output (from Y_1 to Y_2) but an increase in the general price level (from P_1 to P_2).
- The new equilibrium is therefore at point B, where $AD_2 = SRAS$.

Figure 2.10 Short-run equilibrium

Similarly, an outward shift of the *SRAS* curve will tend to increase real national output and reduce the general price level. This might be caused by factors such as improved training opportunities for employees or reduced interest rates.

EXAM PRACTICE *(HL ONLY)*

PAPER 3

3 Using an appropriate diagram, explain how a recession impacts on the short-run equilibrium position of an economy. [4]

4 With the aid of an aggregate demand and aggregate supply diagram, explain what is likely to happen following a temporary reduction in both income tax and corporation tax. [4]

Equilibrium in the monetarist/new classical model

Revised

Full employment exists when the economy is operating at full capacity, i.e. it is not possible to increase real national output as all resources are fully utilised. This can be shown as a point on a production possibility frontier (PPF) or on an *AD-AS* diagram (see Figure 2.11).

Long-run equilibrium, according to monetarists, occurs at the potential or full employment level of real national output. In Figure 2.11, this is shown by the intersection of AD_1 and the *LRAS*, where Y_f represents the full employment level of output.

In reality, it is rather difficult to know precisely the full employment level of output. It can be impractical for every firm in the economy to operate at 100% capacity and it is not easy to determine the number of people who are voluntarily unemployed.

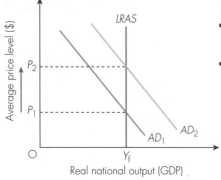

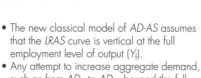

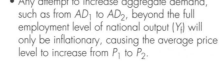

- The new classical model of *AD-AS* assumes that the *LRAS* curve is vertical at the full employment level of output (Y_f).
- Any attempt to increase aggregate demand, such as from AD_1 to AD_2, beyond the full employment level of national output (Y_f) will only be inflationary, causing the average price level to increase from P_1 to P_2.

Figure 2.11 Long-run equilibrium – Monetarist model

In the new classical model, any short term fluctuations in national output will only be temporary as market forces will restore equilibrium to the full employment level of output in the long run. With reference to Figure 2.12:

- Long-run equilibrium is at the full employment level of national output (Y_f) with the average price level at P_1.
- An increase in aggregate demand from AD_1 to AD_2 increases the average price level from P_1 to P_2, causing AS to expand along the $SRAS_1$ curve.
- This temporarily increases national output beyond its capacity, and so raises production costs.
- Hence, aggregate supply shifts from $SRAS_1$ to $SRAS_2$, causing the average price level to rise from P_2 to P_3 and the economy operating back at Y_f.

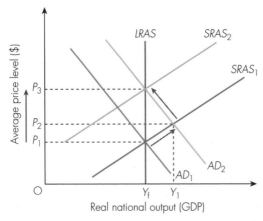

Figure 2.12 Fluctuations in short-run equilibrium (1)

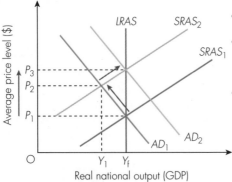

Figure 2.13 Fluctuations in short-run equilibrium (2)

- Long run equilibrium is at Y_f, with the general price level initially at P_1.
- An increase in production costs causes a shift in aggregate supply from $SRAS_1$ to $SRAS_2$, thus raising the average price level to P_2 and resulting in a fall in GDP from Y_f to Y_1.
- Government intervention to raise aggregate demand from AD_1 to AD_2 simply increases the average price level from P_2 to P_3, with the economy operating back at Y_f.

Therefore, monetarists (new classical economists) argue that demand-side policies are ineffective in the long run. They prefer the use of supply-side policies to shift the *LRAS* outwards to achieve economic growth.

Changes in long-run equilibrium are caused by factors that shift the *LRAS* curve rightwards, i.e. supply-side policies. These include: improved productivity of factors of production, technological progress and incentives to stimulate inventions and innovations.

Equilibrium in the Keynesian model

Keynesians believe that wages are 'sticky' downwards, even during a recession, so market forces struggle to restore equilibrium at the full employment level of national output without the need for government intervention (using expansionary fiscal policy and monetary policy).

The Keynesian model of macroeconomic equilibrium suggests that the economy can be in equilibrium at any level of real national output where *AD* intersects with *AS* (see Figure 2.14).

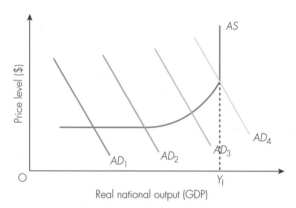

Figure 2.14 Keynesian equilibrium

According to Keynesian economists, an increase in aggregate demand (from AD_1 to AD_2) will not cause inflationary pressures if there is spare capacity in the economy. On the upwards sloping section of the *AS* curve, any increase in aggregate demand (from AD_2 to AD_3 or from AD_3 to AD_4) puts pressure on resources (such as labour shortages) thus pushing up the average price level.

If aggregate supply is perfectly price inelastic (in the long run), any increase in aggregate demand (beyond AD_4) simply increases the average price level as the economy cannot increase national output beyond the full employment level (Y_f).

Contrary to the new classical model, the Keynesian model shows that increases in *AD* need not necessarily cause inflation in the economy, unless it is operating at or near its full employment level of output.

A **deflationary gap** (also known as a **recessionary gap**) exists when the real national output equilibrium (P_e and Y_e in Figure 2.15) is below the full employment level of output (Y_f). Without government intervention, the economy can remain stuck in a deflationary gap.

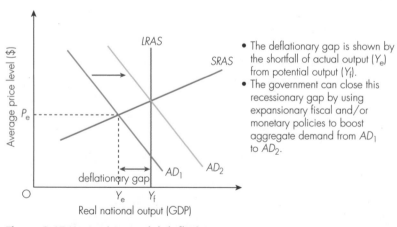

- The deflationary gap is shown by the shortfall of actual output (Y_e) from potential output (Y_f).
- The government can close this recessionary gap by using expansionary fiscal and/or monetary policies to boost aggregate demand from AD_1 to AD_2.

Figure 2.15 Keynesian model deflationary gap

By contrast, an **inflationary gap** exists if actual national output exceeds the full employment level of output, i.e. *AD* increases along the vertical section of the *LRAS* curve (see Figure 2.16), causing an increase in the average price level.

An inflationary gap will occur if the government chooses to maintain full employment, despite rising levels of aggregate demand putting pressure on the ability of the economy to supply goods and services. This will lead to demand-pull inflation, *ceteris paribus*.

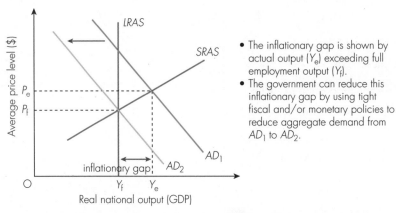

- The inflationary gap is shown by actual output (Y_e) exceeding full employment output (Y_f).
- The government can reduce this inflationary gap by using tight fiscal and/or monetary policies to reduce aggregate demand from AD_1 to AD_2.

Figure 2.16 Keynesian model inflationary gap

The Keynesian multiplier *(HL only)*

Revised ☐

The nature of the Keynesian multiplier *(HL only)*

Revised ☐

Injections to the circular flow (export earnings, government spending and investment) increase the value of the Keynesian multiplier. By contrast, leakages (taxes, import expenditure and savings) cause negative multiplier effects. The larger the value of withdrawals, the lower the value of the multiplier, and vice versa.

The Keynesian multiplier shows the extent to which each additional dollar injected into (or withdrawn from) the economy will increase (or reduce) the value of aggregate demand. It can therefore aid government decisions about macroeconomic policies.

The Keynesian multiplier is calculated using either of the formulae below:

$$\frac{1}{1-MPC} \quad \frac{1}{MPS+MPT+MPM}$$

Note that $\dfrac{1}{1-MPC}$ is equivalent to $\dfrac{1}{MPS+MPT+MPM}$ because the sum of MPC, MPS, MPT and MPM always equals 1.

The scale of the multiplier depends on the shape of the Keynesian AS curve (see Figure 2.8). If the economy is on the horizontal section of the AS curve, the multiplier would increase real national output without any pressure on the average price level due to mass unemployment. If the economy is on the upwards-sloping section of the AS curve, the multiplier will have an impact on both national output and the average price level.

However, if the economy is on the vertical section of the AS curve, the multiplier has no impact on national output, but the associated increase in AD simply leads to an increase in the average price level as the economy is already operating at full employment.

The effectiveness of the multiplier is also subject to time lags, i.e. there is a delay between changes in injections and leakages and any corresponding changes in national output.

> **Keyword definition**
> The **Keynesian multiplier** shows that any increase in the value of injections results in an even greater increase in the value of national income. It also shows that any increase in the value of withdrawals leads to a greater fall in the value of national output.

Keyword definitions

The **marginal propensity to consume** (MPC) measures the proportion of each extra dollar of household income that is spent by consumers, i.e. $MPC = \frac{\Delta C}{\Delta Y}$. An increase in the MPC will tend to increase the value of the multiplier.

The **marginal propensity to save** (MPS) measures the proportion of each extra dollar of income that is saved by households, i.e. $\frac{\Delta S}{\Delta Y}$.

The **marginal propensity to tax** (MPT) measures the proportion of each extra dollar of household income that is levied by the government, i.e. $\frac{\Delta T}{\Delta Y}$.

The **marginal propensity to import** (MPM) measures the proportion of each extra dollar of household income that is spent on imports, i.e. $MPM = \frac{\Delta M}{\Delta Y}$.

EXAM PRACTICE *(HL ONLY)*

PAPER 3

5 If an economy's marginal propensity to consume is known to be 0.85, calculate the size of the Keynesian multiplier. [2]

6 If export earnings increase by $200 million and the multiplier is 2.2, calculate the change in real national income. [2]

7 If government spending increases by $85 million and the marginal propensity to consume is known to be 0.75, calculate the amount by which the aggregate demand curve will shift. [2]

8 Suppose a country in recession has a deflationary gap of $92 billion and its marginal propensity to consume is 0.76. Calculate the amount of government expenditure needed to close the recessionary gap in order to restore equilibrium. [2]

Expert tip

It might be more natural to think about the multiplier leading to positive impacts on the level of national output. However, the Keynesian multiplier also refers to negative multiplier effects caused by a fall in injections or an increase in withdrawals. For example, a rise in marginal rates of income tax will cause negative multiplier effects.

Common mistake

Students should take care when using abbreviations in the exam as understanding is often not shown. For example, 'MPC' can stand for a number of things: monetary policy committee, marginal private costs or the marginal propensity to consume. Be sure to explain any abbreviations that you use in the examinations.

2.3 Macroeconomic objectives

Revised ▢

Low unemployment

Revised ▢

The meaning of unemployment

Revised ▢

Low unemployment is a key macroeconomic objective because it:
- complements economic growth (another macroeconomic objective) – higher employment tends to lead to greater national expenditure. Hence, low unemployment tends to increase the standards of living in an economy.
- increases tax revenues from a range of sources such as income tax (from employment), sales taxes (from increased expenditure) and stamp duty (from the sale and purchase of property)
- reduces the tax burden on the government because there is less of a need for taxpayers to fund welfare benefits as more people are working
- prevents a 'brain drain' from the economy, whereby skilled workers pursue better employment opportunities in other countries.

The **unemployment rate** calculates the percentage of the labour force that is unemployed. It is calculated using the formula:

$$\frac{\text{number of unemployed people}}{\text{labour force}} \times 100$$

The **labour force** consists of the employed, the self-employed and the unemployed, i.e. all those in work and all those actively seeking employment. For example, the unemployment rate in a country with a workforce of 50 million of which 5 million people are actively seeking employment but unable to find employment is:

$$\frac{5\text{m}}{50\text{m}} = 10\%$$

The United Nation's International Labour Organization (ILO) states 15 as the minimum age to enter the labour force. There is no official upper limit, but many countries use a range between 65 and 70 – for example, the official retirement age for women is 67 years in Norway, Poland and the USA.

The ILO measures a country's unemployment based on the number of people who are:
- willing to work, but unable to find it
- actively looking for work, i.e. they have looked for a job in the last 4 weeks, and able to start work within the next 2 weeks, or
- waiting to start a new job within in the next 2 weeks.

Irrespective of the measure or definition of unemployment, it represents an inefficient use of any economy's scarce resources, thereby hindering its potential national output.

> **Keyword definition**
> **Unemployment** occurs when people are willing and able to work and actively seeking employment but are unable to find work.

EXAM PRACTICE (HL ONLY)

PAPER 3

9 Use the data below for Country X to calculate the total number of people unemployed. [2]

LABOUR FORCE	30 million
POPULATION OF WORKING AGE	35 million
UNEMPLOYMENT RATE	7.9%

10 Use the data below to calculate the unemployment rate. [3]

TOTAL POPULATION	100 million
PERCENTAGE OF POPULATION EMPLOYED	74.8%
POPULATION OF UNEMPLOYED	15 million
RETIRED POPULATION	20%

Difficulties in measuring unemployment

Revised

Hidden unemployment – Some people escape the official measure of unemployment, resulting in an underestimation of the true rate of unemployment. For example:

- **discouraged workers** are not willing to work, so are excluded from the calculation of unemployment. The ILO measure of unemployment only considers those who have looked for a job in the past 4 weeks.
- **overstaffing** occurs in firms that employ workers who are not fully utilised, perhaps due to seasonal fluctuations in demand or due to legal constraints such as employment contracts.

Underemployment – This exists when people are inadequately employed, reflecting the underutilisation of the employed population, i.e. they are technically employed but in jobs that do not fully use their skills or abilities, such as:

- involuntary part-time workers who cannot find full-time employment
- overqualified workers, who have education, experience, skills and qualifications beyond the requirements of their jobs.

Regional disparities – The measurement of unemployment is an average measure, so therefore ignores disparities in regional rates of unemployment. For example, unemployment in 2013 for the USA averaged 7.5%, but Nevada recorded 9.6% unemployment, whilst North Dakota saw only 3.1%.

Ethnic disparities – Ethnic minority groups tend to suffer from higher-than-average rates of unemployment, and for longer periods. For example, the unemployment rate for African-Americans in New York is three times higher than the average official unemployment rate.

Age disparities – Unemployment rates among the young and older people are higher than those officially reported for the nation. For example, Greece and Spain experienced unemployment of around 28% in 2013, although youth unemployment reached 58.7% and 56.1% respectively.

Gender disparities – Females tend to experience higher average rates of unemployment than men. On average, men also re-enter the labour market quicker. According to the ILO, gender inequalities in unemployment rates are exceptionally high in the Middle East and North Africa.

Expert tip

Remember that not all people of working age are *willing* or *able* to participate in employment. This will partly depend on the country's welfare benefits scheme and social attitudes towards women in the workforce. For example, women in Saudi Arabia face huge barriers to entering the labour force.

EXAM PRACTICE

PAPER 2

11 According to the International Monetary Fund (IMF), Pakistan's annual unemployment rate between 2007 and 2013 was kept steady at 5–6%. This, according to the Central Intelligence Agency (CIA), meant that Pakistan's gross domestic product grew by 3.7% in 2012 and another 5% in 2013. These changes have helped to reduce some of the poverty in the country.

   a Explain two reasons why it might be difficult at times to know the exact rate of unemployment in a country.   **[4]**

   b Evaluate the possible consequences of low unemployment for the Pakistani economy.   **[8]**

Consequences of unemployment

Revised ▢

The **economic consequences** of unemployment include the following:

■ **A loss of GDP** – Lower gross domestic product (negative economic growth) has detrimental consequences on the economy, including a fall in its international competitiveness (ability to compete in overseas markets).

■ **Loss of tax revenues** – Unemployment results in lower income and expenditure, thus resulting in lower tax revenues for the government.

■ **Increased cost of unemployment benefits** – Unemployment creates an increased opportunity cost of government expenditure on unemployment benefits. Prolonged periods of high unemployment can therefore lead to increased government debts.

■ **Loss of income for individuals** – Unemployment results in lower household income, with negative consequences for individuals and their families. If prolonged, unemployment can cause (or increase) poverty in the economy.

■ **Greater disparities in the distribution of income** – As women, the young, ethnic minority groups and those living in rural areas tend to suffer more from prolonged periods of unemployment, the result will be greater discrepancies in the distribution of income and wealth.

The **social consequences** of unemployment include the following:

■ **Stress** – The unemployed suffer from stress, depression, health problems and low self-esteem. Prolonged periods of unemployment can lead to homelessness and family breakdowns, such as arguments, separation and divorce. In extreme cases, unemployment has led to suicides.

■ **Crime** – The impact of unemployment in individuals can cause deprivation and desperation, thus leading to increased crime, such as theft and vandalism.

■ **Indebtedness** – Lower income, caused by unemployment, leads to increased indebtedness for individuals, firms and the government. Indebtedness can cause bankruptcy, leading to absolute poverty, hunger, disease, homelessness and even suicides.

■ **Social deprivation** – The local community can suffer if there is mass unemployment, for example poverty, falling house prices (and hence asset values) and increased crime rates.

Types and causes unemployment

Revised ▢

Frictional unemployment occurs when people are in transition between jobs due to the time delay between leaving a job and finding or starting a new one. It is always present because it takes time for the labour market to match available jobs with suitable candidates.

    Structural unemployment (see Figure 2.17) occurs when the demand for products in a particular industry continually falls, thus reducing the demand for particular labour skills. It can also be caused by changes in geographical locations of industries (for cost advantages) and labour market rigidities (such as the unwillingness of workers to accept lower wage rates).

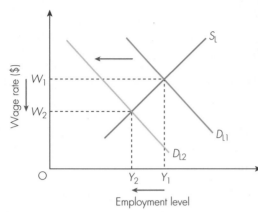

- The decline in the derived demand for labour in an industry from D_{L1} to D_{L2} causes the employment level to fall from N_1 to N_2.
- The industry suffers from structural and long-term changes in demand, with wage rates falling from W_1 to W_2.
- It is usually difficult for those in structural unemployment to find a new job without retraining.
- The UK, for example, has experienced structural unemployment in shipping, textiles, steel production, coal mining and car making.

Figure 2.17 Structural unemployment

Seasonal unemployment is caused by regular and periodical changes in demand for certain products. For example, fruit pickers are in high demand during the summer months whilst retailers in many parts of the world hire more temporary workers during the Christmas holiday season.

Cyclical unemployment (or **demand-deficient unemployment**) is the most severe type of unemployment as it can affect every industry in the economy. It is caused by a lack of aggregate demand, which causes a fall in national income (see Figure 2.18).

> **Expert tip**
>
> The concept of **hidden unemployment** is important to economists. There are plenty of people who are not included in the official calculation of unemployment statistics (due to the choice of measurement rather the core meaning of unemployment – the non-use of factors of production). It includes, for example, **discouraged workers** who have stopped actively searching for employment.

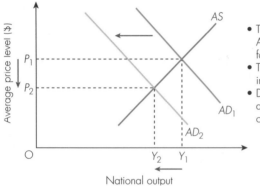

- The decline in aggregate demand from AD_1 to AD_2 causes national output to fall from Y_1 to Y_2.
- This creates widespread unemployment in the economy.
- Demand-deficient unemployment is associated with a decline in the business cycle (during recessions and slumps).

Figure 2.18 Demand deficient unemployment

Government policies to deal with unemployment

Revised ☐

Governments can deal with the problems of unemployment in various ways, depending on the types and causes of unemployment in the economy:

■ **Frictional unemployment** – This type of unemployment can be reduced by improving information services to aid job seekers. However, imperfect information in the labour market can worsen frictional unemployment as people are unaware of available jobs.

■ **Seasonal unemployment** – Improving the skills of seasonally unemployed workers helps to reduce occupational immobility. Policies to improve education and training will give these people a better chance of re-employment and the incentive to find work.

■ **Structural unemployment** – Governments can introduce a broader range of vocational training programmes, greater access to university courses (to allow people to retrain) and offer more job training opportunities. However, this comes at an opportunity cost to taxpayers.

■ **Cyclical unemployment** – To combat this demand-deficient unemployment, the government might choose to use expansionary fiscal policy and/or expansionary monetary policy to stimulate economic activity and hence to reduce the level of unemployment.

There are four generic policies for reducing unemployment as a whole: fiscal policy, monetary policy, supply-side policy and protectionist policies:

■ **Expansionary fiscal policy** – A reduction in taxes and/or increased government expenditure should, all other things being equal, boost aggregate demand and hence the derived demand for labour (see Figure 2.19).

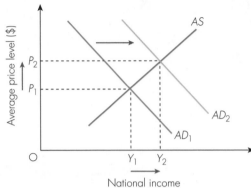

- Fiscal policy (the use of taxation and government spending policies to influence the level of economic activity) can be used to tackle unemployment caused by demand-side issues, such as cyclical and structural unemployment.
- Tax cuts and increased government spending boost aggregate demand from AD_1 to AD_2, thus boosting real national income from Y_1 to Y_2. In turn, this will lead to more employment opportunities.

Figure 2.19 Expansionary fiscal policy to combat unemployment

■ **Expansionary monetary policy** – A cut in interest rates and/or a devaluation of the currency should stimulate consumer and business confidence levels, alongside increased consumption and net exports. In time, this will boost the derived demand for labour in the economy (see Figure 2.20).

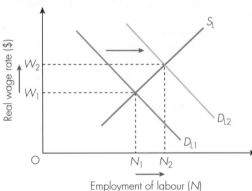

- By lowering interest rates, the cost of borrowing falls, thus encouraging households and firms to spend and invest, i.e. AD increases.
- The higher AD boosts the derived demand for labour curve from D_{L1} to D_{L2}, thus reducing unemployment.
- The resulting rise in real wages from W_1 to W_2 attracts more labour, i.e. there is an expansion along the S_L curve.

Figure 2.20 Expansionary monetary policy and the labour market

■ **Supply-side policies** – These are government policies used to deal with imperfections in the labour market and to reduce unemployment caused by supply-side factors. Examples include the following:

☐ Investment in education and training helps unemployed people to gain new skills so they can find employment – for example, retraining people structurally unemployed in the manufacturing sector so they can find employment in the tertiary sector.

☐ Reduction in trade union powers will mean that labour unions are not in such a strong bargaining position for higher wages in excess of inflation. Government intervention to reduce the influence and power of trade unions can help to reduce unemployment.

☐ Employment incentives can be offered to firms for training and hiring the long-term unemployed – for example, the government can offer these firms tax allowances and/or subsidies to reduce their costs of training and hiring workers.

☐ Reviewing of unemployment benefits can ensure that there are incentives to seek employment rather than to rely on state welfare benefits. By making it more difficult for people to claim unemployment benefits, people become more proactive in searching for jobs.

■ **Protectionist policies** – Trade barriers, such as tariffs and quotas, can be used to safeguard domestic jobs from the threat of international competition. For example, Japan imposes up to 778% import taxes on rice – the highest rate in the world – to protect agricultural jobs in its country.

EXAM PRACTICE

PAPER 2

12 In June 2010, Tesco opened Britain's first supermarket without any checkout workers. Instead, one person is hired to supervise the five checkouts, mainly to assist customers who have not used a self-service checkout before. The UK's largest retailer employs around 221,000 workers in the UK but critics argue that such technological advancement would cause mass job losses.

   a Define the term unemployment.   [2]

   b Explain how the UK government could deal with the 'mass job losses'.   [4]

Low and stable rate of inflation

Revised ☐

The meaning of inflation, disinflation and deflation

Revised ☐

> **Keyword definitions**
>
> **Inflation** is the sustained rise in the average price level in an economy over time. This does not mean that the price of every good and service increases, but on average the prices are rising. Governments set a target inflation rate as a key macroeconomic objective.
>
> **Deflation** refers to the persistent fall in the average price level in an economy over time, i.e. the inflation rate is negative. It is caused by a continual decline in aggregate demand and/or an increase in aggregate supply caused by technological progress.
>
> **Disinflation** occurs when there is a fall in the rate of inflation (i.e. prices are still rising, but at a slower pace) rather than an actual fall in the general price level. Disinflation can lead to deflation if not controlled, with negative consequences for the economy and standards of living in the country.

> **Expert tip**
>
> Make sure you can distinguish between disinflation and deflation. A fall in the rate of inflation (disinflation) means that prices are still rising on average, only at a slower rate. Be clear about the meaning of deflation – an actual fall in the general price level.

    Diagrammatically, deflation results in lower average prices (see Figure 2.21) whereas disinflation is shown by a smaller proportional increase in average prices (see Figure 2.22).

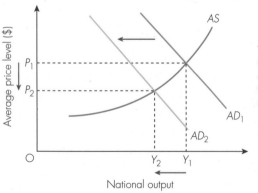

The fall in aggregate demand from AD_1 to AD_2 causes national output to drop from Y_1 to Y_2 with the general price level falling from P_1 to P_2.

Figure 2.21 Deflation

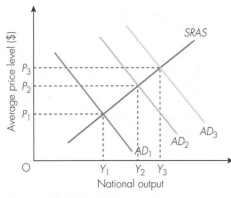

- An increase in aggregate demand from AD_1 to AD_2 causes national output to rise from Y_1 to Y_2 but with prices rising from P_1 to P_2.
- Disinflation occurs when the rate of increase in AD slows down (from AD_2 to AD_3), reducing the rate of increase in the general price level from P_2 to P_3.

Figure 2.22 Disinflation

Inflation and deflation are typically measured by using a **consumer price index (CPI)**. This weighted index measures the change in prices of a representative basket of goods and services consumed by the average household in the economy. The prices of items such as staple food products, clothing, petrol and transportation are likely to be included in the CPI. In the UK in 2013, ebooks and blueberries were among the goods in the CPI basket.

Different statistical weights are applied to reflect the relative importance of the average household's expenditure. For example, a 10% increase in the price of petrol will affect people far more than a 50% increase in the price of light bulbs, batteries or tomatoes.

Measuring inflation and deflation

Revised ☐

The statistical weighting in the CPI is based on the proportion of the average household's income spent on the items in the representative basket. For example, if the typical household spends 15% of its income on food, then 15% of the weighting in the CPI is assigned to food prices. Therefore, items of expenditure that take a greater proportion of income are assigned a larger weighting. Changing fashions and trends, such as greater household expenditure on smartphones and tablet computers, require a review or update of the weighting in the CPI.

However, it must be noted that the CPI does not necessarily measure changes in average price levels (and hence the cost of living) for all stakeholders in the economy:

- The CPI only considers the expenditure of the 'average' household; whatever this might actually mean in a multicultural society in the real world.
- Different income earners can experience a different rate of inflation because their pattern of expenditure is not necessarily or accurately reflected by the CPI. For example, the average pensioner or university student will have different spending habits from a 'typical' family household.
- Inflation figures and calculations may not accurately reflect changes in consumption patterns due to time lags in collecting data to compile the CPI.

Economists calculate an **underlying rate of inflation** (or core rate of inflation), which is an adjusted measure of inflation that eliminates the sudden or volatile fluctuations in prices of essential items of expenditure such as oil, food and energy.

Economists also find the calculation of a **producer price index (PPI)** useful for predicting inflation or deflation by measuring changes in the prices of manufacturers and producers (rather than retailers who sell to consumers). The PPI consists of three price indices:

- raw materials, such as crude oil and copper
- intermediate goods, such as components and other semi-finished goods sold to other manufacturers and producers
- finished goods that are sold to retailers, such as Honda or BMW selling their cars to franchised car showroom dealers (operators).

> **Expert tip**
>
> It should be noted that, as a price index, the CPI ignores changes in the *quality* of goods and services – for example, the higher build quality of modern computers, televisions, cars and smartphones is not represented in the calculation of the CPI.

Calculating inflation *(HL only)*

> Revised ▢

The consumer prices index (CPI) is a weighted index of average consumer prices of goods and services over time. It is the most common method used to measure inflation (and hence changes in the cost of living) for a typical household in the economy.

A **base year**, with an index number of 100, is used as the starting period when calculating a price index such as the CPI. So, a price index of 115.2 means prices have in general increased by 15.2% since the base year.

Percentage changes in the index number are used to show inflation in subsequent years. So, if prices were to rise by another 5% in the following year, the price index number would become 120.96 (i.e. 115.2 × 1.05), or 20.96% higher since the base year.

In practice, price changes in the CPI are measured on a monthly basis but reported for a 12-month period. Calculating changes in the CPI will give the rate of inflation. There are two steps to do this:

- Collection of the price data (for the representative basket of goods and services of the average household), collected on a monthly basis.
- Assigning statistical weighting to each item of expenditure, representing different patterns of spending over time.

> ### Worked example
>
> The simplified example below, with three products in the representative basket of goods and services, shows how a CPI is calculated. Assume 2012 is the base year, when the total price of the basket was $20.
>
> | Product | Price in 2013 | Price in 2014 |
> |---|---|---|
> | Pizza | $9 | $10 |
> | Cinema ticket | $10 | $11 |
> | Petrol | $3 | $3.5 |
> | Total basket price | $22.0 | $24.5 |
>
> To calculate the inflation between 2013 and 2014, first calculate the price indices for the two years:
>
> - 2013: $\frac{\$22}{\$20} \times 100 = 110$ (prices in 2013 were 10% higher on average than in 2012).
>
> - 2014: $\frac{\$24.5}{\$20} \times 100 = 122.5$ (prices in 2014 were 22.5% higher on average than in 2012).
>
> The inflation rate between 2013 and 2014 is the percentage change in the price indices during these two periods:
>
> $$\frac{122.5 - 110}{110} \times 100 = \mathbf{11.36\%}$$

However, the products in the CPI are of different importance to the typical household, so statistical weighting is applied to reflect this. Suppose, for example, that food consumption accounts for 40% of average household spending, entertainment represents 20%, transport equals 25% and all other items account for the remaining 15%. To create a weighted CPI, economists multiply the price index of each item by the statistical weighting for the item. Applying the weights gives the following results:

Product	Price index	Weight	Weighted index
Food	110.0	0.40	$110 \times 0.4 = 44.0$
Entertainment	115.0	0.20	$115 \times 0.2 = 23.0$
Transport	116.4	0.25	$116.4 \times 0.25 = 29.1$
Others	123.3	0.15	$123.3 \times 0.15 = 18.5$
Weighted index			**114.6**

Whilst the price of food has increased the least (only 10%), the spending on food accounts for 40% of the typical household so has a much larger impact on the cost of living. Without using weighting, the average price index would be 116.18, i.e. $\dfrac{110+115+116.4+123.3}{4}$. The weighted index reduces the CPI to 114.6 because the relatively higher prices of non-food items account for a smaller proportion of spending by the typical household. Therefore, the use of a weighted CPI is more accurate in measuring changes in inflation and hence the cost of living.

EXAM PRACTICE *(HL ONLY)*

PAPER 3

13 The data below show the inflation rates for a country over 3 years.

YEAR	1st	2nd	3rd
INFLATION RATE (%)	2.5	1.7	2.3

    a Define the meaning of 'inflation rate'. [2]

    b Explain why inflation was at its highest level in the third year. [3]

14 Calculate the weighted price index from the information below. [3]

ITEM	PRICE INDEX	STATISTICAL WEIGHTING
Food and drink	120	10
Transportation	130	20
Leisure and entertainment	140	30
Housing	150	40

15 Calculate the inflation rate if the consumer price index changes from 123.0 in Year 1 to 129.15 in Year 2. [2]

16 Calculate the consumer price index if there is 3.0% inflation during the year if the price index was previously at 130. [2]

17 Calculate how much a basket of goods and services which is currently priced at $1200 would be if the CPI increased from 125.0 to 135.0. [3]

Expert tip

Although the CPI and RPI are the most widely used price indices for measuring inflation, they only take an average measure. They therefore hide the fact that the prices of some products increase more rapidly than others, whilst the price of other products might have actually fallen.

Expert tip

When evaluating the measurement of inflation, it is worth remembering that there are limitations of using the CPI to measure inflation. For example, the CPI has no relevance for atypical households. Housing costs also vary enormously between countries, making international comparisons difficult. Finally, the CPI does not reflect regional differences and disparities in inflation.

EXAM PRACTICE

PAPER 2

18 The data below are for a hypothetical country, Jukeland.

ITEM	RETAIL PRICE INDEX	WEIGHT
Clothing	110	10
Food	120	20
Housing	130	30
Others	140	40

a Define what is meant by a 'consumer price index' (CPI). [2]

b 'The typical household in Jukeland spends more money on housing than on food or clothing.' Explain this statement. [2]

c Use the data above to calculate a weighted price index for Jukeland. [4]

> **Common mistake**
>
> Students often define the CPI with reference to changes in the average price of a representative basket of *goods*, without acknowledging that *services* are also included in the calculation.

Consequences of inflation

Revised ☐

Inflation can complicate planning and decision making for households, firms and governments, with many consequences:

- **Menu costs** – Inflation impacts on the prices charged by firms. Catalogues, price lists and menus have to be updated regularly and this is costly to businesses.
- **Shoe leather costs** – Inflation causes fluctuations in price levels, so customers spend more time searching for the best deals, be it physically or online. They might also have to make more regular cash withdrawals. Shoe leather costs therefore represent an opportunity cost for customers.
- **Consumers** – The purchasing power of consumers declines when there is inflation, i.e. there is a fall in their real income because money is worth less than before. Therefore, as the cost of living increases, consumers need more money to buy the same amount of goods and services.
- **Savers** – Savers, be they individuals, firms or governments, will lose out from inflation, assuming there is no change in interest rates for savings. Hence, inflation discourages savings as money becomes less effective as a store of value.
- **Lenders** – Creditors, be they individuals, firms or governments, will also lose from inflation. This is because the money lent out to borrowers becomes worth less than before due to inflation.
- **Borrowers** – By contrast, borrowers tend to gain from inflation as the money they need to repay is worth less than when they initially borrowed it. For example, a mortgage at 5% interest with inflation at 3.5% means that the real interest rate is only 1.5%, i.e. the real value of the debt declines.
- **Fixed-income earners** – Fixed-income earners (such as salaried workers and pensioners whose pay does not change with their level of output) are worse off than before as the purchasing power of their fixed income declines with higher prices.
- **Low income earners** – Inflation harms the poorest members of society far more than those on high incomes. They tend to have a high price elasticity of demand for goods and services. By contrast, those on high incomes and accumulated wealth are not so affected by higher prices.
- **Exporters** – The international competitiveness of a country tends to fall when there is domestic inflation as exports become less price-competitive. This causes a drop in profits, leading to a fall in export earnings, lower economic growth and higher unemployment.
- **Importers** – Imports become more expensive for individuals, firms and the government due to the decline in the purchasing power of money. Hence, inflation can cause problems for countries without many natural resources such as petroleum, steel, rice and coffee.

> **Expert tip**
>
> Governments aim to control inflation because it reduces the value of money and the spending power of households, governments and firms. For example, inflation was around 48% in Syria in 2013, meaning that the general price level increased by an average of 48% in a year.

- **Employers** – Workers are likely to demand a pay rise during times of inflation to maintain their level of real income. As a result, labour costs of production rise and profits margins decline, *ceteris paribus*.
- **Business confidence levels** – The combination of uncertainty and the lower expected real rates of return on investment (due to higher costs of production) tends to lower the amount of planned investment in the economy.
- A **wage-price spiral** occurs when trade unions negotiate higher wages to keep income in line with inflation, but this simply fuels inflation as firms raise prices to maintain their profit margins.

Therefore, high inflation makes conditions far less predictable for economic stability, i.e. there is greater uncertainty for consumers, producers and the government.

EXAM PRACTICE *(HL ONLY)*

PAPER 3

19 Study the data below and answer the questions that follow.

YEAR	INFLATION RATE (%)	WAGE INCREASE (%)
1	2.5	3.0
2	3.1	3.5
3	2.9	3.1

   a In which year was there the largest increase in real wages? Explain your answer. **[3]**

   b Explain why average wages were higher in Year 3 than in Year 2. **[3]**

EXAM PRACTICE

PAPER 2

20 Iran's inflation rate climbed above 30% in 2013, having reached 31.5% at the end of the Islamic country's calendar year. The country, with a population of 74.8 million, had experienced double-digit inflation rates for most of the past decade. At the end of 2010, the government reduced food and fuel subsidies, thereby fuelling inflation. In addition, international sanctions due to Iran's disputed nuclear programme forced down the value of the Iranian rial, the country's official currency. This meant added pressure on higher prices in the economy.

Inflation rate in Iran

PERIOD	INFLATION (%)
March 2012	26.4
Dec 2012	27.4
March 2013	31.5

   a With reference to the data above, explain why prices in Iran were generally higher in 2013 than in 2012. **[4]**

   b Explain two reasons why the Iranian government might aim to control the level of inflation in its economy. **[4]**

   c Evaluate how some Iranians are likely to have been more affected than others by the double-digit inflation rates. **[8]**

Consequences of deflation

Revised ▢

The consequences of deflation depend on the cause. **Benign deflation** is generally positive as the economy is able to produce more (an outwards shift of the *LRAS* curve), thus boosting national output and employment, without an increase in the general price level (see Figure 2.23).

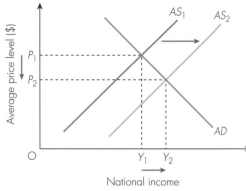

- Deflation can be caused by higher *AS*, i.e. increased productive capacity of the economy.
- This drives down the general price level of goods and services from P_1 to P_2 whlist increasing national income from Y_1 to Y_2.
- Such deflation is called benign deflation (non-threatening deflation), perhaps caused by higher productivity or technological progress.

Figure 2.23 Deflation caused by supply factors

Economists are concerned with **malign deflation**, which is generally harmful to the economy due to a decline in aggregate demand for goods and services, often associated with an economic recession and rising levels of unemployment (see Figure 2.24).

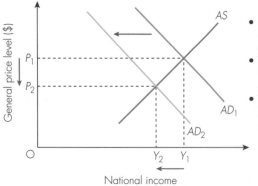

- Deflation can also be caused by a leftwards shift of the aggregate demand curve from AD_1 to AD_2.
- This reduces national income from Y_1 to Y_2, and forces down the general price level from P_1 to P_2.
- This causes malign deflation (deflation that is harmful to the economy).

Figure 2.24 Deflation caused by demand factors

The consequences of malign deflation include the following:
- **Cyclical unemployment** – As deflation usually occurs due to a fall in aggregate demand in the economy, this causes a fall in the derived demand for labour, i.e. deflation can cause huge job losses in the economy.
- **Bankruptcies** – Consumers tend to spend less during periods of deflation, so firms suffer from lower sales revenues and profits. This makes it more difficult for them to pay their costs and liabilities (debts such as mortgages), thus causing a large number of bankruptcies.
- **Lower investment expenditure** – Firms have less of an incentive to invest because they receive lower prices and hence profitability. This can have a detrimental impact on economic growth.
- **A rise in the real value of debts** – The real cost of debts (borrowing) increases when there is deflation because real interest rates rise when the price level falls. For example, if interest rates average 1.0% but the inflation rate is −1.5%, then the real interest rate is 2.5%.
- **A fall in the value of wealth** – Due to declining profitability, share prices fall during times of deflation. This means that dividends and the capital returns on holding shares also fall, thus reducing the wealth of shareholders.
- **Government debt** – With more bankruptcies, unemployment and lower levels of economic activity, tax revenues fall whilst the amount of government spending rises (due to the economic decline associated with malign inflation). This can create a budget deficit for the government.

Expert tip

The extent to which an economy is affected by malign deflation will depend on the severity of deflation. Portugal's experience of zero rate inflation in 2013 would have been very different from Somalia's −15.35% inflation rate in the same year.

■ **Declining confidence levels** – With deflation and the subsequent rising real value of debts, both consumer and business confidence levels fall, further adding to the economic problems in the country – for example, consumers may postpone their spending and firms postpone their investments.

EXAM PRACTICE

PAPER 2

21 For much of the past 20 years, Japan has suffered from deflation (see the chart below).

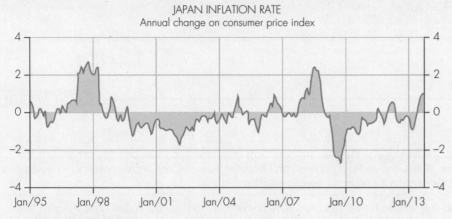

JAPAN INFLATION RATE
Annual change on consumer price index

a Define the term deflation. **[2]**

b Explain what evidence there is in the chart to suggest that Japan has suffered deflation for most of the past 20 years. **[2]**

c Explain the impacts of prolonged deflation for the Japanese economy. **[4]**

Causes of inflation

Revised

There are two main causes of inflation: demand–pull inflation and cost–push inflation. **Demand–pull inflation** is inflation triggered by higher levels of aggregate demand in the economy, which drives up the general price level (see Figure 2.25).

Hence, an increase in any determinant of aggregate demand (changes in consumption, investment, government spending and net exports) will cause demand–pull inflation, for example higher GDP per capita, income tax cuts or lower interest rates.

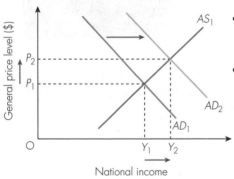

- During an economic boom, consumption of goods and services increases due to higher GDP per capita and higher levels of employment.
- This is shown by a rightwards shift of the aggregate demand curve from AD_1 to AD_2, raising national income from Y_1 to Y_2 and increasing the general price level from P_1 to P_2.

Figure 2.25 Demand–pull inflation

Cost–push inflation is triggered by higher costs of production thus shifting aggregate supply to the left and forcing up average prices (see Figure 2.26).

Causes of cost–push inflation include higher imported prices for raw materials, components (semi-finished goods) and finished goods for sale, higher wages in the economy, increased corporation taxes and soaring rents for commercial properties.

Expert tip

An increase in aggregate demand has a minimal impact on inflation if there is spare capacity in the economy, i.e. if aggregate supply is relatively price elastic.

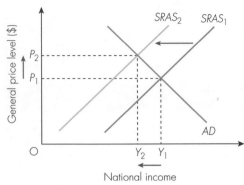

• Higher raw material costs, increased wages, and soaring rents shift the aggregate supply curve from $SRAS_1$ to $SRAS_2$.
• This forces up the average price level from P_1 to P_2 but reduces national income from Y_1 to Y_2.

Figure 2.26 Cost–push inflation

Types of inflation

Table 2.3 Types of inflation

Creeping inflation	Occurs when prices are rising slightly, i.e. very low rates of inflation up to around 3% per annum. It is the mildest form of inflation and presents few problems for the economy. More economically developed countries (MEDCs) tend to experience creeping inflation.	
Moderate inflation	Refers to single-digit inflation rates (less than 10% per year). Professor Paul A. Samuelson argues that moderate inflation represents a stable rate of inflation and is not a serious economic problem.	
Strato inflation	Refers to double-digit, and often triple-digit, rates of inflation. It occurs if moderate inflation persists (continues to increase) and is not controlled. Prolonged periods of strato inflation (sometimes referred to as **chronic inflation**) can lead to hyperinflation.	
Hyperinflation	Refers to extortionately high and uncontrollable rates of inflation – for example, Zimbabwe's macroeconomic mismanagement between 2003 and 2009 resulted in hyperinflation of 231,000,000% in July 2008, resulting in the issue of 100 trillion Zimbabwean dollar banknotes!	

Expert tip

It is difficult for an economy to break out of a downward deflationary spiral (Japan has suffered deflation for much of the past 20 years). Business and consumer confidence levels would need to increase significantly to boost aggregate demand. It might be possible, for example, to cut interest rates to encourage consumer spending and increased investment in the economy.

Common mistake

Students are often quoted stating that demand–pull and cost–push are the two types of inflation. This is incorrect as these are the *causes*, not the *types* of inflation.

Government policies to deal with inflation

In general, inflation can be controlled by limiting the factors that cause demand–pull inflation and cost–push inflation. For example, the government can raise taxes and interest rates to limit consumption and investment expenditure in the economy to control demand–pull inflation.

Policies to deal with demand–pull inflation include the following:

- Deflationary fiscal policy to reduce aggregate demand – for example, raising both direct and indirect taxes to reduce consumption and/or lowering government expenditure.
- Contractionary monetary policy – for example, raising interest rates and/or reducing growth of the money supply to limit consumption and investment expenditure.
- Supply-side policies to boost national output – for example, improving productivity and/or labour relations in order to increase aggregate supply, thus dampening the impact of inflation.
- Import controls to reduce the chances of experiencing imported inflation (caused by higher import prices of essential goods and services such as oil and financial services).

Policies to deal with cost–push inflation include the following:

- Negotiations with labour unions to match any annual wage rises with higher productivity levels, thus limiting inflationary pressures by boosting aggregate supply.
- Government intervention to limit annual nominal wage increases, thus preventing a potential wage-price inflationary spiral.
- Subsidising production to moderate costs, and hence prices. Some countries, such as Iran and France, have used subsidies for food and fuel to reduce price inflation in the economy.
- Revaluation of the currency on the foreign exchange market, as the higher exchange rate helps to lower the cost of imported raw materials, components and finished goods.

Governments are likely to use a combination of contractionary monetary policy, deflationary fiscal policy and supply-side policies to combat inflation.

Collectively, however, contractionary policies are likely to reduce the level of economic activity, thus possibly harming economic growth, employment opportunities and international trade.

Possible relationships between unemployment and inflation *(HL only)*

The short-run **Phillips curve** shows a potential trade-off between inflation and unemployment. A fall in unemployment, due to an increase in aggregate demand, creates more consumption expenditure in the economy, thereby fuelling inflation (see Figure 2.27).

The model is named after New Zealand economist William Phillips (1958) who used data from the UK from 1861 to 1957 to show the trade-off between the unemployment rate and the rate of change in nominal wages (which correlates to price stability).

The short-run Phillips curve shows that there is a **natural rate of unemployment (NRU)** – the unemployment rate that exists when the inflation rate is zero. The NRU is the unemployment rate that exists at full employment, i.e. where the demand for labour equals the supply of labour. It exists at the full employment level of output, i.e. the sum of frictional, seasonal and structural unemployment

When unemployment is above its natural rate, deflation occurs because the inflation rate becomes negative.

An increase in aggregate demand will tend to cause a movement up (to the left) along the short-run Phillips curve because unemployment falls whilst the average price level begins to rise.

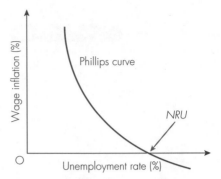

Figure 2.27 The short-run Phillips curve (SRPC)

The Phillips curve can shift over time. For example, a reduction in structural unemployment will tend to shift the Phillips curve to the left.

Supply shocks shift the short-run Phillips curve to the right (creating a higher NRU), for example oil crises, financial crises, natural disasters (such as severe flooding or drought) and the spread of contagious (infectious) diseases.

The Phillips curve lost some credibility in the 1970s due to the existence of **stagflation** – when unemployment rises (due to a fall in real national output) with inflation occurring in the economy. Stagflation is often caused by supply shocks.

Subsequent studies of the Phillips curve showed that the trade-off between inflation and unemployment only seemed to exist in the short-run. In the long run, there is no trade-off (see Figure 2.28) because inflation would be stable.

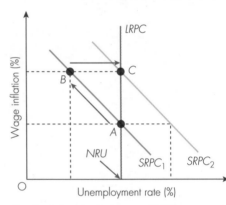

- The movement from point *A* to point *B* can be caused by expansionary fiscal and monetary policies.
- Real wages fall with inflation, so workers push for higher nominal wages.
- This is not sustainable, so the short run Phillips curve shifts from *SRPC*$_1$ to *SRPC*$_2$ with unemployment reverting to the *NRU*.
- Hence, attempts to reduce unemployment below its natural rate will be inflationary in the long run, as shown by the movement from point *B* to point *C*.

Figure 2.28 The long-run Phillips curve (LRPC)

The *SRPC* can shift outwards due to a decrease in *SRAS*, perhaps caused by supply shocks such as an oil shortage, natural disaster or a global financial crisis. In extreme situations, this can lead to stagflation.

Most governments strive to reduce the *NRU* (shifting the *LRPC* to the left) by creating incentives to work and encouraging more (re)training schemes for the unemployed to improve their occupational mobility.

Economic growth

Revised ▢

The meaning of economic growth

Revised ▢

Economists believe that sustained economic growth is an important macroeconomic objective because it is the most practical measure of standards of living in a country. Economic growth represents the long-term expansion in the productive capacity of the economy, i.e. the annual percentage change in GDP.

Diagrammatically, economic growth can be shown by a rightwards shift of the long-run aggregate supply curve (see Figure 2.29) or an outwards shift of the production possibility curve (see Figure 2.30).

Economic growth occurs when there is an increase in the quantity and/or quality of factors of production, such as an increase in labour productivity or improvements in the state of technology. **Negative economic growth** results in a recession in the business cycle.

> **Keyword definition**
> **Economic growth** refers to an increase in a country's real gross domestic product over time, i.e. the annual percentage change in real national output.

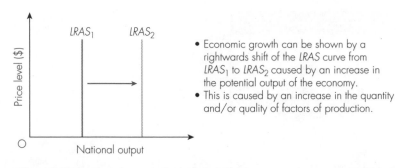

Figure 2.29 Economic growth and the *LRAS*

Figure 2.30 shows that economic growth occurs when there is an increase in the actual output of the economy. This can result from the use of unemployed resources (Point A to Point B) or from improved factor utilisation and increased productive efficiency (Point B to Point C).

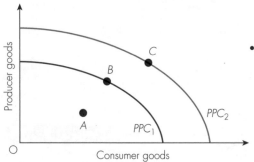

- A combination of an increase in the quantity and quality of factors of production shifts the *PPC* outwards from *PPC₁* to *PPC₂*, creating more producer and consumer goods.

Figure 2.30 Economic growth and the *PPC*

> **Expert tip**
>
> Although economic growth is generally regarded as the key indicator of economic wellbeing or the general standard of living in a country, there are other measures, such as the Human Development Index (HDI). This composite index measures three dimensions of living standards: healthcare (life expectancy), education (years of schooling) and income levels (real GDP per capita).

Calculating economic growth *(HL only)*

Revised ☐

Economic growth is measured by calculating changes in real gross domestic product.

Changes in nominal GDP figures give gross domestic product at **current prices**, whereas changes in real GDP figures give gross domestic product at **constant prices** (allowing economists to compare growth rates over time without the impact of price inflation).

A **GDP deflator** is an index number used to convert nominal GDP to real GDP by eliminating the impact of inflation on the calculation of GDP. It can therefore be seen as a measure of the general level of inflation in the economy.

Real GDP is calculated by dividing nominal GDP by the GDP price deflator and then multiplying the result by 100.

Worked example					
Year	Nominal GDP ($bn)	GDP deflator	Real GDP ($bn)	Nominal growth rate (%)	Real Growth rate (%)
2012	120.0	100.0	120.00	–	–
2013	126.5	102.8	123.05	5.41	2.54
2014	136.2	106.4	128.00	7.67	4.02

With 2012 as the base year, the nominal GDP is equal to real GDP for the year, i.e. $120bn.

With inflation running at 2.8% in 2013, the nominal value of GDP includes higher prices due to inflation. A GDP deflator of 102.8 means that real GDP is actually $\frac{126.5}{102.8} = \$123.05$bn.

Worked example *(Continued)*

The real growth rate between 2012 and 2013 is therefore:

$$\frac{123.05 - 120.0}{120} \times 100 = 2.54\%$$

Note that growth in nominal GDP is higher:

$$\frac{126.05 - 120}{120} \times 100 = 5.41\%$$

Similarly, in 2014 the nominal GDP is deflated to yield:

$$\frac{136.2}{106.4} \times 100 = \$128.0\text{bn}$$

The growth rate between 2013 and 2014 is:

$$\frac{128 - 123.05}{123.05} \times 100 = 4.02\%$$

Note that growth in nominal GDP is again higher:

$$\frac{136.2 - 126.5}{126.5} \times 100 = 7.67\%$$

Causes of economic growth

Revised ☐

Factor endowments refer to the quantity and quality of a country's factors of production – for example, Saudi Arabia is well-endowed in the supply of oil, France has plenty of arable land for its agricultural output, and Australia has many natural resources such as coal, gold and iron ore.

Discovery of raw materials such as oil, or any other tradable commodity in a country, will increase its productive capacity and so tend to shift the PPC outwards.

The size and skills of the labour force impacts on the country's economic growth – for example, India's large labour force and Germany's highly skilled workers have contributed to the economic growth of these countries.

The mobility of labour refers to the extent to which workers are willing and able to change jobs (occupational mobility) and move to different locations for employment (geographical mobility). The more mobile workers are, the greater economic growth tends to be.

Labour productivity refers to the output produced in a given time period. It is determined by several interrelated factors such as the qualifications, experience, training, skills and motivation of the labour force. Higher productivity tends to lead to greater economic growth.

Investment expenditure in capital and human resources is vital for long-term competitiveness and economic growth as it boosts the country's productive capacity – for example, foreign direct investment can stimulate economic growth and development.

EXAM PRACTICE

PAPER 2

22 According to *The Economist's* Economist Intelligence Unit, Macau's economy grew by 14.3% in 2013 – the highest economic growth rate for any country in the year. The island nation had enjoyed 9.8% growth in 2012 with gambling revenue increasing by approximately 14% to about $38 billion, making it the world's biggest gambling market ahead of Las Vegas. In 2011, Macau enjoyed a stunning 20.7% growth rate. The country is also investing huge amounts of money to attract a wider range of tourists with casino giants such as Sands and MGM Resort also investing large sums of money into the economy.

   a Define the term 'economic growth'. [2]

   b Explain how investment in Macau helps to boost its economic growth. [4]

Consequences of economic growth

Revised

Impacts on living standards – Economic growth tends to lead to higher standards of living for the average person. Higher real income per head enables people to spend more money to meet their needs and wants, thus helping to eliminate absolute poverty in the country.

Unemployment – Economic growth leads to higher levels of employment in the economy. This helps to raise consumption and encourages further investment in capital, helping to sustain growth in the economy.

Inflation – If the economy grows rapidly due to excessive aggregate demand in the economy, there is the danger of demand–pull inflation. This can lead to the prices of goods and services rising to unstable levels, with a negative impact on the economy's international competitiveness.

Income distribution – Economic growth often creates greater disparities in the distribution of income and wealth, widening the gap between rich and poor. However, economic growth also leads to greater tax revenues, enabling the government to redistribute income and wealth.

The **current account** of the balance of payments – The current account tends to improve with economic growth due to a higher value of net exports (a component of aggregate demand).

Sustainability – Growth usually creates problems for the sustainability of scarce resources and economic wellbeing, such as resource depletion (e.g. deforestation and overfishing), pollution, congestion, damage to ecosystems, land erosion and climate change.

> **Expert tip**
>
> Whilst economic growth is generally seen as a desirable macroeconomic objective, remember that individuals do not benefit equally from economic growth.

Equity in the distribution of income

Revised

The meaning of equity in the distribution of income

Revised

Equity differs from equality in the distribution of income. Equity is based on the argument that income inequalities (such as wage differentials) are needed to create incentives for people to study and work harder. Equality means equal distribution of income in the economy.

Economies face unequitable distribution of income due to the natural unequal ownership of factors of production in a free market economy. For example, consider the wage differentials between professional footballers, doctors or pilots and those earning the national minimum wage.

> **Keyword definitions**
>
> **Equity** means fairness, such as those with higher levels of qualifications, skills and experience being paid more, so justified inequalities exist.
>
> **Equality** means there is parity in income (earnings) between individuals, i.e. everyone is paid equally, so no inequalities exist.

Indicators of income equality/inequality

Revised

The degree of income equality (or inequality) can be measured by the relative share of national income earned by given percentages of the population.

Deciles refer to the statistical method of splitting data into tenths, with each part accounting for 10% of the population. For example, if the top decile (10%) of the income earners accounted for 45% of the national income, there would be huge income inequalities.

Quintiles are used to divide statistical data into fifths, with each part representing 20% of the population.

The **Lorenz curve**, named after US economist Max Otto Lorenz (1905), is a graphical representation of income distribution in a country. It shows the degree of income inequality, such as the poorest 10% of income earners accounting for just 1% of the nation's income.

In Figure 2.31, the 45° line shows perfect equality in income distribution. For example, at point A the first four deciles account for 40% of the national income.

The Lorenz curve shows the actual income distribution in a country. Point B in Figure 2.31 shows the hypothetical situation where 60% of the population account for just 20% of the nation's income. So, the top four deciles must earn the remaining 80% of the national income.

The greater the area between the 45° line of total income equality and the Lorenz curve (as shown by the area between the two curves), the greater the income inequality in the country.

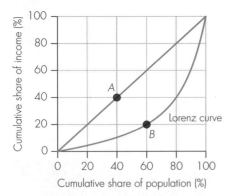

Figure 2.31 The Lorenz curve

The **Gini coefficient**, named after Italian statistician Corrado Gini (1912), is a statistical tool that measures income inequality, with the outcome ranging from 0 (complete equality) to 1 (total inequality). It is a numerical representation of a country's Lorenz curve.

At one extreme, if an individual accounted for all national income, the Lorenz curve would pass through the coordinates (0, 0), (100, 0) and (100,100) leading to a Gini coefficient equal to 1. At the other extreme, there is total equality as shown by the (45°) line of perfect equality. The Gini coefficient is calculated by the ratio of the area under the Lorenz curve to the area under the 45° line of complete equality, which has a total area of
$$\frac{100 \times 100}{2} = 5000.$$

In general, low-income countries and/or those that suffer from a high degree of corruption have a high Gini coefficient, such as Haiti (0.592) and South Africa (0.631). High-income countries tend to have a low Gini coefficient, such as Germany (0.283), Finland (0.269) and Denmark (0.240).

Most governments strive to achieve greater income equality over time. They can use the Gini coefficient to measure whether income distribution is increasing or decreasing.

Common mistake

Do not misinterpret the Gini coefficient as a comparative measure of national income between countries. Different countries with the same Gini coefficient do *not* have the same national income (GDP), as this tool is used simply to measure relative equality in income distribution.

Poverty

Revised

Poverty refers to the state of an individual, household or country being extremely poor, i.e. not having enough money to meet basic human needs such as food, clothing, shelter, healthcare and education. The World Bank describes poverty as a situation people want to escape.

Definitions of poverty are relative because it varies considerably depending on the situation in different countries. Feeling poor in Finland or Norway is different from living in poverty in Sierra Leone or Namibia. Different degrees of poverty also exist within the borders of a country.

The relative poverty in a country is determined by examining the percentage of the population with earnings less than a predetermined percentage of the median income within that country.

Tackling poverty is a key economic issue because, apart from humanitarian reasons, it represents economic inefficiency preventing people and economies from reaching their full potential.

Keyword definitions
Absolute poverty exists when people are deprived of basic human needs for human survival. Those in absolute poverty suffer from malnutrition, hunger, a lack of clean water, poor healthcare and inadequate shelter.

Relative poverty refers to incomes, and hence consumption, below the social norm within a country. It can lead to damaging effects on individuals and families, including social exclusion. It is a comparative measure, so relative poverty will differ from country to country.

Causes of poverty

Revised

Table 2.4 Possible causes of poverty

Low income	Without sufficient money, households will not be able to meet their basic human needs. According to The United Nations and World Health Organization, people earning less than $2 per day suffer from absolute poverty.
Unemployment	Without a job, people are unlikely to be able to sustain their standard of living. The consequences of unemployment include lower self-esteem and depression, and higher rates of crime, violence, health problems and homelessness.
Lack of human capital	The lack of sufficient provision of, and investment in, education and training leads to mass poverty. Without the necessary knowledge and skills, the workforce will be unproductive and national income will be significantly lower than its potential.
Overpopulation	The lack of population control means that GDP per capita will tend to decline, thus causing greater poverty in the country. Larger families also tend to suffer from relative poverty.
Gender inequalities	More women tend to suffer from poverty than men, mainly due to social prejudice against females. For example, women are less likely to be in paid employment on a full-time basis and tend to earn less than men. This represents an inefficient use of labour resources.
Corruption and conflict	Highly corrupt countries and those in political turmoil tend to have a high Gini coefficient, causing mass poverty for the majority of the population.
Lack of natural resources	The lack of natural resources and/or the poor management of these resources will generally reduce a country's potential net export earnings.
Natural disasters	Major disasters such as tsunamis and earthquakes can wipe out much of a country's scarce resources, thus creating mass poverty. Countries can struggle to fully recover from major natural disasters.

Consequences of poverty

Revised

The main causes of poverty are as follows:

■ **Low living standards** – Those in poverty, be it absolute or relative, experience a low quality of life as they are unable to meet their basic needs or to experience a better standard of living.

■ **Lack of access to healthcare and education** – Poverty-stricken people are unable to afford quality healthcare and education. This hinders the human capital of the country and thus compromises prospects of economic growth.

■ **Conflict and war** – History has shown that poverty often leads to political instability and can even lead to war in extreme cases. This can lead to other issues, such as a mass emigration of the population, which undermines the country's ability to recuperate from poverty.

Clearly, poverty hinders the ability of governments to achieve other macroeconomic objectives such as economic growth and low unemployment.

> **Expert tip**
>
> The causes and consequences of poverty can create a **poverty trap**, i.e. the poor become even poorer. For example, low incomes lead to low savings, reduced funds for investments, reduced productivity, lower national output and hence a diminished quality of life. This increases poverty even further. Hence, eradicating poverty is a key macroeconomic priority for many governments.

The role of taxation in promoting equity

Revised

A major role of taxation is to promote income equality by redistributing income to help the relatively less well-off in society.

Direct taxes are taxes on earnings, whereas indirect taxes are taxes on spending. Direct taxes, rather than indirect taxes, are used as a mechanism to redistribute income from the rich to the poor – for example, the highest earners in Belgium pay up to 55% income tax.

To create incentives to work, individuals are granted a **personal tax allowance**, i.e. they can earn up to a certain amount before they are taxed. The allowance tends to rise with inflation – for example, in the UK, the tax allowance for 2013–2014 was £9440 and rose to £10,000 in 2014–2015.

Indirect taxes are often used to moderate spending on demerit goods such as alcohol, tobacco and gambling.

> **Keyword definitions**
>
> A **direct tax** is a government levy on income, such as income tax and corporation tax.
>
> An **indirect tax** is a government levy on expenditure, such as a goods and services tax (GST).

Direct and indirect taxes can be further categorised:

■ **Progressive taxation** charges a higher *percentage* tax as an individual's income rises, i.e. those who earn more pay a greater proportion of their income in tax.

■ **Regressive taxation** charges a greater proportion of tax on lower-income earners – for example, sales taxes, such as value added tax (VAT) and goods and services tax (GST), account for a greater proportion of tax paid by the relatively poor.

■ **Proportional taxation** charges the same flat rate percentage tax, irrespective of how much an individual earns. Whilst more tax is paid in absolute terms as an individual's income rises, the percentage tax paid is fixed.

A drawback in using proportional and progressive taxation to redistribute income is that they can create disincentives to work, thereby harming economic efficiency and economic growth.

> **Common mistake**
>
> Too often, students incorrectly define progressive taxes as a policy whereby individuals pay more taxes as their income level rises. This is true for proportional taxes too, i.e. the more you earn, the more you pay in taxation. Instead, progressive taxation charges more tax as a *percentage* of the individual's income, i.e. the more you earn, the greater the average rate of tax paid.

Calculating the marginal and average rates of tax *(HL only)*

Revised ☐

The **marginal rate of tax** refers to the percentage of direct tax paid on the last dollar of an individual's income, i.e. the change in tax rate paid from a given change in income, or $\dfrac{\Delta T}{\Delta Y}$.

The **average rate of tax** refers to the amount of tax paid compared with the amount of income earned, i.e. the total tax paid divided by the total income for an individual, or $\dfrac{T}{Y}$.

The average rate of tax zincreases under a progressive tax system with higher incomes. Under a regressive tax system, the average rate of tax falls when incomes rise.

Under a progressive tax system, an individual's marginal rate of tax is greater than his/her average rate of tax. Under a proportional tax system, as the rate of tax is fixed, the marginal and average rate of taxation are the same.

EXAM PRACTICE *(HL ONLY)*

PAPER 3

23 Suppose a country taxes an individual $5500 on earnings of $55,000 a year and charges another person $1500 on earnings of $15,000 a year. Explain what type of tax system the country uses. [2]

24 Use the data below to answer the following questions for an individual who earns $40,000 per year.

  a Identify the marginal rate of income tax. [1]

  b Calculate the total amount of tax paid by the individual. [2]

  c Calculate the average rate of income tax. [2]

  d Calculate the average rate of tax for another individual who earns $80,000 per year. [3]

INCOME TIER	TAX RATE (%)
First $10,000	0
Next $20,000	10
Next $20,000	20
Thereafter	30

25 Calculate the average tax rate of individuals who earn $50,000 per year in a country that charges a flat rate of 20% income tax and grants individuals a tax allowance of $15,000. [2]

EXAM PRACTICE (CONTINUED)

26 Calculate the change in the amount of tax paid if an individual faces a marginal tax rate of 45% when her income changes from $47,000 to $55,000 per year. [2]

27 From the data below, calculate the tax paid by an individual who earns $35,000 a year. [2]

INCOME TIER	TAX RATE (%)
$9000	0
$9001–$20,000	10
$20,001–$30,000	20
$30,001 and above	30

Other measures to promote equity

Revised ☐

Apart from taxation policy, **government expenditure** enables socially desirable goods and services to be provided, for example healthcare services, education and infrastructure. They might do this by directly providing the services or by subsidising the output of these services.

Subsidies enable firms to provide socially desirable goods and services in order to redistribute income, by making these merit goods available to everyone, for example education and healthcare.

The provision of essential infrastructure (such as sanitation and clean water supplies) helps to promote equality for those on low incomes and to eradicate absolute poverty.

Transfer payments are another means that the government uses to promote income equality by making payments to the less affluent without any corresponding exchange or change in output. Examples include:

■ old-age pensions – an income support scheme paid monthly to elderly people beyond retirement age who may not have any other form of income
■ unemployment benefits – transfer payments made to unemployed people to enable them to meet their basic human needs
■ child allowances (also known as child benefits) – welfare payment made to parents or guardians of children and teenagers, for spending on items such as food, clothing, schooling, transport and health check-ups.

> ### Expert tip
>
> When making or evaluating recommendations to promote income equity, remember that every government decision has an opportunity cost. For example, redistributing income and wealth by using progressive taxes involves administrative costs to the government.

The relationship between equity and efficiency

Revised ☐

Economists can evaluate government policies to promote equality by assessing their potential positive or negative effects on efficiency in the allocation of scarce resources.

The three main ways of government intervention to promote equality are: taxation policy, government expenditure (through direct provision or through subsidies) and by transfer payments.

Whilst taxation provides necessary funds to pay for government expenditure (direct provision and/or subsidies), it puts extra pressure on taxpayers and can cause disincentives to work. The effectiveness of a country's taxation policy can be evaluated using the following criteria:

■ Equitable – Taxes should be based on the principle of the taxpayer's ability to pay, otherwise it creates huge disincentive effects.
■ Economic – The cost of collecting the tax should be a relatively small proportion of the tax yield.
■ Convenience – The methods and timing of tax payments should be made as easy as possible for people to pay.

■ Certainty – The amount and the deadline of the tax due should be unquestionably clear, thus limiting late payments and the number of tax evaders.

Transfer payments are costly and drain the limited budgets of governments. Austerity measures following the global financial crisis of 2008 caused severe economic problems for countries such as Portugal, Ireland, Greece and Spain. They can also cause laziness amongst the workforce.

There is an opportunity cost in the direct provision of goods and services to redistribute income.

Subsidies, apart from being costly to taxpayers, can encourage firms to become reliant on government funding, thus hindering economic efficiency in the allocation of resources.

2.4 Fiscal policy

Revised ☐

The government budget

Revised ☐

Taxation policies can be used to redistribute income and wealth to benefit less wealthy members of society. Taxation can also be used to help control the rate of inflation in the economy, thus affecting its international competitiveness.

Government spending can then be used to improve standards of living, such as by building schools, hospitals and transportation networks. Government expenditure is also a key component of aggregate demand, so an increase in government spending helps to boost national output, jobs and economic growth.

> **Keyword definition**
> **Fiscal policy** is the use of taxation and government expenditure policies to influence the level of economic activity and macroeconomic objectives.

Sources of government revenue

Revised ☐

The main source of government revenue is from taxes. These can be classified as either **direct taxes** (levied on earnings and income) or **indirect taxes** (levied on expenditure).

Table 2.5 Examples of direct taxes

Income tax	Levied on personal incomes, i.e. wages, interest, rent and dividends. In most countries, this is the main source of tax revenue for the government.
Corporation tax	Direct tax on the profits of businesses.
Capital gains tax	Levy on the earnings made from investments such as buying shares and private property.
Inheritance tax	Tax on the transfer of income and wealth, such as money or property bequeathed (passed onto) another person.
Windfall tax	Charged on individuals and firms that gain an unexpected one-off amount of money, such as a person winning the lottery or the gains from a takeover bid for a firm.

Table 2.6 Examples of indirect taxes

Sales tax	Indirect tax, such as value added tax (VAT) or goods and services tax (GST), charged on the manufacturing, sale and consumption of goods and services.
Excise duties	Indirect inland taxes imposed on certain produces. Depending on the country, these might include alcohol, tobacco, petrol, soft drinks and gambling.
Customs duties	Indirect cross-border taxes on foreign imports.
Stamp duty	Progressive tax paid on the sale of commercial or residential property.
Carbon tax	Tax on vehicle manufacturers or firms that produce excessive carbon emissions.

Other sources of government revenue include the following:

- The **sale of goods and services**. These come from state-owned enterprises, such as national providers of postal services, the national broadcasting corporation, the airport authority and nationwide railway operators.
- The **sale of state-owned enterprises**. Privatisation proceeds can be earned by selling government-owned assets and enterprises. However, this is a short-term policy as state-owned assets can only be sold once to the private sector.
- **Sovereign wealth funds** (SWF) are state-owned investment funds such as stocks and shares, the bonds of other governments, investment in property and gold reserves. These sources help to generate income to fund government spending.
- **Public-sector borrowing** is used by government when its   sources of revenue (from taxes, state-owned enterprises and privatisation proceeds) do not meet its spending needs.

Types of government expenditure

Government spending can be classified as:

- **current expenditure** – government spending on goods and services consumed within the (current) year, i.e. it is expenditure for immediate operations and benefits, for example wages and salaries for public-sector workers or current expenditure on education.
- **capital expenditure** – long-term items of government spending (investment) that boost the economy's productive capacity, for example infrastructure (e.g. as the building of new roads and airports).
- **transfer payments** – welfare payments from the government to third parties without any corresponding return, for example unemployment benefits, old-aged pensions and child allowances.

> **Expert tip**
>
> Ideally, the government would only borrow money to fund capital expenditure (i.e. to fund investment in the economy) and never to pay for transfer payments or current expenditure.

> **Expert tip**
>
> Ensure you understand the meaning of transfer payments. They are considered to be part of government spending but do not appear as part of the national income statistics as there is no corresponding output for transfer payments.

The budget outcome

The government's revenues and expenditure are recorded in its annual budget. There are three possible outcomes:

- A **budget deficit** exists if government spending is greater than government revenue. This might occur during a recession when welfare payments tend to rise whilst tax revenues fall due to rising unemployment.
- A **budget surplus** exists if government revenue exceeds public-sector expenditure. This might occur during an economic boom when tax revenues will be higher (due to increased earnings and consumption), whilst government spending on transfer payments will tend to fall.
- A **balanced budget** occurs when the amount of government spending equals the value of its revenues.

Governments strive to balance their budgets in the long run. Budget surpluses tend to be politically unpopular with taxpayers. Budget deficits require government borrowing, which can be rather expensive due to interest charges on the loans.

There is a negative correlation between government debt and the budget, i.e. the more money a government owes, the more likely that its budget will be in deficit.

A budget surplus can help to reduce public-sector debt caused by budget deficits in previous years, whereas a budget deficit will tend to increase government debt.

> **Common mistake**
>
> Some students seem to think that a budget deficit is 'bad' for the economy. It is important to remember that a government might deliberately spend more than it collects in revenue in order to stimulate the level of aggregate demand, especially during an economic recession.

The role of fiscal policy

Fiscal policy and short-term demand management

Government expenditure (G) is a component of aggregate demand $(AD = C + I + G + (X - M))$. Thus, changes in the level of government expenditure will influence the level of AD in the economy, *ceteris paribus*.

Similarly, consumption (C) is a component of aggregate demand. Changes in taxes will influence the level of consumption, thus affecting the level of AD in the economy.

Expansionary fiscal policy is used to stimulate the economy, by increasing government spending and/or lowering taxes. This can boost domestic consumption during an economic recession, thereby helping to close a deflationary (recessionary) gap. By contrast, **contractionary fiscal policy** is used to reduce the level of economic activity by decreasing government spending and/or raising taxes. It is used to reduce inflationary pressures during an economic boom, thus helping to close an inflationary gap.

The potential effects of expansionary fiscal policy or contractionary fiscal policy will depend on the shape of the aggregate supply curve (see Figure 2.32):

- An increase in aggregate demand from AD_1 to AD_2 has no impact on the price level as there is spare capacity. Thus expansionary policy is effective in increasing real national output only.
- If the economy is operating on the upwards-sloping section of the AS curve, an increase in aggregate demand from AD_2 to AD_3 will cause an increase in both national output and the general price level.
- However, if expansionary fiscal policy is used when the economy is at full capacity (i.e. the AS curve is perfectly price inelastic at Y_f), then attempts to boost aggregate demand beyond AD_4 will simply cause inflation without any corresponding increase in national output.
- The three opposite outcomes apply when analysing contractionary fiscal policy, i.e. the consequences depend on the shape of the economy's AS curve.

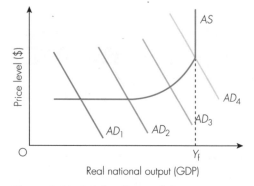

Figure 2.32 Fiscal policy and the *AS* curve

> **Expert tip**
>
> Ensure that you can explain the difference between a deflationary gap and an inflationary gap. The former occurs when the economy is below full employment, i.e. fiscal stimulus (tax cuts and/or increased government spending) is needed to close the recessionary gap. The opposite applies to an inflationary gap (when real GDP exceeds potential GDP), so contractionary fiscal measures are needed to combat the subsequent inflationary pressures.

EXAM PRACTICE

PAPER 1

28 With the aid of an appropriate diagram, explain how the effectiveness of expansionary fiscal policies depends on the shape of the aggregate supply curve. **[10]**

29 Explain why expansionary fiscal policy can cause a budget deficit for the government. **[10]**

The impact of automatic stabilisers

A progressive tax system and welfare benefits for the unemployed are good examples of automatic fiscal stabilisers that help to cushion short-term fluctuations in economic activity:

- During an economic boom, a progressive tax system means that the government automatically receives more tax revenue, from increased tax revenues on income and spending.
- At the same time, government spending on welfare benefits falls due to rising levels of economic activity, thus dampening the increase in consumption expenditure.
- Thus, automatic stabilisers (higher tax revenues and lower welfare benefits caused by higher levels of employment) help to reduce the growth rate, thereby avoiding the risks of an unsustainable economic boom and uncontrollable inflation.

Conversely, economic growth is negative in a recession, but automatic stabilisers (such as more government spending on unemployment benefits) help to limit the fall in economic growth. This helps to inject some money into the circular flow of income to boost aggregate demand.

The effectiveness of automatic stabilisers in reducing fluctuations in economic activity is dependent on:

- the size of the government sector, i.e. government spending as a percentage of GDP – the greater the level of government involvement, the more effective are automatic stabilisers
- the degree of progressivity of the tax system – the more progressive the tax system of the country, the more effective automatic stabilisers tend to be
- the scope of the welfare benefits system – automatic stabilisers will be more effective in countries like Australia and the UK with a wide-reaching welfare system.

> **Keyword definition**
> An **automatic stabiliser** is a part of fiscal policy that automatically influences national income, thus helping to even out short-term fluctuations in the level of economic activity.

Fiscal policy and its impact on potential output

Government spending (G) and consumption (C) are the two components of aggregate demand most directly affected by fiscal policy.

Capital expenditure can help to promote long-term economic growth (the increase in potential national output), for example investment in the country's infrastructure such as railways, road networks, airports and telecommunications networks.

Fiscal policy can be used to directly promote long-term economic growth in three main ways:

- Government spending on physical capital goods – Capital goods are tangible assets used to produce other goods and services, for example machinery, buildings and commercial vehicles.
- Government spending on human capital formation – Human capital formation is the transformation process of using education and/or training to create knowledge and skills to create a more skilled labour force.
- Provision of incentives for firms to invest – Government provision of tax breaks and tax incentives helps to create an economic environment that is conducive to investment. Government spending on infrastructure can also help to encourage foreign direct investment.

Fiscal policy can be used indirectly to promote long-term economic growth by creating an environment of low taxation that is favourable to private sector investment by domestic and foreign firms.

Expansionary fiscal policy can also help to increase both consumer and business confidence levels. This creates further incentives for firms to invest in their labour force and in the economy. However, critics argue that the effectiveness of expansionary fiscal policy depends on the (shape of the) AS curve. It is also debatable whether demand-side policies alone are sufficient to achieve long-term economic growth; there is certainly a case for the use of supply-side policies.

> **Expert tip**
> When evaluating the use of fiscal policy, it is worth noting any potential conflicts in the government's macroeconomic objectives. For example, the government might choose to use contractionary fiscal policy to deal with cost–push inflation, but unemployment is likely to occur as a consequence.

PAPER 1

30 Explain how fiscal policy can be used to affect the level of aggregate demand in an economy. **[10]**

> **Expert tip**
>
> HL students should be able to include the concept of the Keynesian multiplier when evaluating the effectiveness of contractionary or expansionary fiscal policies.

Evaluation of fiscal policy

Revised

The effectiveness of fiscal policy can be evaluated by consideration of various factors:

- The ability to target sectors of the economy – Fiscal policy measures will have a greater impact on some areas of the country than others due to regional disparities in income and spending habits.
- The **direct impact on aggregate demand** – Expansionary fiscal policy can help to achieve economic growth but tax cuts and increased government spending can fuel demand–pull inflation.
- By contrast, contractionary measures to control inflation can cause disincentives to work, lower productivity and unemployment.
- **Spillover effects** of government expenditure – Contractionary fiscal policy via reduced public-sector spending can have detrimental effects on public transportation, healthcare services and educational services. This can lead to economic inefficiencies and market failure.
- The effectiveness of promoting economic activity in a recession – The global financial crisis of 2008 saw governments across the world inject trillions of dollars to stimulate the economy. However, the effectiveness of such policies was hindered by the severity of the global recession.
- **Budgetary constraints** – The effectiveness of fiscal policy will depend on the extent to which the government can afford to sustain a budget deficit. Austerity measures in Greece and Spain were inevitable following the huge debts incurred by the countries during the global financial crisis.
- **Time lags** – There are three problems with the timing of fiscal policy:
  - Recognition time lags – There is a time lag before recognising that government intervention is needed to affect the level of economic activity. This is because governments do not necessarily know if the economy is growing too fast (or declining too quickly).
  - Administrative time lags – There is a time delay between recognising the need for fiscal policy intervention and the time to actually implement an appropriate action, such as approving tax changes or alterations to the government budget.
  - Impact time lags – There is a time lag from implementation of fiscal policy to seeing the actual effects on the economy. A cut in income tax, for example, will take time to have a significant impact on the spending habits of households.
- **Political constraints** – The political cycle (of re-electing political leaders and political parties) can cause artificial shocks to the business cycle – for example, large tax cuts might be used prior to a general election to gain political votes, rather than to tackle fundamental economic problems.
- **Crowding out** – Financial crowding out occurs when increased government borrowing (to finance its spending) causes interest rates to rise, thereby reducing private-sector investment expenditure due to the higher costs.
- **Supply-side shocks** – Fiscal policy is unable to deal with supply-side causes of instability to the economy, for example oil crises, outbreak of infectious diseases and major natural disasters.

> **Expert tip**
>
> It is incorrect to assume that fiscal policy cannot impact on the supply-side of the economy. For example, income tax cuts can create incentives for people to seek employment and to work harder. Lower rates of corporation tax can help to attract foreign direct investment in the country, thereby boosting the economy's potential output.

EXAM PRACTICE

PAPER 1

31 Evaluate the extent to which fiscal policy is effective in achieving long-term economic growth. **[15]**

EXAM PRACTICE *(HL ONLY)*

PAPER 3

32

	INCOME TAX RATE – TOP TAX BAND (%)	CORPORATE TAX RATE (%)	SALES TAX – STANDARD RATE (%)
China	45	25	17
Singapore	20	17–19	7
UK	45	21	20
United Arab Emirates	0	0	0

a Explain one drawback of the low tax rates in the United Arab Emirates (UAE). **[2]**

b From the data above, explain two disadvantages for firms based in China and the UK compared with those based in Singapore or the UAE. **[4]**

2.5 Monetary policy

Revised ☐

Interest rates

Revised ☐

Interest rates can refer to the price of borrowing money or the return from saving money at financial institutions such as banks. The **money supply** refers to the entire quantity of money circulating an economy, including notes and coins, loans and savings deposits at banks.

Like fiscal policy, governments use monetary policy to either expand or contract economic activity to achieve their macroeconomic goals. For instance, interest rate policy and manipulation of the money supply can be used to stabilise inflation.

Direct control of the money supply is relatively difficult as the definition of money is quite loose and banks can create credit fairly easily. Hence, most governments rely on interest rate policy to achieve economic stability.

> Keyword definition
> **Monetary policy** refers to the government's use of interest rates and the money supply to influence the level of aggregate demand and economic activity.

Common mistake

When defining demand-side policies, students do not always refer to these as macroeconomic policies in terms of both fiscal and monetary policy, i.e. both policies are used to influence aggregate demand.

Interest rate determination

Revised ☐

The **interest rate** can be described as the return for lenders of money or the price of borrowing money. It is expressed as a percentage of the money loaned to or borrowed by others.

The price of money is called the **interest rate** and the quantity of money is called the **money supply**. The equilibrium interest rate is determined by the intersection of the demand for, and supply of, money (see Figure 2.33).

The **demand for money** refers to the desire to hold money (rather than saving it) to finance consumption and current expenditure. Interest rates tend to rise when the quantity of money demanded exceeds the quantity supplied. The **supply of money** refers to the total amount of money circulating in the economy at any point in time. It will include bank notes and coins, bank deposits, loans and credit. An increase in the money supply will tend to decrease interest rates, and vice versa.

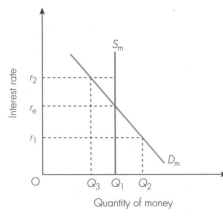

- The supply of money curve (S_m) is vertical at Q_1 quantity of money because the supply of money is fixed by the central bank at any one point in time.
- At interest rates below the equilibrium, there is excess demand for money. At an interest rate of r_1, excess demand is shown by the distance $Q_1 - Q_2$.
- When interest rates are higher than the equilibrium, more money is available than people wish to hold. At r_2, excess supply of money is $Q_1 - Q_3$.

Figure 2.33 The demand for, and supply of, money

A change in either the demand for money or the supply of money will change the equilibrium interest rate. For example, an increase in the money supply caused by an inflow of funds from abroad or due to a lower cash reserve ratio, lowers the interest rate, *ceteris paribus*.

The opportunity cost of holding money varies directly with the level of interest rates, i.e. a fall in interest rates will reduce the opportunity cost of holding money (there is not much of an opportunity cost if, like in Japan and Hong Kong, interest rates have been close to 0%).

Whilst the central bank does not control the demand for money, it has a key role in influencing the supply of money by manipulating interest rates. There are several factors a central bank will consider when setting interest rates:

- The state of the economy – For example, a deflationary gap may require a reduction in interest rates to prevent the economy from going into a deep recession.
- The rate of growth of nominal wages – For example, higher costs of labour usually mean that firms will increase prices. Higher interest rates might then be used to combat inflationary pressures.
- Business confidence levels – Lower interest rates tend to create incentives for investment expenditure due to the lower costs and hence risks of investment.
- House prices – In many countries, house prices (the most valuable asset of typical households) have a direct impact on the level of consumer confidence and hence the value of consumption and potential economic growth in the economy.
- The exchange rate – For example, lower interest rates might be needed to reduce the demand for the currency on the foreign exchange market. This will encourage the sale of exports, *ceteris paribus*.

EXAM PRACTICE

PAPER 1

33 Explain how monetary policy can be used to influence the level of economic activity. **[10]**

Expert tip

In reality, there is no single interest 'rate' in an economy but a structure of different interest rates. This is because there are separate markets for different kinds of loan – such as bank overdrafts, credit cards and mortgages – all of which charge different rates of interest. Borrowers also have different levels of risk – for example, lending to governments and large multinationals tends to be less risky than lending to private individuals.

Common mistake

It is incorrect to assume that low interest rates *will* stimulate aggregate demand and pull an economy out of recession. For example, Japan's interest rates have been close to zero since the mid-1990s yet firms have struggled to survive despite the easy access to money at almost zero cost. Low interest rates do not solve macroeconomic problems on their own.

The role of central banks

Executor of monetary policy – In most countries, the central bank or the country's monetary authority, is responsible for managing interest rates and the exchange rate for its currency in order to achieve macroeconomic objectives.

Government's bank – The central bank is responsible for the money of the government, including its foreign currency reserves. It maintains the accounts of the government in the same way that commercial banks maintain the accounts of their customers.

Bankers' bank – The central bank is the regulator of the country's commercial banking system. For example, commercial banks must keep a certain percentage of their cash reserves at the central bank so that it can control the money supply and use these reserves in times of financial emergency.

Sole issuer of legal tender – As the supreme bank, the central bank is the sole issuer of bank notes and coins within the country. This helps to control the money supply and brings uniformity and confidence to the monetary system.

Lender of last resort – The central bank provides loans to commercial banks when necessary to prevent the risks of a financial crisis caused by limited cash reserves and liquidity problems. Thus, this function helps to ensure that the banking system runs smoothly.

Credit control – By controlling the cash reserves that commercial banks must hold at the central bank, credit creation is managed more effectively. For example, the central bank would raise the cash reserve ratio during an economic boom to limit over-lending by commercial banks.

> **Keyword definition**
> A **central bank** (or **reserve bank**) is the monetary authority of a country that oversees the entire banking system by managing the money supply, the nation's currency and interest rates.

> **Expert tip**
> The central bank will consider a range of factors before making a decision about changing interest rates in the economy. For example, it will consider the level of economic activity, the level of inflation in the economy, and the outlook for the global economy.

The role of monetary policy and short-term demand management

Monetary policy is used to influence the level of economic activity. For example, interest rate policy is often used to influence the level of aggregate demand (recall that $AD = C + I + G + (X - M)$). Lower interest rates will tend to shift the aggregate demand curve to the right for the following reasons:

- Consumption (C), investment (I) and government spending (G) are likely to rise due to the cheaper cost of borrowing money. Households and firms with existing loans might also benefit from lower interest repayments.
- Net exports (the value of exports minus imports) are likely to increase because lower interest rates tend to cause a fall in the exchange rate. This should make exports more attractive to foreign buyers, thus helping to increase aggregate demand.

Expansionary monetary policy (or **easy monetary policy**) aims to increase economic activity by reducing interest rates and/or expanding the money supply. This makes borrowing more attractive because lower interest repayments are charged on the loans. Therefore, expansionary monetary policy will shift the aggregate demand curve to the right, *ceteris paribus* (see Figure 2.34), thereby helping to close a deflationary (recessionary) gap.

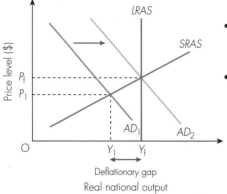

- Expansionary monetary policy (such as a cut in interest rates) shifts aggregate demand from AD_1 to AD_2, *ceteris paribus*.
- This increases real national output from Y_1 to Y_f, thereby closing the deflationary gap (the difference between equilibrium national output and the full employment level of national output).

Figure 2.34 Expansionary monetary policy and deflationary gaps

If the economy operates at less than the full employment level (i.e. it is operating on its *SRAS* curve), then expansionary monetary policy will tend to increase aggregate demand with a corresponding rise in real national output. However, a consequence of easy monetary policy is the potential emergence of inflationary pressures. This can be seen in Figure 2.34, with the average price level rising from P_1 to P_f. This is particularly the case if the economy is operating on the vertical part of its *LRAS* curve.

Contractionary monetary policy (or **tight monetary policy**) can help to close an inflationary gap. An increase in interest rates, for example, tends to reduce consumption and investment in the economy, thereby reducing real national output (see Figure 2.35).

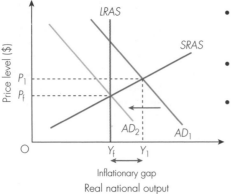

- Tight monetary policy (such as higher interest rates) shifts the aggregate demand curve leftwards from AD_1 to AD_2, *ceteris paribus*.
- This shrinks real national output from Y_1 to Y_f, so that actual output no longer exceeds potential output.
- Thus, contractionary monetary policy helps to close the inflationary gap, restoring prices back to P_f fom P_1.

Figure 2.35 Contractionary monetary policy and inflationary gaps

Tight monetary policy can be used to control the threat of inflation, although higher interest rates can harm economic growth and therefore cause job losses in the long run.

Monetary policy and inflation targeting

Revised

An **inflation rate target** (or **inflation targeting**) refers to the practice of central banks in some countries (such as Canada, Finland, New Zealand, South Africa and the UK) to use monetary policy to achieve a specific rate of inflation. An inflation target is used to provide a transparent goal in order to help control inflation. This is because price stability will enhance confidence in the economy.

Central banks use monetary policy to *influence* rather than to directly determine rate of inflation.

It is the role of the government, rather than a monetary authority, to focus on achieving and maintaining full employment and a low rate of inflation (although monetary policy is used to achieve an inflation target, be it explicit or implicit). If inflation is predicted to be higher than the target rate of inflation, perhaps due to a housing boom or increased consumer confidence in the economy, then contractionary monetary policy can be used, and vice versa.

Evaluation of monetary policy

Revised ☐

The effectiveness of monetary policy can be evaluated through consideration of the following factors:

- Independence of the central bank allows decision makers, in theory, to act in the best interest of the economy, without political interferences.
- The ability to adjust interest rates incrementally means that policy makers can monitor the effectiveness of monetary policy. It is common for interest rates to change in increments of 0.25%, thus reducing the risks of causing huge disruptions to the economy.
- The ability to implement changes in interest rates relatively quickly means that monetary policy can be used to influence and fine-tune macroeconomic objectives. Central banks review the state of the economy and adjust interest rates accordingly, often on a monthly basis.
- Monetary policy may be preferred to fiscal policy because it can be implemented more quickly. Tax changes require careful planning and are time consuming, whilst government spending can be costly.
- However, there are time lags to the reaction of households and firms to changes in interest rates in the economy. This can make the effectiveness of monetary policy less certain.
- Changes in interest rates and the money supply can be destabilising to the economy. For example, whilst the property (housing) market in many countries is a key determinant of consumer confidence levels, it is highly vulnerable to changes in interest rates.
- Consumption and investment are not entirely dependent on interest rates. The 2008 financial crisis meant interest rates were close to 0% in Japan, the USA and Hong Kong, but the lack of business and consumer confidence led to a prolonged economic recession.
- In addition, households and firms have different interest elasticity of demand, i.e. some groups are more affected by changes in interest rates than others. This can make it difficult to estimate the extent to which monetary policy is effective in influencing macroeconomic objectives.
- The effectiveness of monetary policies aimed at increasing aggregate demand is limited if the economy is in a deep recession because confidence levels are low. Firms will not borrow money to invest, even at low rates of interest, if the demand for their products remains low.
- The effectiveness of monetary policies aimed at reducing aggregate demand is limited too, as 'hot money' (the flow of money into the country to gain from higher rates of interest) will increase the exchange rate. This makes exports more expensive and so worsens the trade balance.
- Conflict among government economic objectives exist, so a cut in interest rates or an increase in the money supply (to influence the level of economic activity, for example) can conflict with other macroeconomic objectives, such as inflation (price stability).
- The use of tight monetary policy can be counterproductive as it restricts economic activity and discourages foreign direct investment in the country – for example, higher interest rates raise the costs of production, which negatively impacts on profits, jobs and economic growth.
- Monetary policy influences aggregate demand rather than having a direct impact on the economy's long-run aggregate supply.
- In the short run, monetary policy is generally more effective in dealing with demand–pull inflation than in getting an economy out of an economic depression, which might require the use of fiscal and supply-side policies.

EXAM PRACTICE *(HL ONLY)*

PAPER 3

34 With the aid of an appropriate diagram, explain how the use of monetary policy can help to close a deflationary (recessionary) gap. **[4]**

35 The diagram below shows the market for money in an economy, where D_m is the demand for money and S_m shows the supply of money at varying rates of interest.

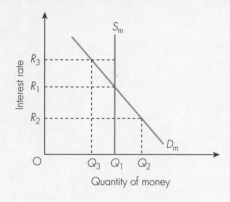

a Outline why the supply of money curve (S_m) is vertical at the Q_1 quantity of money. **[2]**

b With reference to the diagram, explain which interest rate would cause excess demand for money. **[2]**

2.6 Supply-side policies

Revised ☐

The role of supply-side policies

Revised ☐

Supply-side policies and the economy

Revised ☐

Supply-side policies are aimed at increasing the production side of an economy, i.e. boosting aggregate supply. This is achieved by improving the institutional framework (the country's system of rules and regulations) and the economy's productive capacity to produce.

The **productive capacity** of the economy is improved by increasing the quantity and quality of the factors of production – for example, investment in education and training can improve labour mobility and enhance labour productivity.

Supply-side policies are used because increases in the productive capacity of the economy can only be achieved through an increase in the economy's long-run aggregate supply, i.e. they are designed to make the economy more productively efficient in the long run.

Examples of supply-side policies include the following:

- Cuts in welfare benefits, such as unemployment benefits, to create incentives to work.
- Labour market reforms, such as greater spending on education and training to improve the quality and/or quantity of labour.
- Using tax cuts to create incentives to work.
- Removal of labour market imperfections, such as reducing the power of trade unions.

Supply-side policies can be categorised as either market-based or interventionist, although both aim to shift the *LRAC* curve outwards, i.e. increasing the economy's potential output.

> **Keyword definition**
> **Supply-side policies** are government strategies aimed at boosting the productive capacity of the economy by increasing the quality and/or quantity of factors of production, for example spending on education and training to improve the economy's human capital.

Interventionist supply-side policies

The **potential output** of the economy refers to the productive capacity (maximum possible output) if all factors of production are used efficiently. Diagrammatically, the potential output of an economy is shown on its production possibility curve (*PPC*).

The **institutional framework** refers to established systems, structures and contexts that shape the economic behaviour in a country, for example cultural norms and the legal system.

In the short run, interventionist supply-side policies (such as investment in human capital and new technology) increase aggregate demand but in the long run will increase the economy's aggregate supply.

> **Keyword definition**
> **Interventionist supply-side policies** are the deliberate attempts by a government to deal with market imperfections in the economy, for example government retraining programmes to improve the occupational mobility of the structurally unemployed.

Investment in human capital

Human capital refers to the stock of knowledge, skills, expertise and experiences of the workforce.

An important interventionist supply-side policy to increase human capital is to spend on education and training to raise the skills, mobility and productivity of the labour force. Government intervention in labour markets strives to enhance the demand for and supply of labour. It also aims to improve labour mobility.

Investment in human capital increases national income as the expenditure increases aggregate demand in the short run. In the long run, investment in human capital improves the productive capacity of the economy as it increases a country's long-run aggregate supply.

Improved communication in the job market can help to reduce frictional unemployment in the economy.

The increase in aggregate demand in the short run and the greater productive capacity in the long run mean that investment in human capital is vital for economic growth and development.

Investment in new technology

Policies that encourage investment in new technology have a short-term effect on aggregate demand because such expenditure will increase *AD*, *ceteris paribus*. Such policies include low interest rates and tax rebates, both of which can also encourage foreign direct investment. However, in the long run, investment in new technology can increase the productive capacity and productivity of the economy, i.e. it shifts the country's *LRAS* curve outwards.

Spending on research and development (R&D) can improve work processes, thereby enhancing efficiency, for example automation in the car making industry or the use of wireless technology to improve operations in the workplace. R&D can also generate new products for consumption and export, for example energy-saving light bulbs, daily disposable contact lenses, electric cars, smartphones and tablet computers.

Therefore, investment in new technology can be an important source of international competitive advantage.

Investment in infrastructure

As investment (*I*) is a key component of aggregate demand ($AD = C + I + G + (X - M)$), the expenditure on improving the nation's infrastructure will increase *AD* in the short run, thus boosting economic growth, *ceteris paribus*. In the long run, investment in infrastructure shifts the economy's *LRAS* curve to the right and attracts foreign direct investment. This helps the economy to flourish further.

Examples of such investments include spending money on transportation networks, telecommunications networks, electricity grids, waste disposal systems and sewerage systems.

Industrial policies

Revised ☐

Industrial policies are those that target specific key industries to promote economic growth – for example, tax allowances can be used to protect domestic infant industries from larger, well-known foreign rivals. Tax cuts targeted at strategic industries can help to revive these industries, helping them to grow in the long run.

A combination of tax breaks and subsidies on commercial loans can create incentives for firms to locate in less prosperous areas of a country, thus reducing unemployment and increasing the economy's long-run aggregate supply.

Subsidies can also be granted to firms that hire youth workers, mature staff and discouraged workers (those suffering from long-term unemployment). Subsidies might also be offered on loans to encourage business start-ups.

Industrial policies, like all supply-side policies, can improve economic welfare in terms of lower unemployment and increased earnings for those working in these industries. Thus, industrial policies improve the likelihood of sustainable economic growth.

EXAM PRACTICE

PAPER 1

36 Examine how supply-side policies can help to achieve any **two** macroeconomic objectives. **[10]**

> **Common mistake**
>
> Some students seem to think that industrial policy is used primarily to increase competition in an economy. This is incorrect as industrial policy is an interventionist supply-side policy.

Market-based supply-side policies

Revised ☐

Both interventionist and market-based supply-side policies can be used to increase the long-run aggregate supply (LRAS) of the economy, thereby boosting its potential output. Examples of market-based supply-side policies include the following:

- income tax reforms to improve the incentive to work
- labour market reforms to increase aggregate supply
- policies to encourage competition and efficiency
- tax incentives to encourage foreign direct investment.

> **Keyword definition**
> **Market-based supply-side policies** focus on allowing the free market to operate with minimal government intervention by improving market incentives to increase investment and productivity.

Policies to encourage competition

Revised ☐

Privatisation is the sale or transfer of state-owned assets and operations to the private sector. It can make firms become more efficient in order to make a profit and to survive.

Deregulation is the reduction or removal of barriers to entry into certain industries to make markets more competitive and efficient, for example getting rid of government rules and directives in a certain industry to promote competition and greater efficiency.

Anti-monopoly regulation can also be used to promote competition in targeted industries. This refers to competition law that controls the restrictive practices of monopolists, hence limiting their market power in the industry.

On an international scale, **trade liberalisation** involves the reduction or removal of trade barriers, such as tariffs and subsidies, to encourage competition and efficiency. Allowing the free movement of capital flows and encouraging foreign direct investment are further examples.

Labour market reforms

Revised ☐

Supply-side economists argue that the underlying causes of imperfections in the labour market are high rates of income tax and excessive regulations that reduce incentives to work. Supply-side policies that target labour market reforms, such as lower rates of income tax, create incentives to work, i.e. they motivate people to seek employment opportunities.

Market-based supply-side policies aim to make the labour market more efficient, i.e. responsive to changes in the market forces of demand and supply. A flexible labour force is responsive to changes in the economy – for example, workers are able to adapt from declining industries to growing industries.

Reducing unemployment benefits can make the labour market more responsive to market forces, as the unemployed can no longer rely on welfare payments and so have a greater incentive or need to seek employment.

Reducing the power of trade unions improves the efficiency of the labour market. For example, trade unions push for a (higher) national minimum wage but this can be highly costly to firms, thereby artificially reducing their international competitiveness.

> **Keyword definitions**
> **Labour market reforms** are government policies designed to create greater flexibility and efficiency in the labour market, for example reducing the power of labour unions, cutting unemployment benefits and abolishing the national minimum wage.
>
> A **trade union** is an organisation that represents the common interest of its members in work-related matters, for example in negotiations over wages and working conditions.

Incentive-related policies

Revised ☐

Reducing direct taxes, such as cutting personal income tax for those earning low incomes, can create incentives for people to work or to seek employment opportunities. Hence, such market-based supply-side policies are designed to reduce the level of unemployment.

Cuts in business taxes are used to create incentives to invest by reducing the financial risks of investments. Similarly, cuts in capital gains taxes (imposed on the profit of an asset once sold) can also encourage risk taking and investments in the economy.

Evaluation of supply-side policies

Revised ☐

The strengths and weaknesses of supply-side policies

Revised ☐

The advantages of supply-side policies are summarised in Table 2.7.

Table 2.7 The advantages of using supply-side policies to achieve macroeconomic objectives

Improved economic growth	Supply-side policies can be used to achieve sustainable economic growth by increasing the potential capacity of the economy over time.
Lower inflation	As supply-side policies increase the productive potential of the economy, they help to prevent the general price level from rising beyond control.
Lower unemployment	An increase in the productive capacity will tend to increase national output, thereby creating jobs in the economy in the long term. Supply-side policies can also help to reduce both frictional and structural unemployment.
Improved balance of payments	Since supply-side policies can improve productivity and national output without pressures on the general price level, the international competitiveness of the country should improve, thus helping to increase exports.
Improved equity	Interventionist supply-side policies can lower the natural rate of unemployment in the economy, thus reducing inequality.

The limitations of using supply-side policies are outlined in Table 2.8.

Table 2.8 The limitations of using supply-side policies

Time lag	The main criticism of supply-side policies is the time that it takes to reap the benefits. For example, it might take decades for a nation to enjoy the benefits of an improved education system or infrastructure in the country.
Decreased equity	Interventionist supply-side policies do not necessarily improve equity in the distribution of income in the economy, i.e. economic growth can create greater disparities (inequalities) in income distribution.
Effect on the environment	Supply-side policies strive to increase the potential output of the economy but this can come at a huge opportunity cost to the natural environment.

3.1 International trade

Free trade

The benefits of trade

International trade is the exchange of goods and services beyond national borders. It involves the sale of **exports** (goods and services sold to overseas buyers) and **imports** (foreign goods and services bought by domestic households and firms). Countries need to trade because scarce resources are unevenly distributed between countries, i.e. countries have different factor endowments.

Economists believe that the benefits of free international trade tend to exceed the costs, i.e. although not everyone gains from free international trade, or gains equally, the net benefits to society are positive. The benefits of international trade are outlined below:

- **Lower prices** for consumers – Free trade reduces the costs of trading. For example, unfavourable weather conditions in Sweden mean it is better off importing tropical fruits from Jamaica.
- **Greater choice** for consumers – Free trade enables consumers and firms to access a larger variety of goods and services from different producers around the world. For example, Germans can choose to buy Lexus cars from Japan rather than being limited to Audi, BMW or Mercedes models.
- The ability of producers to benefit from **economies of scale** – By operating on a larger scale in international markets, free trade enables firms to benefit from economies of scale, i.e. cost savings that can be passed onto consumers in the form of lower prices.
- The ability to **acquire needed resources** – Through trade, countries can access natural resources and capital goods that are not available domestically to further their production. For example, the Maldives can purchase laptops, motor vehicles and Hollywood movies from the USA.
- A more **efficient allocation of resources** – Free trade benefits the economy as it encourages an efficient allocation of the world's scarce resources. Free trade forces domestic firms to focus on improving the quality of their output due to foreign competition.
- **Increased competition** – Trade ensures that domestic firms become exposed to competition from foreign firms. Hence, domestic firms are forced to become more efficient, i.e. to produce goods and services at the lowest possible cost.
- A **source of foreign exchange** – When countries sell exports, firms and governments acquire foreign exchange (foreign currencies). This enables them to make payments to other countries for the purchase of foreign goods and services.
- **Increased market size** – International trade enables firms to earn more revenues and profits. For example, American firms can sell products to a domestic market of 316 million people, but can sell to a much larger market of more than 2.4 billion potential customers in China and India.
- **Improved international relations** – The absence of trade barriers encourages international trade and cooperation between countries. By contrast, if a country uses trade barriers, then other countries are likely to retaliate by doing the same.

> **Keyword definition**
> **Free trade** occurs when nations can exchange goods and services without any trade barriers, such as quantitative limits or taxes being imposed on imports.

> **Expert tip**
> Make sure you can distinguish between the merits of *international trade* and the merits of *free trade* – they are not quite the same because not all international trade entails free trade. Thus, the merits of free trade (without any trade barriers) are greater than the benefits of international trade (which may involve some trade barriers).

Absolute and comparative advantage *(HL only)*

Revised ☐

An absolute advantage in the production of a good or service gives a country a competitive edge because it is more productive and efficient. If country A spends $10m to make 40,000 units of output of a particular good whilst country B can only produce 30,000 units with the same amount of money, then country A has an absolute advantage in the output of that product. By specialising in the output of the goods or service, the result is increased production and consumption (see Figure 3.1).

The concept of absolute advantage was coined by Scottish economist Adam Smith (1723–90), extending his doctrine of specialisation and the division of labour. If countries specialised in the output of what they are most efficient at producing, world output would subsequently increase.

Absolute advantage occurs mainly because different countries have different factor endowments – for example, Saudi Arabia is well endowed with oil, whilst Thailand has the natural climate suitable for harvesting rice.

By contrast, some countries have an absolute disadvantage, i.e. they are inefficient and unproductive in the output of given goods or services relative to their trading partners.

> **Keyword definitions**
> **Absolute advantage** occurs when a country can produce more of a good or service than another country using the same amount of resources (or is able to produce the same amount of a good or service using fewer resources).
>
> The term **factor endowments** refers to the quantity and quality of factors of production available in a country, such as natural resources and human capital. Countries well-endowed in natural resources tend to have a comparative advantage in products using such resources.

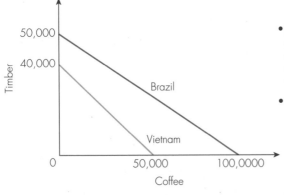

- Brazil's production possibility frontier (*PPF*) shows that it can produce 100,000 units of coffee (compared with Vietnam's 50,000 units) or 50,000 units of timber (compared with Vietnam's 40,000 units).

- Thus, Brazil has an absolute advantage in the output of both coffee and timber.

Figure 3.1 Absolute advantage

Worked example

Suppose two countries, with the same amount of resources, produce books and clothes. Also assume that both countries divide their resources equally between the production of books and clothes. The pre-trade situation is shown below:

Country	Books (units)	Clothes (units)
Alpha	1000	500
Beta	750	1500
Total output	1750	2000

From the above, we can see that Alpha has an absolute advantage in producing books (it is more productive in producing books), whilst Beta has an absolute advantage in the output of clothes (1500 units compared with Alpha's 500 units).

If both countries decide to specialise based on their absolute advantage, then Alpha gives up 500 units of clothes to produce an extra 1000 units of books. Similarly, Beta gives up 750 units of books to specialise in the production of clothes, increasing its total output by an extra 1500 units:

Country	Books (units)	Clothes (units)
Alpha	2000	0
Beta	0	3000
Total output	2000	3000

Therefore, total output increases via the countries specialising in the output of the product in which they hold an absolute advantage. If Alpha and Beta now trade 800 units of their surplus with each other, the post-trade situation now looks like this:

Country	Books (units)	Clothes (units)
Alpha	1200	800
Beta	800	2200
Total output	2000	3000

Through trade, Alpha has an extra 200 units of books and an extra 300 units of clothes. Similarly, Beta has 50 more units of books and 700 more units of clothes.

The theory of comparative advantage was put forward by British economist David Ricardo (1772–1823), who suggested that countries should specialise in goods and services in which they have a comparative advantage (relatively lower unit costs of production). The theory suggests that countries should produce and trade products in which they have a comparatively low opportunity cost, even if the trading partner has an absolute advantage in the output of both products (see Figure 3.2).

> **Keyword definition**
> **Comparative advantage** exists when a country can produce a given amount of output at a lower opportunity cost than another country, i.e. it gives up less resources than other countries in producing a certain good or service.

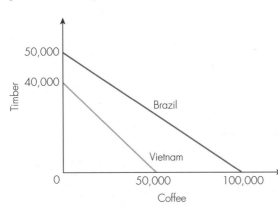

- Despite Brazil having an absolute advantage in the output of both coffee and timber, comparative advantage exist.
- Brazil's opportunity cost of producing timber is 2 units of coffee, whereas Vietnam's opportunity cost is only 1.25 units of coffee.
- Similarly, Vietnam's opportunity cost of coffee is 0.8 units of timber but it is only 0.5 for Brazil. Hence it is cheaper for Brazil to give up producing timber.
- Therefore, Brazil should specialise in and export coffee, whilst Vietnam should specialise in the output of timber.

Figure 3.2 Comparative advantage

Sources of comparative advantage include differences in:

- factor endowments – for example, major oil exporting countries such as Saudi Arabia, Russia and the United Arab Emirates are well endowed in oil supply. These countries can increase production and consumption through specialisation and international trade.
- levels of technology – for example, workers with access to the latest machinery and technology will be far more productive than those using outdated techniques.
- investment in research and development (R&D) – this can give countries a competitive advantage in terms of innovation and inventions. R&D expenditure can also generate new work processes that reduce the relative costs of production.
- inflation – this can damage the comparative cost advantages of a country as higher prices mean that foreign buyers are less willing and able to purchase the exports of domestic firms.
- exchange rate fluctuations – these can affect the relative prices of exports and imports. A long-term unfavourable change in the exchange rate can cause a reduction in demand from domestic and overseas customers.

Worked example

Suppose that two countries, with the same amount of resources, produce books and clothes. Also assume that both countries divide their resources equally between the production of fruits and toys. The pre-trade situation is shown below:

Country	Fruits (units)	Toys (units)
Delta	3000	1500
Gamma	500	1000
Total output	3500	2500

Delta has an absolute advantage in the production of both toys and fruits, i.e. it is better at producing these goods than country Gamma. However, Gamma can produce toys at a lower opportunity cost:

Country	Fruits (units)	Toys (units)	Opportunity cost
Delta	3000	1500	2.0:1
Gamma	500	1000	0.5:1

Whilst Delta has to give up 2 units of fruits to gain 1 unit of toys, Gamma only has to give up 0.5 units of fruits to produce 1 unit of toys. Hence, Gamma should specialise in the output of toys. Likewise, if Delta gives up 1 unit of toys, it can produce 2 units of fruits, whereas Gamma can only gain 0.5 units of fruits. Hence, Delta should specialise in the output of fruits.

Suppose Gamma specialises entirely in toys and Delta decides to switch 500 units of toys to produce (1000 extra units of) fruits instead. Hence, the total output increases by 500 units of both fruits and toys:

Country	Fruits (units)	Toys (units)
Delta	4000	1000
Gamma	0	2000
Total output	4000	3000

If the countries trade their surpluses, say 700 units of each product, both countries now have more of fruits and toys compared with what they started with, when there was no international trade:

Country	Fruits (units)	Toys (units)
Delta	3300	1700
Gamma	700	1300
Total output	4000	3000

EXAM PRACTICE *(HL ONLY)*

PAPER 3

2 Use the production possibilities data below and an appropriate diagram to explain which country should specialise in the production of Aris and which country should specialise in the output of Walkers. **[4]**

COUNTRY	ARIS (UNITS)	WALKERS (UNITS)
Farrowland	1500	600
Mayland	2000	500

Limitations of the theory of comparative advantage *(HL only)*

Revised

The theory has several limitations:

- It assumes that comparative advantage is fixed, whereas in reality it is not. For example, Hong Kong no longer has a comparative advantage in textiles and the UK no longer has a relative cost advantage in the output of steel and coal.
- It assumes that there are no barriers to international trade, although this is not necessarily the case in the real world, with tariffs and quotas still being imposed by countries.
- It is a static model, which ignores the fact that comparative advantages can shift between countries over time.
- Whilst the theory explains how countries can gain from trade, it ignores the disparities of the relative gains from trade, i.e. some countries will gain more than others due to their better bargaining position and terms of trade.
- Transportation costs of trade are ignored in the calculation of comparative advantage. So, even if Australia is able to produce textbooks relatively cheaper than the EU, transportation costs to Europe could mean Australia has a comparative disadvantage.
- It is assumed that there is perfect occupational mobility of resources, i.e. factors of production can be switched between different industries without any loss of efficiency. This contradicts the idea of increased gains from trade through specialisation.

Expert tip

When evaluating the real-world relevance and limitations of comparative advantage, ensure that you do two things: (1) discuss the shortcomings of the assumptions of the model of comparative advantage and (2) consider the arguments for and against free trade.

The World Trade Organization (WTO)

Revised

The **World Trade Organization (WTO)** was established in 1995 to promote trade liberalisation, to oversee multilateral trade agreements (free trade agreements between multiple countries) and to resolve trade disputes between member states.

The **objectives** of the WTO are as follows:

- To encourage free international trade. Member states are obliged to reduce and remove artificial trade barriers such as subsidies (which reduce production costs for domestic firms).
- To remove discriminatory treatment in trade relations between member nations (except for those in trading blocs that have their own set of agreed trade rules).
- To help provide trade opportunities for economically developing countries in order to enhance their growth and development prospects.

The WTO has six **functions**:

- Administering WTO trade agreements – The WTO provides a forum for members to negotiate trade rules and agreements, which become binding contracts for governments to keep their trade policies within agreed parameters.

- Forum for trade negotiations – Members of the WTO are involved in 'Rounds' of negotiations. There have been nine Rounds so far, with the first one focusing on lowering tariffs on imported goods. The latest Doha Round of negotiations started back in 2001.
- Handling trade disputes – The WTO acts as an arbitrator in trade disputes between member states. It acts to settle such disputes in a quick and objective manner.
- Monitoring national trade policies – The WTO regularly monitors the national trade policies of its member states through its Trade Policy Review Mechanism. This serves to encourage accountability and transparency on trade policies on a multilateral level.
- Technical assistance and training for economically developing countries – Trade-related technical support and training are provided to help low-income countries to better understand WTO obligations and agreements and thus build their capacity to trade.
- Cooperation with other international organisations – The WTO collaborates with other organisations to promote economic cooperation and growth, such as the World Bank and the Organization for Economic Cooperation and Development (OECD).

> **Expert tip**
>
> Note that in some special circumstances the WTO will support maintaining trade barriers (rather than promoting free trade), for example to protect consumers from the spread of disease (e.g. bird flu and swine flu).

Restrictions on free trade: trade protection

`Revised` ☐

> Keyword definitions
>
> **Trade protection** is the use of barriers to trade to safeguard a country from excessive international trade and foreign competition.
>
> **Barriers to trade** are obstacles to free trade, imposed by a government to safeguard national interests by reducing the competitiveness of foreign firms.

Types of trade protection

`Revised` ☐

Tariffs are import taxes – for example, the USA has used a 35% tariff on all tyres imported from China. Tariffs raise the costs of production to importers, thus raising the price of foreign goods in the domestic market, and thereby lowering the amount of imported products (see Figure 3.3).

A tariff increases costs of production, thus shifting the supply curve up from $S_{world \, (free \, trade)}$ to $S_{+tariff}$, forcing the price up from P_1 to P_2. Figure 3.3 shows the effects of tariffs (or **customs duties**) on various stakeholders:

- Domestic producers – Domestic firms will tend to gain from the tariff as they will receive a higher price (P_2 rather than P_1), and sell a larger quantity (Q_2 rather than Q_1). The higher price also means that producer surplus increases by the area a.
- Foreign producers – Importers tend to lose out as the tariff reduces their price competitiveness and they are only able to sell a reduced amount; they could sell $Q_1 - Q_4$ output before the tariff, but are only able to sell $Q_2 - Q_3$ after the imposition of the tariff.
- Consumers – The value of consumer expenditure on imports is shown by the area $c + e$. As consumers now pay a higher price of P_2, there is a loss in consumer surplus, as shown by the area $a + b + c + d$. Hence, consumers lose out from the imposition of a tariff.
- The government – Tariffs help to raise revenue for the government. The tariff is shown by the vertical distance between P_1 and P_2, and as the amount imported is shown by the distance $Q_2 - Q_3$, the government gains area c as tax revenue.
- Society – There is a **welfare loss** as a result of the imposition of the tariff, as shown by the areas $b + d$.

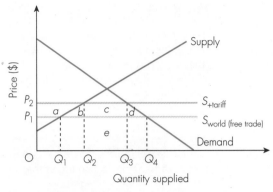

Figure 3.3 The effects of tariffs *(HL only)*

Expert tip

Only higher level students need to be able to use the tariff diagram (Figure 3.3) to *calculate* the effects on domestic producers, foreign producers, consumers and the government.

EXAM PRACTICE *(HL ONLY)*

PAPER 3

3 Use the diagram below to calculate the following:

  a Consumer surplus before the imposition of the tariff. **[2]**

  b Producer surplus before the imposition of the tariff. **[2]**

  c Consumer surplus after the imposition of the tariff. **[2]**

  d Producer surplus after the imposition of the tariff. **[2]**

  e Revenue to the government after the imposition of the tariff. **[2]**

  f The welfare loss after the imposition of the tariff. **[2]**

Quotas are quantitative limits on the sale of a foreign good into a country – for example, Indonesia imposes import quotas on fruits and vegetables from Thailand. This limits the quantity imported and so causes an increase in the market price of the foreign goods (see Figure 3.4).

Prior to protection, the volume of imports is shown by the distance $Q_1 - Q_4$. The quota is shown by the horizontal distance between $S_{domestic}$ and $S_{domestic + quota}$ (or Q_1 and Q_2). This limits the amount of imports to $Q_2 - Q_3$. It is not possible to import the product below a price of P_{quota}.

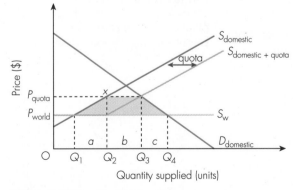

Figure 3.4 The effects of quotas

Figure 3.4 shows the effects of import quotas on various stakeholders:

- Domestic producers – The quota on imports enables domestic firms to supply more to the market (Q_2 rather than Q_1). They are also able to charge a higher price of P_{quota}, raising their revenue to the area $P_{quota}, x, Q_2, 0$. This can have a positive impact on domestic jobs.
- Foreign producers – Before the imposition of the quota, revenue was $a + b + c$. After the quota is imposed, imports are reduced, so revenue falls to b. Hence, they will lose out from the imposition of a quota.
- Consumers – Domestic consumers lose from the imposition of a quota as they are charged a higher price (P_{quota} rather than P_{world}). In addition, they could previously buy Q_4 under free trade, but can only buy Q_4 after the quota is enforced.
- The government – Whilst the effects of a quota are similar to those of a tariff, there is no direct impact on the government as the quota does not generate any tax revenue.
- Society – The reduced consumption resulting from the quota shifts production away from more efficient imported products towards less efficient domestically produced goods. This misallocation of resources results in a net welfare loss, as shown by the shaded green area.

Expert tip

Higher level students need to be able to use the quota diagram to *calculate* the effects on domestic producers, foreign producers, consumers and the government.

Expert tip

Critics of trade protection argue that tariffs and quotas are regressive in nature as consumers are forced to pay higher prices than under free trade. The higher prices account for a larger proportion of spending for low-income earners, thus there is a detrimental impact on the distribution of income.

EXAM PRACTICE *(HL ONLY)*

PAPER 3

4 Use the diagram below to identify the following:
  a Consumer surplus before the imposition of a quota. **[1]**
  b Producer surplus for domestic firms before the imposition of a quota. **[1]**
  c Consumer surplus after the imposition of a quota. **[1]**
  d Producer surplus for domestic firms after the imposition of a quota. **[1]**
  e The welfare loss following the imposition of the quota. **[1]**

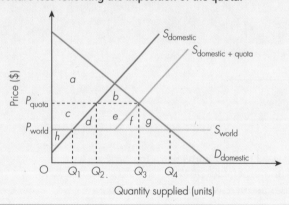

Subsidies are a form of financial assistance to local firms to help them compete against foreign imports by lowering the costs of production. This helps to protect local jobs – for example, the European Union subsidises its farmers to encourage agricultural output (see Figure 3.5).

There are two types of subsidy that can be used to protect domestic industries:

- **Production subsidies,** the most common form, help to reduce the production costs for domestic firms. The analysis below refers to production subsidies.
- **Export subsidies** are less wide-ranging as they are targeted at protecting specific export-orientated firms.

Like quotas, the use of subsidies does not create any revenue for the government. Instead, subsidies use up the government's budget.

Figure 3.5 shows the effects of subsidies on various stakeholders:

- Domestic producers – Domestic firms gain from the subsidy as they are able to supply more (Q_2 rather than Q_1). The amount received by domestic firms is shown by the green shaded area. Note that they would still sell at the world price of P_w after receiving the subsidy.

Expert tip

Higher level students need to be able to use the subsidy diagram to *calculate* the effects on domestic producers, foreign producers, consumers and the government.

- Foreign producers – Before trade protection, foreign firms were able to sell $Q_3 - Q_1$ amount of imports. However, the subsidy reduces the amount of imports to $Q_3 - Q_2$.
- Consumers – The consumption of the product is not affected as the price remains at the world price, P_w, so Q_3 is traded. Consumers do, however, buy more domestic goods, so whether they gain or lose depends on the relative quality of the foreign goods.
- The government – There is a negative impact on the government's budget due to the expenditure on production subsidies. Taxpayers are also worse off (shown by the green shaded area) as there is an opportunity cost of using this money for subsidies.

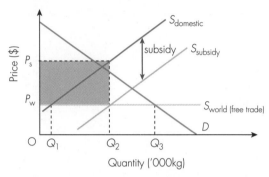

Figure 3.5 The effects of subsidies on domestic producers

EXAM PRACTICE *(HL ONLY)*

PAPER 3

5   Use the diagram below to calculate the following:

   a   The cost of the subsidy to the government.   **[2]**

   b   The amount of imports before government intervention.   **[2]**

   c   The amount of imports after government intervention.   **[2]**

   d   The total amount spent by domestic consumers under free trade.   **[2]**

   e   The total amount spent by domestic consumers after the imposition
       of the subsidy.   **[2]**

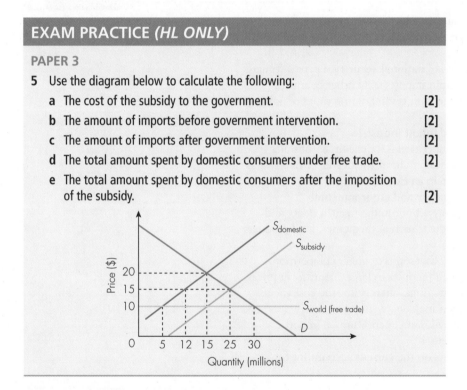

Administrative barriers are bureaucratic rules and regulations that countries use as a form of protection, for example strict rules regarding food safety, environmental standards and product quality. Complying with these administrative barriers increases the costs for foreign firms.

Embargoes are bans on trade with a certain country, often due to political and/or economic disputes (although they can be used for health and safety reasons). An embargo rarely benefits local consumers, who suffer from a lack of choice and higher prices due to the lack of supply.

Exchange controls are restrictions on the quantity of foreign exchange that can be bought or sold by domestic residents, for example daily limits on the amount of foreign currency that tourists or investors can exchange, thus limiting the amount of foreign exchange available to importers.

EXAM PRACTICE

PAPER 2

6   Since 2009, China has been the world's largest producer, consumer and exporter of tyres, accounting for over 25% of the world's output of car tyres. The China Passenger Car Association reported that over 20 million new cars were sold in China in 2013, with annual sales growth of over 10% expected over the next few years.

According to the USA's Bureau of Labor Statistics, the average US employer had to pay about $35 per hour (salary and benefits) to hire a production line worker whereas an employer in China could do the same for just $1.36 per hour. America simply could not compete, thus prompting the need for protectionist measures.

a   With reference to the above information, explain two reasons why countries use trade protection. [4]

b   Discuss which method of trade protection would be best for the USA to impose. Justify your answer. [8]

Arguments for trade protection (arguments against free trade)

Revised ☐

Trade protection can help to protect **domestic jobs**. In extreme cases, fierce competition from foreign rivals can even force domestic firms out of business if there is no trade protection.

Protectionism might be used for reasons of **national security**, i.e. to safeguard the country from being too reliant on certain imports from other countries (such as weapons and war machines). Protection is vital during times of political conflict and turmoil such as a war.

Protectionist measures help to safeguard **infant industries** (new, unestablished businesses) from foreign competition – for example, subsidies help to reduce costs of production, quotas help to limit the degree of rivalry and tariffs help domestic sunrise industries to gain a price advantage.

Protection is used to maintain **health, safety and environmental standards** in the country. Governments may set minimum health, safety and environmental standards for imported products such as medicines, food products and motor vehicles to protect its citizens.

Trade protection prevents **dumping** and other forms of unfair competition. Dumping occurs when foreign firms sell their products in large quantities at prices deliberately below those charged by domestic firms, often below the cost value.

The impacts of anti-dumping protection include:

- Higher domestic consumption caused by lower expenditure on imports.
- Higher sales and profits for domestic firms.
- Improvement in the balance of payments on the current account for the protected country.

Protection is a means of overcoming a **balance of payments deficit**. If a country's expenditure on imports exceeds the revenue earned from its exports, protectionist measures can be used to rectify this imbalance.

Protection can also be a source of **government revenue**. For example, India imposes a $535 per 10 gram tariff on the import of gold, thus helping to raise tax revenue for the government.

Expert tip

The most common form of trade protection is the use of **tariffs**. All other types of trade protection are collectively known as **non-tariff barriers**.

Arguments against trade protection (arguments for free trade)

A **misallocation of resources** – Government intervention can distort market signals and so lead to a global misallocation of resources. For example, protected firms and industries can become too reliant on the government and thus become inefficient.

The danger of **retaliation** and trade wars – Other countries are likely to react by retaliating and imposing their own trade barriers. Such actions can cause trade wars (trade disputes), which ultimately hinder global economic growth and prosperity.

The potential for **corruption** – Trade restrictions can create opportunities for bribes and the illegal smuggling of goods into a country.

Increased costs of production due to lack of competition – Protection can create a lack of incentives for domestic firms and industries to control their costs of production.

Higher prices for domestic consumers – Protectionist measures mean that domestic consumers might not be able to purchase lower-priced imports, which could be of higher quality than those produced domestically.

Increased costs of imported factors of production – Due to trade protection, domestic producers might need to pay higher prices for vital imported raw materials and components. This could lead to **imported inflation**, thus leading to higher domestic prices.

Reduced export competitiveness – The lack of foreign competition and incentives to be innovative means that the protection of domestic producers can lead to inefficiencies and hence a decline in the country's international competitiveness.

> **Expert tip**
>
> Whilst trade protection can provide short-term benefits for a country, most economists believe that it is detrimental to economic growth and development in the long term. Indeed, such a view is supported by the World Trade Organization.

3.2 Exchange rates

Freely floating exchange rates

Exchange rates are fundamental to international trade simply because different countries use different currencies. The demand for exports of goods and services falls if they become dearer, *ceteris paribus*. Similarly, the demand for exports should rise if the price of imports becomes more expensive.

The foreign exchange market is the marketplace where national currencies can be bought and sold.

> **Keyword definition**
>
> An **exchange rate** is the price of one currency measured in terms of other currencies – for example, the exchange rate of Australian dollars (AUD) to Chinese yuan (CNY) might be AUD1 = CNY5.5 (or 1 yuan = AUD0.18).

EXAM PRACTICE *(HL ONLY)*

PAPER 2

7   With reference to the diagram below, calculate the exchange rate in terms of US dollars.   [2]

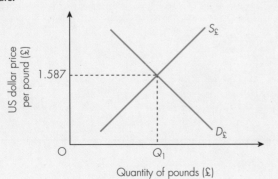

EXAM PRACTICE *(HL ONLY)*

PAPER 3

8 Suppose the exchange rate between the British pound (GBP) and the US dollar (USD) is GBP1 = USD1.55. Calculate the price for customers in Britain buying American cars priced at USD35,500. **[2]**

9 a If the exchange rate of the US dollar to pounds sterling is $1 = £0.65, calculate the price paid in pounds sterling by a British tourist spending $45 on a theme park ticket in Florida, USA. **[2]**

b If the US dollar falls against the pound sterling to $1 = £0.6, calculate the new amount that British tourists would have to pay in pounds sterling for the same entrance ticket. **[2]**

10 a Suppose the exchange rate between the Australian dollar (AUD) and the Chinese yuan renminbi (CNY) is AUD1 = CNY6.5. Calculate the price for customers in China of buying textbooks priced at AUD65 from Australia. **[2]**

b Suppose that the exchange rate between the Canadian dollar ($) and the British pound (£) is $1 = £0.65 and the euro (€) is $1 = €0.75. Calculate the exchange rate of the British pound against the euro. **[2]**

Determination of freely floating exchange rates

Revised ☐

In a **freely floating exchange rate** system, the value of a currency is determined by the demand for, and supply of, the currency on the foreign exchange market – for example, overseas tourists buy (demand) the currency by selling their own (foreign) currencies.

An **appreciation** of the currency occurs when there is an increase in the value of the exchange rate relative to another currency operating in a floating exchange rate system. Exports will tend to become more expensive whilst imports will tend to become relatively cheaper.

A **depreciation** of the currency occurs when there is a fall in the value of the exchange rate relative to another currency operating in a floating exchange rate system.

An exchange rate that is set above the equilibrium level causes excess supply of the currency, causing a subsequent fall in the exchange rate, i.e. equilibrium is restored by market forces.

Countries that adopt a freely floating exchange rate system include: Belgium, Chile, Luxembourg, Spain, Japan, New Zealand, Sweden and the United Kingdom.

In Figure 3.6, higher demand for the Canadian dollar (CAD), perhaps due to higher interest rates than in Brazil, is shown by a shift in demand from D_1 to D_2. This raises the exchange rate of the CAD from 2.05 Brazilian real (BRL) to 2.25.

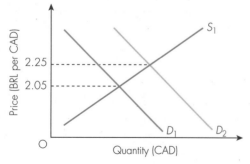

Figure 3.6 Currency appreciation of Canadian dollar

Causes of changes in the exchange rate

Revised

A change in any factor that affects the demand for, or supply of, a currency will have an influence on the exchange rate. These factors include the following:

- Foreign demand for a country's exports – An increase in the demand for exports, perhaps due to improved quality or successful advertising, will increase the demand for the country's currency. Hence, there is an appreciation of the currency, *ceteris paribus*.
- Domestic demand for imports – An increase in the demand for imports, perhaps due to an increase in the competitiveness of foreign firms, causes an appreciation of the foreign currency. The higher demand is required to facilitate the purchase of foreign goods and services.
- Relative interest rates – A cut in interest rates in the economy will tend to reduce incentives for investors, so they sell the domestic currency in search of investments with better returns. This reduces the exchange rate, *ceteris paribus*.
- Relative inflation rates – An increase in the price of goods and services caused by domestic inflation will tend to decrease the demand for exports. Therefore, the exchange rate will tend to fall in value as a result of inflation.
- Investment from overseas in a country's firms, including:
  - foreign direct investment (FDI) – Inward FDI boosts the demand for a currency – for example, Nissan's factories in India require the Japanese carmaker to buy Indian rupees to pay for labour and other production costs. By contrast, outward FDI increases the supply of a currency.
  - portfolio investment – Foreign currency is demanded for the purchase of financial investments abroad, such as stocks, shares and bonds of overseas firms and governments. Domestic currency is supplied when banks and the government lend money to overseas firms and governments.

Expert tip

All these factors can affect the exchange rate under a freely floating exchange rate system. In addition, **government intervention** in the foreign exchange market can affect the exchange rate. For example, if increased demand for US goods causes an appreciation of the dollar, the US Federal Reserve can sell its dollar reserves (increasing its supply), causing a fall in the value of its currency.

■ Speculation – Foreign exchange traders and investment companies move money around the world to take advantage of higher interest rates and variations in exchange rates to earn a profit. As huge sums of money are involved, it can cause exchange rate fluctuations.

An appreciation of the currency is caused by an increase in the demand for the currency and/or a fall in the supply of the currency (see Figure 3.7).

A depreciation of the currency is caused by a decline in the demand for the currency and/or an increase in the supply of the currency (see Figure 3.8).

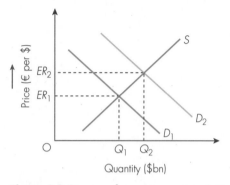

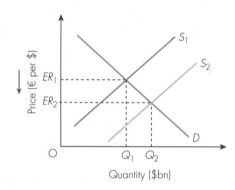

Figure 3.7 Causes of currency appreciation

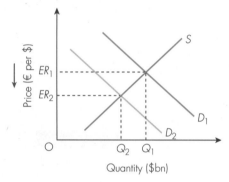

Figure 3.8 Causes of currency depreciation

The effects of exchange rate changes

Revised ☐

Exchange rate fluctuations have an impact on macroeconomic objectives:
■ **Employment** – An appreciation of the currency will tend to reduce the demand for exports, leading to deteriorating profits. In the long run, this will cause job losses (unemployment) in export-oriented industries.
■ **Inflation** – Unemployment caused by the currency appreciation leads to lower consumption in the economy, thus reducing the inflation rate. If the country relies heavily on certain imports, such as oil or food supplies, the higher exchange rate helps to reduce the general price level even further.
■ **Economic growth** – In the long run, economic growth is likely to fall due to the combination of lower export sales and higher unemployment resulting from the higher exchange rate.
■ **Balance of payments** – A currency appreciation tends to cause a fall in exports because it is more difficult to sell goods and services in overseas markets at a higher price. Cheaper imports leads to rising import penetration. Therefore the current account balance worsens.

Exchange rate fluctuations also affect different stakeholders in different ways:
■ **Customers** have greater purchasing power when the exchange rate increases – for example, if the exchange rate changes from $1.6 = £1 to $1.4 = £1, then Americans would need fewer dollars to buy British goods and services.

> **Expert tip**
>
> When analysing the impact of changes in exchange rates, students should consider time lags. Whilst fluctuations in the exchange rate affect the economy, the impacts take time to happen, i.e. there is a time delay between a change in the exchange rate and its impact on economic growth, employment, inflation and the balance of payments.

- **Exporters** face more difficult trading conditions when the exchange rate increases because the prices of their goods and services become more expensive for foreign customers.
- **Importers** potentially gain from a stronger currency as this makes it cheaper for firms to import raw materials, components and finished goods from abroad.

EXAM PRACTICE

PAPER 2

13 Since China's admission to the World Trade Organization in November 2001, the USA has complained that the Chinese government has deliberately kept its exchange rate artificially low. The low value of the yuan compared with the dollar has contributed to the economic problems of the US economy.

a Define the term exchange rate. **[2]**

b Explain **two** advantages of an undervalued yuan for the Chinese economy. **[4]**

Government intervention

Revised ▢

Fixed exchange rates

Revised ▢

A **fixed exchange rate system** exists when the central bank (or monetary authority) buys and sells foreign currencies to ensure that the value of its currency stays at the pegged value, i.e. a single fixed rate.

Revaluation occurs when the price of a currency operating in a fixed exchange rate system is officially and deliberately increased.

Devaluation occurs when the price of a currency operating in a fixed exchange rate system is officially and deliberately lowered. The international competitiveness of a country can be improved by a currency devaluation, as exports become relatively cheaper.

The government intervenes in foreign exchange markets to maintain its fixed exchange rate at a predetermined level by buying (demanding) or selling (supplying) foreign currency reserves.

It is possible to change the pegged (fixed) rate over time – for example, the Hong Kong dollar (HKD) was originally fixed at HK\$5.65 = USD1 back in 1972. As the USA's economy developed, its currency was revalued to HK\$7.8 in 1983 and has since been fixed at that rate (see Figure 3.9).

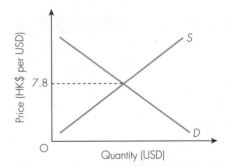

Figure 3.9 The fixed exchange rate system

The fixed exchange rate is achieved by the respective governments buying and selling foreign currencies to maintain the 'peg'. For example, if the HKD falls in value the Hong Kong Monetary Authority can buy (demand) enough HKD (thus raising its price) to maintain the fixed exchange rate.

Managed exchange rates (managed float)

Revised ☐

In a **managed exchange rate system**, the government or central monetary authority intervenes periodically in the foreign exchange market to influence the exchange rate by affecting the demand for, and supply of, the domestic currency.

Intervention is used to prevent large and sudden fluctuations in the exchange rate, which could happen if currencies were left entirely to the market forces of demand and supply. This helps to create certainty and confidence in the economy.

China's currency, the yuan (CNY), is pegged to the US dollar (USD), although the rate has been allowed to appreciate slowly over time (from CNY6.8 in January 2009 to CNY6.15 5 years later). The managed float has helped to control China's export growth and to offset its inflation.

Table 3.1 The advantages and disadvantages of over- and undervalued exchange rates

	Advantages	Disadvantages
Overvalued currency	Imported goods become cheaper so there is downward pressure on the rate of inflation. Domestic producers are forced to be more efficient to compete with the cheaper foreign imports.	Exports become less competitive, causing lower profits in export industries. As imports become cheaper and exports more expensive, there is a negative impact on the balance of payments.
Undervalued currency	Exports become cheaper, leading to growth and employment in export industries. Imports become more expensive for consumers, so they switch to buying domestic goods.	Imports become more expensive, which can lead to imported inflation, i.e. imported raw materials and components are more costly, thus affecting the general price level.

Evaluation of different exchange rate systems

Revised ☐

The main advantage of fixing exchange rates is that it reduces uncertainties for international trade. This allows firms, both foreign and domestic, to be certain about future costs and prices, thereby encouraging international trade and exchange. Similarly, fixed exchange rates remove uncertainties and volatility caused by currency fluctuations due to speculation in the foreign exchange market.

However, fixing exchange rates reduces the country's ability to use monetary policy to affect the economy (which would be particularly useful during an economic recession). There is also a huge opportunity cost in using large amounts of foreign exchange reserves on a daily basis to maintain the fixed rate.

The opposite impacts apply to floating exchange rates – for example, they can create instability and uncertainties to international trade, although exchange rates are more responsive to changes in the economy.

3.3 The balance of payments

Revised

The structure of the balance of payments

Revised

The meaning of the balance of payments

Revised

The role of the balance of payments (BOP) is to record **credit items** (all payments received from other countries) and **debit items** (all payments made to other nations).

Credit items on the BOP include revenues earned from the export of goods and services, foreign direct investment and capital transfers. For example, the expenditure of French tourists visiting the UK would be recorded as a credit item on the UK's balance of payments (see Table 3.2).

Debit items on the BOP include the purchase of imports of foreign goods and services, income transfers overseas, and the repatriation of profits from multinational companies in the economy. These transactions have a corresponding outflow of money from the domestic economy.

Essentially, the balance of payments is a record of a country's sources and uses of foreign exchange with its trading partners.

In theory, the balance of payments (BOP) must always balance over time because a country, like an individual, can only spend what it earns.

> **Keyword definition**
> The **balance of payments** is a financial record of a country's transactions with the rest of the world for a given time period, usually over 1 year. This includes the country's trade in goods and services with other countries.

Table 3.2 Examples of credit and debit items for the UK economy

Credit (inflow or export earning)	Debit (outflow or import expenditure)
The purchase of UK-produced chemical products by German companies	UK Government maintaining foreign embassies overseas
American tourists flying to the UK on British Airways	UK supermarkets' purchase of Australian wine and meat products
Global sales of *Harry Potter* books by British author J. K. Rowling	A large British firm buying a fleet of lorries (trucks) from Japan
French tourists buying theatre tickets to see *Les Misérables* in London	The UK government paying interest on its borrowing (debts)

The components of the balance of payments accounts

Revised

The balance of payments consists of three accounts: the current account, the capital account and the financial account.

The structure of the balance of payments accounts is shown in Table 3.3. This can vary from one country to another. However, the version here is used in the IB Economics curriculum and assessment.

Table 3.3 The structure of the balance of payments

1. Current account	2. Capital account	3. Financial account
■ Balance of trade in goods ■ Balance of trade in services ■ Income ■ Current transfers	■ Capital transfers ■ Transactions in non-produced, non-financial assets	■ Direct investment ■ Portfolio investment ■ Reserve assets
current account = capital account + financial account + errors and omissions		

Source: *IB Economics Guide*, first examinations 2013, page 98

The current account

The **current account** is a record of all exports and imports of goods and services, plus its net investment income from overseas assets and the net balance of transfers made between countries by individuals and governments. The account is usually reported per year.

There are four components of the current account:

■ **Balance of trade in goods** – this records all exports and imports of physical goods (e.g. rice, computers and motor vehicles) between a country and the rest of the world.

■ **Balance of trade in services** – this records all exports and imports of services (e.g. insurance, banking, management consultancy and tourism) between a country and the rest of the world.

■ **Income** – this records the **income receipts** (inflows) earned from foreign investments minus the **income payments** (outflow) of factor incomes paid to foreign investors. Investment income consists of the inflows and outflows of wages, rent, interest and profit.

■ **Current transfers** – this records the inflows and outflows of payments that are not made in exchange for anything (e.g. official development assistance, grants, concessionary loans and donations) between a country and the rest of the world.

The **balance of trade** (or **trade balance**) is the difference between a country's total export earnings and its total import expenditure on both goods and services. The balance of trade is typically the largest component of the current account.

A **current account deficit** occurs when a country spends more money than it earns, i.e. the sum of money flowing out of a country exceeds the money flowing into the country. A **current account surplus** exists if a country has a positive net balance on its current account. A current account deficit can occur due to a combination of two factors:

■ **Lower demand for exports** – This is mainly caused by exports being relatively more expensive to foreign buyers. It can be caused by higher labour costs in the domestic economy, falling incomes (perhaps due to a recession) or a higher exchange rate making exports dearer.

■ **Increased demand for imports** – Domestic buyers tend to buy more imports if they are relatively cheaper and/or of better quality – for example, a higher exchange makes it cheaper to buy foreign goods and services.

Expert tip

Remember the **GIST** of the current account, i.e. that it is made up of four components:
■ **G**oods – the trade in physical goods
■ **I**ncome – investment income from overseas assets
■ **S**ervices – the trade in services
■ **T**ransfers – current transfers (of private individuals and government) between countries

EXAM PRACTICE *(HL ONLY)*

Expert tip

Higher-level students must be able to calculate elements of the balance of payments from a set of data, as in these Paper 3 practice questions.

PAPER 3

14 Use the data below to calculate the balance of trade.　　　　　**[2]**

BALANCE OF TRADE IN GOODS ($m)	2014
Food, beverages and tobacco	−3558
Oil	4305
Finished manufactured goods	−685
Others	−1886
BALANCE OF TRADE IN SERVICES ($m)	**2014**
Transportation	−632
Communications	−531
Insurance	1450
Others	3776

15 Use the data below to calculate the current account balance.　　　**[4]**

2014	BALANCE OF TRADE IN GOODS	BALANCE OF TRADE IN SERVICES	INVESTMENT INCOME	CURRENT TRANSFERS
CREDIT (+)	$736m	$336m	$295m	$106m
DEBIT (−)	$663m	$277m	$261m	$119m

16 Study the data below and answer the questions that follow.

Balance of trade for country K ($billion), 2014

Exports	**85**
Goods	57
Services	28
Imports	.....
Goods	88
Services	15
Balance of trade in goods	.....
Balance of trade in services	.....
Trade balance	.....

　a Define the term 'balance of trade in services'.　　　　　　　**[2]**

　b Calculate the missing figures in the data above.　　　　　　　**[4]**

17 Study the data below and answer the questions that follow.

- Trade in goods =　　　− $18.3bn
- Trade in services =　　+ $21.8bn
- Net income =　　　　　+ $6.7bn
- Net current transfers =　− $5.6bn

　a Outline what is meant by 'net income'.　　　　　　　　　　**[2]**

　b Calculate the value of the balance of trade on the balance of payments.　**[2]**

　c Calculate the value of the current account on the balance of payments.　**[2]**

The capital account

Revised

The **capital account** is the smallest component of the balance of payments. It records the different forms of capital inflows and outflows of a country during a given time period, for example foreign currency flows and bank deposits. Here are some examples:

- If Indian citizens buy shares in American banks, this is recorded as a credit item on the USA's capital account and a debit item on India's capital account. However, the dividends earned by the Indian shareholders would be a credit item for India and a debit item for the USA.
- If Chinese citizens purchase US government bonds, the USA receives a capital injection of money (credit item) whereas China will have a debit (outflow) on its capital account.

The two components of the capital account are:

- **Capital transfers** – These are the net monetary movements of capital goods used in the production process (e.g. machinery and equipment) and financial assets (e.g. investment grants and debt forgiveness, i.e. the cancellation of debts for highly indebted poor countries).
- **Transactions in non-produced, non-financial assets** – The exchange of money in non-produced assets, i.e. natural resources (e.g. commodities such as minerals) and intangible assets (e.g. patents, copyrights, trademarks and internet domain names).

Financial assets, such as money or bonds, are of little physical value (the paper they are printed on is of little value). Instead, their value is based on what the asset represents. By contrast, **non-financial assets** (such as gold) are assets with physical value.

Less economically developed countries (LEDCs) tend to have a capital account deficit as there is financial instability and mounting government debts and loans.

The financial account

Revised

The **financial account** records a country's net transactions in external financial assets and liabilities, for example foreign direct investment, the purchase or sale of real estate (land), and investments in stock markets. It records the difference between sales of domestic assets to foreign buyers and purchases of foreign assets by domestic buyers.

A financial capital inflow occurs when foreigners loan money to domestic citizens by acquiring domestic assets.

The three main components of the financial account are:

- **Direct investment** – This refers to the inflows and outflows of long-term investments in physical capital, for example foreign ownership of domestic assets such as property and land. Direct investments are mainly undertaken by multinational corporations (MNCs).
- **Portfolio investment** – The buying and selling of stocks, shares, government bonds, pension funds and other financial investments in foreign companies is collectively known as portfolio investment. Essentially, these assets represent international borrowing and lending.
- **Reserve assets** – This refers to official reserves that are readily available to a government for direct financing of international payments imbalances and to affect its exchange rate, for example gold reserves and foreign exchange assets.

The relationship between the accounts

Revised

In theory, the overall balance of payments (BOP) must always balance because in the long term a country can only spend what it earns, i.e. the sum of all credit items equals the sum of debit items. However, it is possible to run a deficit in one component of its BOP so long as it can 'balance' this by having a surplus on another account. For example:

- Hong Kong has a deficit on its current account but funds this by having a surplus on its financial account due to favourable conditions for FDI, i.e. it must have a surplus to provide it with the foreign exchange to pay for the excess of imports over exports.
- China, Norway, Germany and Saudi Arabia have a current account surplus but can run a deficit on their capital account or financial account by directly investing the surplus in foreign countries and/or accumulating foreign currency reserves.

This means that the current account and the financial account are interdependent. A country with a current account deficit consumes more than it produces so has to pay for this extra output somehow, i.e. through a surplus on its financial account (and vice versa).

In reality, the balance of payments will not balance as there are too many transactions to account for. To resolve this problem, **errors and omissions** are used to represent statistical discrepancies when compiling the accounts. Therefore the following condition must hold:

current account = capital account + financial account + errors and omissions

Current account deficits

Revised ☐

The relationship between the current account and the exchange rate

Revised ☐

A **current account deficit** exists when the sum of the outflows from the current account exceeds the inflows into the account – for example, net import expenditure on goods and services is greater than net export earnings. A current account deficit shows the country is spending more than it is earning, so it must require more foreign exchange whilst it faces lower demand for its own currency as exports decline.

In theory, the deficit is automatically resolved under a freely floating exchange rate system because it makes exports relatively cheaper and imports relatively more expensive. Export earnings should rise and import expenditure should fall, restoring equilibrium.

However, this is more problematic in a fixed exchange rate system unless a devaluation of the currency is approved. If so, this should improve the current account in the same way, as with a depreciation of the currency.

In a managed exchange rate system, a current account deficit is resolved by combining market forces and central bank intervention by buying and selling of foreign currencies to reduce the value of the domestic currency in overseas markets.

> **Expert tip**
>
> This analysis refers to a current account deficit. The opposite would apply to a current account surplus, for example, it would put upwards pressure on the exchange rate so, in theory, a currency appreciation should eventually automatically reduce the surplus.

Implications of a persistent current account deficit *(HL only)*

Revised ☐

Foreign ownership of domestic assets – A current account deficit has to be financed by a surplus on the financial account, often in the form of FDI, i.e. more domestic assets become owned by foreign MNCs. There are opposing implications of this:

- FDI can help to boost aggregate demand in the economy, thus boosting economic growth.
- FDI and foreign ownership of domestic assets can cause leakages in the circular flow of income as MNCs remit income and profits back to their home countries.

Exchange rates – A persistent deficit on the current account will deplete the country's foreign currency reserves. For countries reliant on key imports such as oil, a declining currency can fuel imported inflation, with its negative impacts on GDP and employment.

Interest rates – As a persistent current account deficit puts downward pressure on the exchange rate, governments may be tempted to raise interest rates to attract foreign currency and capital inflows. However, higher interest rates can be contractionary and reduce aggregate demand.

Indebtedness – If a country does not have sufficient financial reserves to fund its persistent current account deficit, it will have to borrow money from abroad. The country therefore goes into debt, with its related problems, for example mounting interest repayments, lower growth and job losses.

International credit ratings – Credit rating refers to the credit worthiness of a borrower based on the likely ability to repay the debt. A persistent current account deficit tends to reduce a country's credit rating as it can signal underlining structural problems for the economy.

Demand management – Contractionary demand management policies might be used to reduce the demand for imports to correct a persistent current account deficit. However, this can negatively affect growth and employment.

> **Expert tip**
>
> In general, a large and persistent current account deficit suggests that the country is uncompetitive in international markets, which causes detrimental consequences for the domestic economy such as lower aggregate demand and job losses. Thus, current account deficits will have a negative impact on economic growth and standards of living.

EXAM PRACTICE

PAPER 2

18 Sri Lanka is a major exporter of tea and coconuts. The chart below shows the balance of trade for Sri Lanka from 2004–2013.

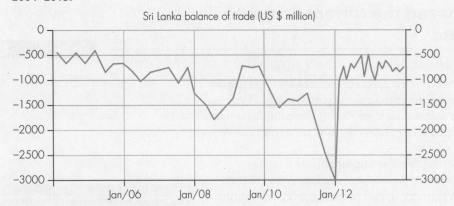

Sri Lanka balance of trade (US $ million)

a Define the term 'balance of trade'. [2]

b Explain **two** possible causes of Sri Lanka's persistent balance of trade deficit. [4]

EXAM PRACTICE *(HL ONLY)*

PAPER 3

19 'A current account deficit on the balance of payments is undesirable during a recession but is not really a problem during periods of economic growth.'

a Define the term 'current account deficit'. [2]

b Explain the validity of the above statement. [4]

> **Common mistake**
>
> Students seem to regularly confuse the concept of *budget deficits* with *balance of payments deficits*. It is incorrect to say that a budget deficit means that a country's import spending is greater than its export earnings (as budget deficits are concerned with government fiscal policies).

> **Expert tip**
>
> A deficit on the current account that is manageable is not necessarily a bad thing. For example, the deficit might be the result of strong economic growth, with residents purchasing more foreign goods and services. This allows the country's residents to enjoy a higher standard of living, as they are able to benefit from access to a wider range of good quality imports.

Methods to correct a persistent current account deficit *(HL only)*

Expenditure switching policies – These policies are intended to encourage households and firms to buy domestically produced goods and services rather than imported alternatives by raising the relative price of imports or reducing the relative price of exports. Examples include the following:

- **Export promotion** – These are policies that stimulate the demand for exports, for example export subsidies and tax concessions for export-orientated firms.
- **Trade protection** – These measures reduce the competiveness of imports, thereby making domestic consumption more attractive – for example, tariffs (import taxes) raise the price of imports, whilst quotas are quantitative limits on the amount of available imports.
- **Currency devaluation** – The central bank can devalue its exchange rate to reduce the price of exports and make imports more expensive.

Expenditure reducing policies – These policies are designed to cut a current account deficit by lowering disposable income to limit aggregate demand and import expenditure in particular. This is usually achieved through use of contractionary fiscal and monetary policies:

- **Contractionary fiscal policy** – These measures use a combination of higher taxes and reduced government spending to reduce consumption, including the amount of money available to spend on imports.
- **Contractionary monetary policy** – Higher interest rates make new and existing loans more expensive, so both households and firms reduce their demand for imports.

Supply-side policies – These policies strive to raise the productive capacity of the economy and to increase its international competitiveness. Examples include:

- investment in education and healthcare to improve the economy's human capital (investment to improve the skills and productivity of the workforce), thereby raising the quality of exports and improving the country's long-term international competitiveness
- investment in infrastructure to support businesses and industries, especially those engaged in export-orientated markets
- measures to encourage export-driven business start-ups and industries, such as the use of government subsidies and tax incentives.

Expenditure-switching policies do not always work because:

- price is not always the deciding factor in determining the level of demand for goods and services. Customers will consider non-price factors that determine the demand for products, for example quality, functionality and brand loyalty.
- trade protection can cause other countries to retaliate by creating their own trade barriers. Such disharmony will reduce the benefits of free international trade.
- currency devaluations only work under a system of fixed exchange rates, yet the falling value of the currency can cause imported inflation (higher-priced imports of essential products such as crude oil, raw materials and foodstuff).

Expenditure-reducing policies such as higher taxes can cause huge disincentive effects, negatively affecting economic growth and development. Contractionary policies can also cause mass-scale unemployment in the economy.

Whilst supply-side policies aim to make domestically produced goods and services more competitive, they tend to take a long time to materialise. Hence, the implementation of supply-side policies to rectify a persistent current account deficit tends to be very costly.

The Marshall-Lerner condition and the J-curve effect *(HL only)*

Under a fixed exchange rate system, a government can devalue its exchange rate to resolve a current account deficit. In theory, this will make exports relatively more attractive to overseas buyers and make imports more expensive for domestic citizens, thus improving the account.

Similarly, a country with a current account deficit and operating under a floating exchange rate system should experience an improvement if there is downward pressure (depreciation) on its exchange rate.

However, a devaluation or depreciation of the currency will only work in rectifying a current account deficit if the sum of the price elasticities of demand for exports (X) and imports (M) is greater than 1, i.e. price elastic. This rule is called the **Marshall-Lerner condition**:

$$PED_X + PED_M > 1$$

Hence, if $PED_X + PED_M = 1$ then a currency devaluation or depreciation has no impact on the current account deficit. Likewise, if $PED_X + PED_M < 1$ then the fall in the exchange rate will actually worsen the deficit further.

The **J-curve effect** is an economic model that shows that following a currency depreciation the balance of trade worsens before it gets better (see Figure 3.10). The effect is caused by time lags, such as:

- limited access to information – people are not aware of the currency devaluation
- ongoing contracts – so firms cannot take advantage of the currency devaluation
- existing habits and tastes – in the short run, buyers might not be responsive to the currency devaluation and so continue to buy imports at a higher price (and export at a lower price).

In other words, households and firms in both domestic and foreign markets need time to adjust to the changes in the price of exports and imports.

The J curve will only materialise (i.e. a fall in the value of the exchange rate in rectifying a current account deficit) if the Marshall-Lerner condition holds.

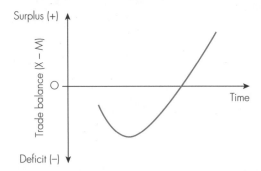

- The lower exchange rate causes a rise in the price of imports and a fall in the price of exports.
- This worsens the deficit as the PED_X and PED_M remain price inelastic in the short term.
- In the long term, the PED_X and PED_M will increase as households and firms adjust to the relative price changes, with the lower exchange rate boosting exports and reducing imports.

Figure 3.10 The J curve

Expert tip

The previous analysis can work for countries with a persistent current account surplus (an 'upside-down' J curve) that they want to eliminate by raising the value of the exchange rate.

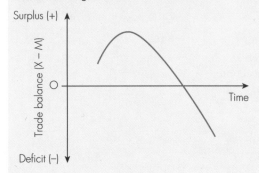

Current account surpluses

Revised ☐

The relationship between the current account and the exchange rate

Revised ☐

A **current account surplus** exists when the sum of the inflows from the current account exceeds the outflows into the account – for example, the value of net export earnings on goods and services is greater than the value of net import expenditure.

A surplus on the current account can occur due to a combination of two factors:

- **Higher demand for exports** – This could be caused by improved domestic manufacturing competitiveness, higher labour productivity or higher incomes in overseas markets (foreign households and firms have more disposable income to spend on the country's exports).
- **Reduced demand for imports** – Domestic buyers will tend to buy fewer imports if they are more expensive or of lower quality than those provided by domestic firms, choosing instead to buy more home-produced goods and services.

A current account surplus shows that the country is earning more than it is spending, so there is a greater demand for its currency as exports increase. Hence, there is greater upwards pressure on its exchange rate.

In general, a current account surplus means that the country is a net lender to the rest of the world, whereas it would be a net borrower from the rest of the world if it ran a current account deficit.

A current account surplus is generally seen as positive for an economy, especially if it is due to export-orientated growth and development strategies, as used in countries such as China, India, Mexico, Indonesia, South Korea and Turkey.

Alternatively, the current account surplus could signify that the country is spending less on imports than its trading partners because of relatively lower incomes. Thus, households have a relatively lower standard of living as they are unable to access a wider range of goods and services.

In addition, many countries with a persistent or rising current account surplus (such as Kuwait and Qatar) are heavily dependent on export earnings and a high savings rate, but with weak domestic aggregate demand.

In a freely floating exchange rate system, the currency appreciation, caused by a persistent current account surplus, results in a fall in the demand for exports and a rise in the demand for imports. Thus, the fall in the exchange rate automatically eliminates the current account surplus.

> **Expert tip**
>
> A surplus on the current account is not necessarily a good thing. For example, Romania, a former communist nation, had a trade surplus by using trade protection. This limited access to foreign goods and services, thus lowering living standards.

Implications of a rising current account surplus (*HL only*)

Revised ☐

Lower domestic consumption – A current account surplus can be caused by lower domestic expenditure on imports, which is not necessarily good for households and firms if it is due to a lower level of income.

Lower domestic investment – Domestic investment is likely to fall due to inflationary pressures caused by the current account surplus. A higher exchange rate, associated with a current account surplus, is also likely to reduce foreign direct investment.

Currency appreciation – The higher demand for exports can cause the domestic currency to appreciate in value. Subsequently, exporters will find it increasingly difficult to sell to foreign buyers who have to pay higher prices for the products.

Reduced export competitiveness – Higher demand for exports and a higher exchange rate can lead to higher export prices. Therefore, a current account surplus can diminish the international competitiveness of the country over time.

EXAM PRACTICE

PAPER 2

20 Kuwait is one of the world's largest net exporters of oil. The chart below shows the ratio of the country's current account balance relative to its gross domestic product (GDP) from 2000 to 2013.

Kuwait current account to GDP

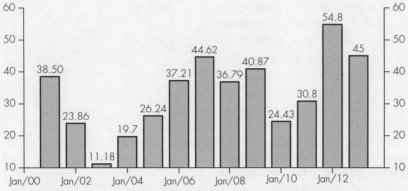

    a Define the term 'current account surplus'. [2]

    b Explain two consequences of Kuwait's persistent current account surplus from 2000 to 2013. [4]

3.4 Economic integration

Forms of economic integration

Forms of economic integration include:

- preferential bilateral and multilateral trade agreements
- trading blocs, such as free trade areas, customs unions and common markets
- monetary union
- foreign direct investment (FDI)
- globalisation and expansion of multinational corporations.

> **Keyword definition**
> **Economic integration** refers to the process of countries becoming more interdependent and economically unified. It can be achieved by preferential trade agreements between member governments to remove trade barriers.

Preferential trade agreements

A **bilateral trade agreement** is a contractual trade arrangement between two countries, such as closer economic partnership agreements (CEPAs). For example, Hong Kong and China's CEPA signed in 2004 created improved cross-border trade and investment between the two countries.

A **multilateral trade agreement** is a legally binding trade deal between more than two countries, for example in a free trade area. Such trade agreements are made within the guidelines of the World Trade Organization (WTO), i.e. an agreement to reduce or remove international trade barriers.

As bilateral trade agreements are made between two countries only, they have far greater flexibility than multilateral trade agreements. The latter can involve many countries, so they are far more complex.

Preferential trade agreements (PTAs) give certain countries special and easier access to specific products in a market due to advantages such as the reduction or removal of tariffs and non-tariff barriers to international trade.

In line with WTO rules, PTAs must adhere to the principle of **non-discrimination**. This means that a country cannot discriminate against other WTO member countries by imposing higher trade barriers on one country whilst reducing the trade barriers on imports from another country.

The two exemptions to the principle of non-discrimination are bilateral trade agreements and regional trading blocs such as the European Union. In both cases, non-member countries can have higher trade barriers imposed.

> **Keyword definition**
> A **preferential trade agreement** is a trade deal between two or more countries that gives special or favourable terms and conditions, such as tax exemptions or tax concessions.

Trading blocs

Economic integration within a trading bloc will intensify the degree of competition for producers within the member countries. However, firms can benefit from access to a larger market without trade barriers, thereby benefiting from economies of scale. Whilst a trading bloc promotes free trade with its member countries, the bloc imposes trade barriers for non-member states.

There are three categories of trading bloc, with varying degrees of economic integration:

- A **free trade area** (FTA) is the least economically integrated trading bloc, where member countries agree to remove trade barriers with one another, but impose *separate* trade barriers with non-member countries, for example the North American Free Trade Agreement (NAFTA).
- A **customs union** is a group of member countries that engage in free trade and impose a **common external tariff** for non-member countries, i.e. all members impose the same trade restrictions on non-member states.
- A **common market** is the most integrated trading bloc. This is a customs union that, in addition to imposing the same trade restrictions on non-member nations, allows the free movement of goods, services, capital and labour between its member countries.

> **Keyword definition**
> A **trading bloc** is a group of countries that agree to economic integration and freer international trade by removing trade barriers with one another.

Some economists argue that economic integration, especially common markets, causes a loss of national economic sovereignty, i.e. the lost opportunity to enjoy economic independence. For instance, trading blocs might impose stricter environmental legislation and labour laws.

In addition, detrimental changes in the economic conditions of one member country (such as inflationary pressures or an economic recession) are likely to affect the economic performance of all member countries.

Another drawback of joining a trading bloc is that it could lead to more unemployment in the short run. This is due to the increased intensity of competition facing domestic firms in the trading bloc.

Nevertheless, most economists believe that trade protection, rather than economic integration, is harmful to households and firms. This is due to the dynamic efficiency gains from free trade and because of the reduced choice and higher prices under trade protection.

Expert tip

Make sure you can use real-world examples in the external examinations. This means that you should be able to give examples of the various categories of trade bloc:

- Free trade areas include the North American Free Trade Agreement (NAFTA), a trilateral trade agreement between the USA, Canada and Mexico to promote trade and investment.

- Customs unions include the European Union (EU), or the five member countries of the Southern African Customs Union (SACU) – Botswana, Lesotho, Namibia, South Africa and Swaziland.

- Common markets include the Caribbean Community (CARICOM), which promotes economic integration and cooperation among its 15 member countries.

Trade creation and trade diversion *(HL only)*

The formation of a customs union is likely to cause both trade creation and trade diversion. Economic integration improves the welfare of the economy if it leads to more trade creation than trade diversion.

Trade creation occurs when economic integration shifts trade deals away from higher-cost producers from outside the trading bloc to lower-cost producers within the trading bloc, due to the removal of trade barriers.

Trade diversion occurs when economic integration shifts trade deals away from lower-cost producers outside the trading bloc to higher-cost producers within the trading bloc due to the trade agreements of the customs union.

Economic integration allows multinational corporations (MNCs) to locate overseas in member states and to export without trade barriers. Thus, MNCs can gain easier access to larger markets and operate on a much larger scale. Trade creation therefore helps them towards economies of scale.

Arguments for limiting the degree of economic integration include: the need to protect domestic infant industries from international rivals, political and strategic reasons (economic and political sovereignty) and the protection of domestic employment.

Expert tip

Higher level students need to be able to distinguish between trade diversion and trade creation. Remember that a disadvantage of joining a regional trading bloc is trade diversion, whereas a key benefit of joining is trade creation with member countries.

Monetary union

To achieve monetary union, members of a common market must first agree to permanently fix their exchange rates to use a common currency and to establish a common central bank to be responsible for monetary policy. This means that there is convergence of interest rates within the monetary union, so member states do not have flexibility in exercising their own monetary policy.

A well-known example of monetary union is the 17 member states (collectively called the 'eurozone') of the European Union that use the euro

Keyword definition

A **monetary union** exists when member states of a common market adopt a single currency and hence a common central bank that oversees monetary policy.

as their common currency. Monetary policy is exercised through the European Central Bank (ECB).

For full monetary union, a single (common) currency is used by all member countries. This is not the case within the European Union member states.

Advantages of monetary union

Revised ☐

There is exchange rate certainty as a common currency is used. This eliminates the risks associated with international trade due to exchange rate fluctuations and uncertainties.

Trade creation will occur between members of a single currency area due to the preferential trade agreement and the confidence in the use of a common currency. The use of a common currency also eliminates transaction costs as there is no need to exchange foreign currencies between members of the monetary union.

Similarly, the use of a common currency attracts inward investment from non-member states due to the removed risks associated with exchange rate fluctuations. Inward investment will have a positive impact on economic growth and employment in the monetary union.

There is price transparency, i.e. households and firms can compare prices across different member states at a glance.

Disadvantages of monetary union

Revised ☐

There is a loss of economic freedom and flexibility as countries within the monetary union are unable to adjust macroeconomic policies to deal with their own specific economic problems. For example, a country with relatively high unemployment cannot reduce interest rates to stimulate its economy.

Similarly, the actions taken by the common central bank have an asymmetric impact on different countries due to their varying circumstances. For example, contrasting rates of inflation and unemployment in Greece and Germany mean that a common monetary policy might not work for either country.

Members of a monetary union are also deprived of exercising their own exchange rate policy. With independence, the country can depreciate its currency during a recession or to combat a balance of payments deficit. This autonomy is not possible in a monetary union.

EXAM PRACTICE

PAPER 2

21 Using appropriate examples, differentiate between a customs union and a monetary union. [4]

22 Using an appropriate diagram, explain how economic integration can benefit the economy. [4]

3.5 The terms of trade *(HL only)*

Revised ☐

The meaning of the terms of trade *(HL only)*

Revised ☐

The terms of trade (TOT) is measured using the same currency, by comparing the index of average export prices against the index of average import prices, i.e.:

$$\text{terms of trade (TOT)} = \frac{\text{index of average export prices}}{\text{index of average import prices}} \times 100$$

Thus, when the average price of exports rises, the TOT increases – economists call this an improvement in the terms of trade because the country can potentially buy more imports with the same amount of exports (it can import more products than before as its exports are worth more).

The TOT differs from the exchange rate, which measures the price of exports in terms of foreign currencies.

Note that the TOT only indicates relative *price movements* of imports and exports; it does not tell us anything about the *volume* of trade (which depends on the price elasticity of demand for both exports and imports) or the *quality* of the exports and imports.

> **Keyword definition**
> The **terms of trade** (TOT) is an index number that expresses the value of average export prices divided by the average of import prices, per time period. An increase in the ratio indicates an improvement the terms of trade, i.e. the country can buy more imports for the same amount of exports as before. By contrast, a fall in the ratio means a deterioration in the terms of trade.

Measurement *(HL only)*

Revised ☐

As countries trade a huge amount of goods and services, the terms of trade are measured using a weighted price index of average prices of exports and imports. Index numbers are used to calculate the terms of trade, as this simplifies the calculations and allows for easier comparisons rather than expressing prices in different currencies (which tend to fluctuate over time).

In general, the more imports that a country can purchase from each sale of exports, the better off it will be.

Worked example						
Year	Average price of oil ($ per unit)	Price index (oil)	Average price of tea ($ per unit)	Price index (tea)	TOT (USA)	TOT (Sri Lanka)
2011	98	94.2	320	111.1	84.8	117.9
2012	104	100.0	288	100.0	100.0	100.0
2013	109	104.8	254	88.2	118.8	84.2

In the above table, 2012 is base year, so the price indices of oil and tea are assigned an index number of 100. The price index for tea in 2011 is calculated as:

$$\frac{320}{288} \times 100 = 111.1$$

Similarly, the price index for oil in 2013 is calculated as:

$$\frac{109}{104} \times 100 = 104.8$$

Finally, to work out the terms of trade for the USA, we need to divide the price index of the export (oil) by the index price of imports (tea). So, the TOT for 2013 is:

$$\frac{104.8}{88.2} \times 100 = 118.8$$

The TOT for Sri Lanka is calculated by dividing the price index for its export (tea) by its import (oil), so for example its TOT in 2011 was:

$$\frac{111.1}{94.2} \times 100 = 117.9$$

So, in this worked example, the terms of trade have improved for the US economy between 2011 and 2013.

EXAM PRACTICE *(HL ONLY)*

PAPER 3

23 a Suppose the price index for exports is 110 and that for imports is 105. If export prices rise on average by 10% whilst import prices rise by 5%, calculate the terms of trade. **[2]**

b Comment on the change in the terms of trade. **[2]**

24 Refer to the information below for a given country and answer the questions that follow. Assume that 2012 is the base year.

YEAR	PRICE OF RICE EXPORTS ($ PER UNIT)	PRICE OF MILK IMPORTS ($ PER UNIT)
2012	430.0	19.2
2013	481.6	22.6
2014	505.7	23.7

a Calculate the price index of rice exports in 2013. **[2]**

b Calculate the price index of milk imports in 2013. **[2]**

c Calculate the terms of trade in 2013. **[2]**

d Comment on the change in the terms of trade for the country. **[2]**

Causes of changes in the terms of trade *(HL only)*

Revised ☐

There are essentially two main causes of a change in the terms of trade – changes in the average price of exports or changes in the average price of imports. Examples of such changes in the short term include the following:

- Changes in the demand for exports and imports – A fall in the demand for exports will tend to reduce the relative price of exports thereby worsening the terms of trade, i.e. each unit of exports buys fewer units of imports.
- Changes in the global supply of key inputs – An increase in the price of important inputs to the production process, such as oil, will improve the TOT for countries that export such products and deteriorate the TOT for countries that need to import such commodities.
- Changes in relative inflation rates – Demand–pull inflation, for example, can cause domestic prices to rise, thereby improving the country's TOT because the relative price of exports will rise. Note that this does not mean that inflation itself is necessarily good for the country.
- Changes in relative exchange rates – A currency depreciation will reduce the relative price of exports, thus worsening the terms of trade.

In the long term, there are three main causes of changes in the terms of trade:

- Changes in world income levels – Typically, higher household incomes will lead to an increase in the demand for goods and services, especially those that are relatively income elastic in demand. This helps to improve the TOT for countries that produce and export such products.
- Changes in productivity – Long-term changes in supply cause the productive capacity of the economy to increase, so national output rises. This results in exports being produced at a lower cost and hence price, consequently deteriorating the terms of trade.
- Technological developments – Advances in technology help to achieve productivity gains and hence boost the productive capacity of the economy. Although this deteriorates the TOT, the improved competitiveness of domestic firms is a positive impact on the economy.

Expert tip

Whilst most students seem to be able to define the terms of trade, they are often unable to use real-world examples to substantiate their answers. Use a well-known example to help – for example, the price inelastic demand for oil and its low supply mean that the terms of trade will tend to improve in the short-term for oil-rich countries such as Kuwait.

Consequences of changes in the terms of trade *(HL only)*

Revised ☐

Long-term changes in the terms of trade can cause a global redistribution of income and wealth – for example, China's improved TOT over the past few decades has led the nation to economic supremacy.

There are higher costs of debt servicing (repayment of loans plus interest charges) if the TOT deteriorates. This is because more exports are needed to pay off the foreign loans following deterioration in the TOT. This is because a larger volume of exports is now needed to pay for the purchase of imports.

The demand for primary-sector products produced in less economically developed countries (LEDCs) tends to be highly price inelastic, but they often face deteriorating terms of trade. In addition, the income elasticity of demand (YED) is low for primary-sector output. Hence, LEDCs that focus on primary industries lose out as consumers will spend proportionately more on manufacturing and tertiary-sector jobs as their incomes rise.

Changes in the terms of trade can improve or worsen the balance of payments current account depending on the price elasticity of demand (PED) for both imports and exports:

- A deteriorating TOT due to lower export prices (caused by a lower exchange rate) will increase export revenues if the demand for exports is price elastic, i.e. there is a proportionally higher amount of spending on exports following the fall in average export prices.
- An improvement in the TOT due to higher export prices is beneficial to the economy if the demand for exports is price inelastic, i.e. foreign customers are relatively unresponsive to the higher average price of exports.

The advantages and disadvantages of changes in the TOT are outlined in Tables 3.4 and 3.5:

Table 3.4 Advantages and disadvantages of an improvement in the TOT

Advantages	Disadvantages
■ Export revenues will increase if demand for exports is price inelastic. This improves the current account balance. ■ The country can consume more imports, giving citizens greater choice. ■ Debt servicing is made easier as the country can repay its borrowing more easily.	■ If demand for exports is price elastic, export revenues will fall, thereby worsening the current account balance. ■ If demand for imports is price elastic, import expenditure will rise, thus worsening the current account balance. ■ An improvement in the TOT can lower both national income and employment.

Table 3.5 Advantages and disadvantages of a deterioration in the TOT

Advantages	Disadvantages
■ If demand for exports is price elastic, a deterioration in the TOT will lead to an improvement in the current account. ■ A deterioration in the TOT can lead to higher demand for exports as export prices are relatively lower. ■ A deterioration in the TOT can lead to higher aggregate demand and more job opportunities as export earnings rise.	■ If demand for imports is price inelastic, a deterioration in the TOT will cause a negative effect on the current account. ■ If the demand for exports is price inelastic, a deterioration in the TOT will cause a negative effect on the current account. ■ Higher-priced imports can cause imported inflation in the economy if the country relies on certain foreign imports, such as oil.

Expert tip

Whether or not a change in the TOT is beneficial to the economy depends on the price elasticity of demand for exports and imports. Lower export prices (which cause a deterioration in the TOT) can cause an *increase* in export revenues if the PED for exports and imports is elastic. This improves the current account on the balance of payment, so can be beneficial to the economy.

Common mistake

Students often mistake an improvement in the terms of trade to be beneficial to the domestic economy. Whilst this *might* be the case, relatively higher exports prices (which led to the improved terms of trade) are not necessarily beneficial to the economy.

4.1 Economic development

The nature of economic growth and economic development

Economic growth and economic development

Economic growth is the increase in the value of real gross domestic product (GDP) per capita over time. It is therefore a quantitative variable of economic wellbeing.

Economic development is an intangible concept that considers qualitative variables. It is multidimensional, encompassing factors that raise the general standard of living in a country, for example political freedom, reduced income inequalities, greater self-esteem, and the reduction of poverty.

There is a positive relationship between a country's economic growth and its economic development, i.e. the wealthier a country is, the higher its standards of living tend to be.

However, it is possible for some people to live happier lives in the absence of higher incomes as economic growth can bring about negative consequences such as pollution, climate change and environmental damage. In addition, economic growth does not always lead to a higher standard of living for the majority of people, so there is no economic development in such cases. For example, if a country spends significantly more on national defence then growth may occur but not necessarily development.

Economic growth can also lead to greater income inequality (as in the case of Hong Kong, which has the world's largest wealth gap).

Economic growth can be caused by productivity gains caused by the increased use of technology and automation (such as self-service checkouts in supermarkets) but this results in technological unemployment. Thus, economic growth does not necessarily lead to economic development. Nevertheless, economic growth is usually needed over the long term for there to be economic development. After all, to meet their infinite wants, people need to earn more income.

Economists prefer to use real GDP per capita figures rather than real GNP per capita as a measure of growth and development in LEDCs. This is because real GDP per head measures the national income (level of economic activity) earned within the borders of the LEDC.

Sustainable economic development refers to development that meets the needs of the present generation without compromising the ability of future generations to meet their needs.

> **Keyword definition**
> **Economic development** includes economic growth in addition to qualitative determinants of quality of life, for example a reduction in: poverty, income inequality, gender inequality, political oppression and unemployment.

> **Expert tip**
> It is incorrect to use the terms 'economic growth' and 'economic development' interchangeably. Economic growth is often regarded as a prerequisite to economic development but there are far more factors that contribute to development than simply an increase in real incomes.

Sources of economic growth and development in LEDCs

- An increase in the quantity and quality of physical capital through foreign direct investment (FDI). This helps to create jobs and to boost the productive capacity of the economy.
- An increase in the quantity and quality of human capital through improved education and healthcare, to boost the productivity of the labour force.
- The development and adoption of technology that is appropriate to the context of the LEDC, for example farming technologies and capital investments that increase the productivity and competitiveness of agricultural industries.
- Institutional changes to the banking, legal and political systems of the country to enable economic transactions to be carried out with relative ease. These changes are required to facilitate trade, attract FDI and boost both consumer and business confidence.

Common characteristics of LEDCs

Low levels of GDP per capita – LEDCs have a low national income per head of the population, partly due to their relatively low GDP and partly due to their relatively high birth rate. The World Bank classifies countries according to their level of gross national income (GNI) per capita.

High levels of poverty – LEDCs suffer from high levels of extreme poverty. According to the United Nations, 1.2 billion people still live in extreme poverty, with most of these living in LEDCs.

Relatively large agricultural sectors – In general, LEDCs have a relatively large primary sector, in particular, agriculture. However, the income elasticity of demand for agricultural products is relatively low, making it difficult for LEDCs to develop.

Large urban informal sectors – LEDCs have a large **informal sector**, i.e. where economic activities are not officially registered or recorded. In LEDCs, the informal sector is important for many people's survival and accounts for a large proportion of employment in urban areas.

High birth rates – Whilst most LEDCs experience low rates of economic growth they suffer from relatively high rates of population growth. This will tend to cause a fall in the GDP per capita, thus limiting economic development.

> **Expert tip**
>
> Whilst these characteristics are common to many LEDCs, it is wrong to assume that *all* LEDCs have the same features and that there are no exceptions to these generalisations. For example, although GDP per capita may be low in LEDCs, there can certainly be extremely wealthy individuals in the country.

EXAM PRACTICE (HL ONLY)

PAPER 3

1 Assume that a less economically developed country has a real GDP per capita of $2000 compared with $35,000 in a wealthier country. If both countries have economic growth of 2.5%, calculate the change in the per capita income gap between the two countries. **[2]**

2 Assume that in a less economically developed country the real gross national income (GNI) increases from $50 billion to $54 billion and that the population increases from 68 million to 71 million. Calculate the change in the LEDC's real GNI per capita. **[2]**

The poverty trap

Revised

The **poverty trap** (or **poverty cycle**) is a vicious cycle of poverty causing greater poverty. Low-income earners spend most, if not all, of their income on meeting their essential needs, so they have insufficient funds to invest in their future and are trapped in poverty (see Figure 4.1).

Low levels of GDP per capita will tend to cause LEDCs to suffer from a low **savings ratio**. This means that such countries have limited funds from savings for investment expenditure, thereby hindering their future productive capacity and economic development.

Low-income countries are often unable to break the poverty cycle as they have little, if any, savings to fund the necessary investment in factors needed for economic development. These include:

- physical capital, for example tools, machinery, transportation networks and sewerage systems
- human capital, leading to low levels of education and skills, and poor health. This will have an impact on rates of infant mortality, maternal mortality and life expectancy.
- natural capital, i.e. the stock of indispensable natural resources from the Earth's ecosystems will be depleted and will not be replenished without the necessary capital investments.

Low-income households also struggle to break the poverty trap because banks are unlikely to lend money to very poor families, as there is a high risk of them defaulting on the loans.

It is common that poverty is transmitted from generation to generation – for example, a poor family that is unable to access education has a relatively low chance of getting out of poverty. This leads to malnutrition and a physically weak labour force.

Because of this poverty trap, government intervention is required to bring people out of extreme poverty, for example through investment in education to increase human capital or improving employment opportunities for women. If a country is so poor that government intervention is not possible, then it will need to rely on foreign aid.

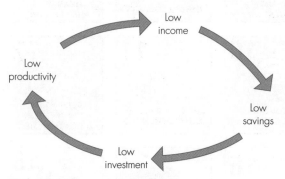

Figure 4.1 The poverty cycle

Diversity among LEDCs

Revised

The differences between LEDCs can be extreme:

- Resource endowment – Countries have different quantities and qualities of natural resources. For many LEDCs, the main exports consist of agricultural products, whilst some LEDCs, such as Angola, have oil and mineral reserves.
- History (colonial or otherwise) – Many LEDCs were former colonies of countries such as Spain and Britain. Colonisation often meant wealthier countries extracting marketable resources from LEDCs rather than investing in the countries for economic development.
- Political systems – LEDCs have a range of political systems, including dictatorship (e.g. North Korea) and democracy (e.g. Botswana, Ghana and Peru).
- Political stability – political turmoil and corruption can hinder economic development.

- Climate – LEDCs have varying weather conditions, which can directly impact on production. Agricultural output is clearly dependent on the climate, but climate can also affect people's productivity levels in other economic activities.
- Population – whilst LEDCs tend to have large and/or growing populations (e.g. Bangladesh and Ethiopia), others do not (e.g. Mali and Burkina Faso). Some LEDCs have very fast-growing populations (e.g. Niger and Rwanda.)

International development goals

Revised

The Millennium Development Goals (MDGs) of the United Nations consist of eight international anti-poverty development targets, to be achieved by all 193 UN member countries by 2015.

Find out more about the eight MDGs here: www.un.org/millenniumgoals.

In 2016, the UN launched the 2030 Agenda for Sustainable Development. The new Agenda calls on countries to begin efforts to achieve 17 Sustainable Development Goals (SDGs) over the next 15 years.

'The seventeen Sustainable Development Goals are our shared vision of humanity and a social contract between the world's leaders and the people,' said UN Secretary-General Ban Ki-moon. 'They are a to-do list for people and planet, and a blueprint for success.'

THE GLOBAL GOALS
For Sustainable Development

 1 NO POVERTY

 2 ZERO HUNGER

 3 GOOD HEALTH AND WELL-BEING

 4 QUALITY EDUCATION

 5 GENDER EQUALITY

 6 CLEAN WATER AND SANITATION

 7 AFFORDABLE AND CLEAN ENERGY

 8 DECENT WORK AND ECONOMIC GROWTH

 9 INDUSTRY, INNOVATION AND INFRASTUCTURE

 10 REDUCED INEQUALITIES

 11 SUSTAINABLE CITIES AND COMMUNITIES

 12 RESPONSIBLE CONSUMPTION AND PRODUCTION

 13 CLIMATE ACTION

 14 LIFE BELOW WATER

 15 LIFE ON LAND

 16 PEACE AND JUSTICE STRONG INSTITUTIONS

 17 PARTNERSHIPS FOR THE GOALS

 18 THE GLOBAL GOALS FOR SUSTAINABLE DEVELOPMENT

- The goals address the needs of people in both developed and developing countries, emphasizing that no one should be left behind.
- The Agenda addresses the three dimensions of sustainable development: social, economic and environmental, as well as aspects related to peace, justice and effective institutions.

The 17 SDGs build on the eight MDGs, which specifically sought:
- to eradicate extreme poverty and hunger
- achieve universal primary education
- promote gender equality and empower women

- reduce child mortality
- improve maternal health
- combat HIV/AIDS, malaria and other diseases
- ensure environmental sustainability
- develop a global partnership for development.

Expert tip

Remember that economic growth does not always lead to economic development. Indeed, economic growth can help to eradicate extreme poverty, but it does not necessarily promote gender equality or other international development goals.

EXAM PRACTICE

PAPER 2

3

	NOMINAL GDP (US$BN)	JOBLESS RATE (%)	POPULATION (MILLION)	DEBT TO GDP RATIO (%)	INFLATION (%)
USA	15,685	7.3	315	101.6	1.5
China	8,230	4.1	1,354	23.0	2.6
Japan	5,960	4.1	128	211.7	0.9
Bangladesh	116	4.5	152	22.8	7.1
Azerbaijan	67	5.2	9	11.2	2.2
Kenya	37	40.0	43	46.5	8.3
Zambia	21	8.1	14	31.2	7.0
Burundi	2	35.0	10	18.8	10.4

a Define the term nominal GDP.   [2]

b Using the above data, explain the multidimensional nature of economic development.   [4]

4.2 Measuring development

Revised ☐

Measurement methods

Revised ☐

Single indicators of measuring development

Revised ☐

Real GDP per capita – This is a single indicator of economic development that calculates the value of national output of a country (its gross domestic product) divided by its population. It is the most used single indicator of standards of living within a country (see Table 4.1).

Table 4.1 GDP per capita (selected countries)

Country	GDP ($bn)	GDP per capita ($)	Population (million)
China	8,250.0	6,094	1,353.82
Sweden	538.3	56,956	9.54
Luxembourg	58.42	113,533	0.524

Real GNI per capita – As an alternative single indicator, this measure also calculates real GDP per person but includes the net value of what the country earns from overseas investments, i.e. net property incomes earned abroad by nationals of the country.

Keyword definition
A **single indicator** refers to a statistical measure of economic development that uses one particular gauge, such as literacy rate, income per capita or life expectancy.

Expert tip
Using GDP per capita to gauge the level of economic development in LEDCs can be misleading, as the value of parallel markets (unofficial transactions) is unrecorded.

The most common single measure of the standard of living (or wellbeing) of a nation is to calculate its gross national income per capita, adjusted for differences in the cost of living between countries.

If a country's GDP is greater than its GNI, as in the case of many LEDCs, this means that it has debts owed to foreign creditors and/or it has productive assets owned by foreign individuals and firms. Hence, GNI tends to be a better measure than GDP to measure development in LEDCs. For example, many migrant workers from the Philippines, Indonesia and Sri Lanka remit large amounts of money from their employment in overseas countries back to their home country, so the GNI exceeds the GDP.

Comparing GDP and GNI figures of different countries can be meaningless due to variations in exchange rates and costs of living. Hence, **purchasing power parity** (PPP) is used – the exchange rate that equates the price of a basket of the same traded goods and services in different countries.

Hence, PPP equates the cost of living across countries, so that GDP per capita at PPP exchange rates enables a more meaningful comparison of differing costs of living (and hence standards of living) across different countries.

LEDCs tend to have a higher GDP per capita when measured using PPP because prices of similar goods and services (and hence the costs of living) in these countries tend to be lower than in MEDCs.

EXAM PRACTICE (HL ONLY)

PAPER 3

4 Suppose the exchange rate between Demland and Danland is 1 dems to 3.5 dans. If a Big Mac burger costs 3.5 dems and there is purchasing power parity, calculate the price of a Big Mac burger in Danland. **[2]**

Expert tip

Whichever measure of income is used to measure economic development (real GDP/GNI per capita or PPP exchange rate of GDP/GNI), it is worth noting that other essential components of development are ignored, such as income and wealth inequalities, gender inequalities, political freedom and environmental issues.

Health indicators measure health-related measures of the quality of life, such as:
- longevity (life expectancy at birth)
- expenditure on healthcare as a percentage of GDP
- mortality rates, for example of children aged 5 and below per 1000 of the population (see Table 4.2).

Table 4.2 Health indicators: life expectancy and mortality rates for selected countries

Health indicators	Life expectancy at birth (years)	Under-5 mortality rate (per 1000 live births)
Japan	83.6	3
Hong Kong	83.0	3
Switzerland	82.5	5
Lesotho	48.7	85
Guinea-Bissau	48.6	150
Sierra Leone	48.1	174

Education indicators measure education-related quality-of-life factors, such as literacy rates and the mean average years of schooling (see Table 4.3).

Table 4.3 Education indicators: years of schooling and literacy rates for selected countries

Education indicators	Mean years of schooling (years)	Adult literacy rate (% of population aged 15+)
USA	13.3	99.0
Norway	12.6	100.0
New Zealand	12.5	99.0
Ethiopia	2.0	35.1
Niger	1.4	28.7
Mozambique	1.2	56.1

Composite indicators of measuring development

Revised ☐

Composite indicators are more complicated to compile as they include more than one measure of economic development. However, they are considered to be better measures of economic development than single indicators as they are more comprehensive.

The most widely used composite indicator of economic development is the Human Development Index (HDI), created by Pakistani economist Mahbub ul Haq and Indian economist Amartya Sen in 1990 as part of the United Nations Development Programme.

In general, there is a direct correlation between a country's GDP/GNI per capita and its ranking of economic development using composite indicators.

> **Keyword definition**
> A **composite indicator** is a statistical method that combines single indicators of economic development into a combined index such as the Human Development Index.

The Human Development Index (HDI)

Revised ☐

The **Human Development Index** (HDI) is a composite indicator (of life expectancy, educational attainment and income) used as an alternative to real GDP or GNI per capita as a measure of economic development. The HDI measures three dimensions of human development:

- Healthcare – this measures life expectancy at birth. The better the healthcare in a country, the greater social and economic wellbeing tends to be.
- Education – this indicator measures the mean (average) years of schooling and the expected years of schooling in the country.
- Income levels – the higher the national income (using purchasing power parity) of a country, the greater human development tends to be.

The three dimensions of the HDI are assigned equal statistical weighting in the index. The value of the HDI is between 0 (extreme underdevelopment) and 1 (very high human development), for example Australia's HDI might be 0.981, whereas Sierra Leone's HDI might be 0.336. LEDCs such as Niger, Mozambique, Chad, Burkina Faso and Mali have a very low HDI. MEDCs such as Norway, Australia, Germany, Canada and Japan have a very high HDI.

Economic development can occur if there is a reduction in inequality and absolute poverty. This improves the HDI, but it does not mean that the country's GDP/GNI necessarily increases. Similarly, although a country's GDP/GNI can increase without any improvement in the provision of healthcare and education, its HDI ranking will fall relative to its GDP/GNI ranking.

However, there are limitations in using the HDI as a composite measure of development and standards of living:

- **Qualitative factors** – the HDI ignores qualitative measures affecting standards of living, such as gender inequalities and human rights.
- **Income distribution** – the HDI does not take account of inequitable income distribution, and so is less accurate in measuring living standards and human development for the 'average' person.
- **Environmental issues** – the HDI ignores environmental and resource depletion as a consequence of economic growth. This includes the negative externalities associated with increased output and consumption, such as pollution and environmental degradation.
- **Cultural differences** – although the HDI is a composite indicator, it ignores cultural differences and interpretations of the meaning of 'standards of living' and 'quality of life'; both vital aspects of human development.
- **Sustainable development** – the HDI ignores the concept of sustainable development, i.e. consuming more now can mean a lower standard of living for future generations.

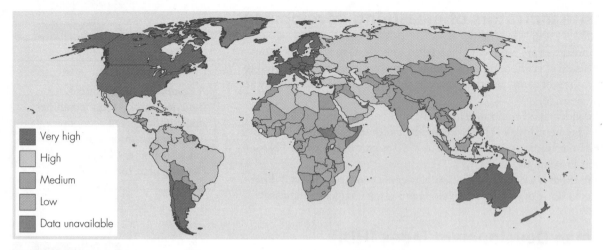

Figure 4.2 HDI in 2013

EXAM PRACTICE

PAPER 2

5 Study the information below, which shows the Human Development Index for four countries: Australia, Ethiopia, Russia and Vietnam.

Country	HDI	Country	HDI
A	0.929	C	0.593
B	0.755	D	0.363

  a Define the term 'Human Development Index'. [2]

  b Identify the four countries based on the given HDI figures in the table and explain the reasoning behind your answers. [4]

Common mistake

It is incorrect to assume that countries with a high GNI per capita have a high HDI. This is not necessarily the case – for example, Kuwait, Qatar and Liechtenstein have a higher GNI per capita than the USA and Hong Kong, but a lower HDI.

4.3 The role of domestic factors

Revised ☐

Domestic factors and economic development

Revised ☐

There are five domestic factors (those within the control of the country in question) that contribute to the economic development of LEDCs:

■ education and health
■ use of appropriate technology
■ access to credit and micro-credit
■ empowerment of women
■ income distribution.

All five domestic factors have positive externalities of production and consumption for LEDCs.

Education and health

Revised ☐

Education and healthcare provision can help to increase labour productivity (output per worker). The quality of labour is clearly dependent on its level of educational attainment, skills, training and health. It will also depend on the use of appropriate technology such as the capital used.

Investment in education and healthcare will shift an economy's long-run aggregate supply curve to the right, *ceteris paribus*. Alternatively, the subsequent increase in the economy's productive capacity can be shown using a production possibility frontier diagram (see Figure 4.3).

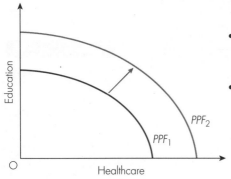

- Investment in education and healthcare are prerequisites for economic development in LEDCs.

- Investment in education and healthcare will increase labour productivity, thus shifting the economy's productive capacity outwards from PPF_1 to PPF_2, *ceteris paribus*.

Figure 4.3 Education, healthcare and economic development

According to the children's charity UNICEF, educated women are at least twice as likely to encourage their children to attend school at *primary* level. In some cultures, parents prefer boys to attend school whilst girls are expected to remain at home to help with household responsibilities.

Individuals who have greater access to healthcare have better nutrition, so are more productive and enjoy a better quality of life.

> **Expert tip**
>
> Remember that education and health are important aspects of the United Nations Millennium Development Goals (MDG), for example eradicating extreme poverty and hunger, reducing child mortality, improving maternal health and combating diseases such as HIV/AIDS.

> **EXAM PRACTICE**
>
> **PAPER 2**
>
> **6** Using an appropriate diagram, explain how investment in education and healthcare can affect a country's real national income. **[4]**

The use of appropriate technology

Revised ☐

The use of appropriate technology is a key domestic factor determining the scope of economic development. For example, micro-credit schemes allow individuals to invest in technologies that increase the productive capacity of the economy (see Figure 4.4).

Technology can be classified as capital-intensive technologies or labour-intensive technologies:

- **Capital-intensive technologies** rely on the use of capital in the production process, such as in oil refining, telecommunications and motor manufacturing.
- **Labour-intensive technologies** rely more on the use of labour, for example basic tools and equipment such as bicycles, wheelbarrows and hand-powered water pumps.

Economic development in LEDCs relies more on labour-intensive technologies to create jobs and income for the population of the country to escape from extreme poverty. For example, women in LEDCs can use sewing machines to be far more productive than when doing the same jobs by hand.

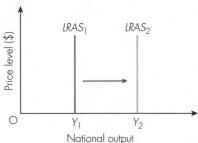

- Advances in technology and the use of appropriate technologies lead to a favourable change in the productive capacity of the economy.
- This is shown by an outwards shift of the economy's long run aggregate supply from $LRAS_1$ to $LRAS_2$, thus increasing national income from Y_1 to Y_2.

> **Expert tip**
>
> Remember that not all economic growth leads to economic development. For example, technological progress that boosts capital productivity and causes mass unemployment (technological unemployment) can create economic growth, but this does not equate to human development.

Figure 4.4 Productive capacity and the use of appropriate technology

However, economic development can be interrupted if foreign currencies are required to purchase spare parts or to maintain the technologies.

Many LEDCs suffer from a lack of infrastructure, such as transportation and telecommunications networks. This hinders their chances of economic growth and development.

Access to credit and micro-credit

Revised

Credit schemes offer access to borrowed money. The provision of credit is important to economic development because individuals and firms that cannot borrow simply cannot invest in any physical, human or natural capital – all essential for economic development.

Micro-credit schemes are loans of small amounts to individuals on low incomes in LEDCs for self-employment projects that generate income, so they can care for themselves and their families. They promote an entrepreneurial culture, and so help to stimulate economic growth and development.

The idea of micro-credit financing was developed by Bangladeshi banker, economist and Nobel peace prize winner Muhammed Yunus (2006). The system grants small-sized loans to those (especially women) who cannot ordinarily borrow money from financial institutions.

Commercial banks and non-government organisations (NGOs) are the main providers of micro-loans. Most banks will charge relatively high interest rates due to the high risks of lending money to the poor. NGOs tend to charge lower interest rates, striving instead to stimulate development.

Criteria used to determine which individuals qualify for micro-credit include:
- the borrower's credit rating (past record of ability to pay debts)
- the value of the borrower's assets
- how much debt the borrower can afford.

Those who qualify for micro-credit schemes are required to attend classes on financial management. Thus, such schemes have educational and social benefits to the economy.

The key advantage of micro-credit schemes is that they can simultaneously enhance gender equality and income distribution. The World Bank and United Nations are supporters of micro-credit schemes as a form of economic and human development, especially as they can be used to empower women.

However, the lack of property rights in LEDCs is a major source of poverty because individuals have little, if any, collateral (financial security on their assets) to borrow money to fund development projects.

Arguments against the use of micro-credit schemes include the following:
- They do not create job opportunities on a large enough scale to increase the LEDC's productive capacity.
- High interest rates are charged by commercial banks because those on low incomes are usually not credit-worthy.
- Micro-entrepreneurs in LEDCs are extremely vulnerable to external shocks (unexpected changes) in the economy, such as adverse weather conditions affecting supply. These firms may not be maintainable, so micro-credit does little for sustainable economic development.
- Micro-entrepreneurs tend to have limited qualifications, skills, training and experience (as they lack opportunities and access to education). Hence, there is a high chance of the funds being misused or ineffectively used, thus leading to business failures.
- The self-employed in LEDCs often have unstable incomes yet endure a huge degree of risk, so many people who qualify for micro-credit choose to take jobs at factories instead, as there is greater financial stability. This clearly defeats the purpose of micro-credit schemes.

The empowerment of women

Revised

Gender inequality is a barrier to economic and human development because it limits the quantity and quality of labour resources in the production process. Economists therefore believe that empowering women is a vital development strategy in reducing poverty in LEDCs. Ignoring gender disparities is detrimental to people's wellbeing and to the economic and human development of all countries, but LEDCs in particular.

The empowerment of women (gender equality) helps to end social and cultural discrimination against females – for example, women in Saudi Arabia are not allowed to work with men, vote or drive, which hinders labour productivity and national output.

Empowerment of women can have a huge impact on their self-esteem and productivity. In the long term, this has positive effects on maternal health and reducing child mortality (both Millennium Development Goals of the United Nations).

Countries that fail to empower women and promote gender equality, such as Ghana and Rwanda, face the problem of lower productivity, and slower economic and human development, as approximately half of their population are denied opportunities to improve their standard of living.

The World Development Report from the World Bank recommends four priorities to promote gender equality and to empower women:

- Reducing excess female mortality and closing education gaps where they remain. Improving healthcare provision for women and educating females are two of the most significant investments for fostering human development in LEDCs.
- Improving access to economic opportunities for women – for example, increasing opportunities for women to participate in the labour force and improving women's access to credit and other productive resources.
- Increasing women's voice and agency in the household and society, i.e. improving the ability of females to make effective choices and to transform their choices into desired outcomes, including decision making over family formation and freedom from the risk of violence.
- Limiting the reproduction of gender inequality across generations. For example, China's one-child policy (since 1979) was used to alleviate social, economic and environmental problems. However, as a consequence of this policy there has been a major gender imbalance in favour of boys.

Income distribution

Revised

Income distribution refers to how the national income of a country is spread among its population. Unequal distribution of national income exists when the relatively rich minority account for the majority of the country's national income, i.e. it is not distributed proportionately.

Economic development depends not only on growth in national income but also on the *distribution* of income. Income inequalities hinder economic development as the poor do not have access to education, healthcare, credit or micro-credit.

A high and rising degree of income inequality in many LEDCs is seen as a major barrier to economic development. After all, the eradication of poverty does not only depend on growth in national income but also on how that income is distributed.

A more equal distribution of income will mean that those in extreme poverty are more likely to be able to access education and healthcare. This helps to improve human development and raise the level of productivity in the economy.

Greater income equality also reduces the likelihood of corruption, which is a major obstacle to human development in many LEDCs. Corruption and civil unrest distort market forces and create disincentives for individuals and firms to take entrepreneurial risks.

Common mistake

It is incorrect to assume that all trading activities in unofficial (parallel) markets are illegal. Whilst these are unrecorded, many of these trades in LEDCs may be in the form of barter (swapping) or payments made in kind (using goods and services to trade rather than money). Hence, unofficial trade is not necessarily illegal trade, but has an indirect impact on income distribution.

The main way to redistribute income from the rich to the poor is to implement an effective progressive tax system, i.e. increasing marginal tax bands as income levels rise. However, there are three key reasons why it is difficult for LEDCs to raise tax revenues:

- Only a small proportion of the population pay income taxes, as so many people are poor and because LEDCs tend to have a large unofficial (parallel) market.
- Similarly, as the level of official economic activity is low, the revenue collected from corporation tax tends to be low. This is especially the case if LEDCs offer financial assistance to domestic firms and/or tax incentives to encourage foreign direct investment (FDI).
- Low incomes and the lack of international trade in many LEDCs mean that there is minimal tax revenue earned from tariffs (taxes on imports).

Ineffective tax systems in LEDCs have hindered income redistribution and hence economic and human development.

> **Expert tip**
>
> All five domestic factors affecting economic development are affected by the political regime of the country in question, i.e. political instability and conflict impact on the economic development of a country. For example, corruption in many LEDCs has reduced the effectiveness of domestic policies aimed at improving development. In some countries, such as Angola, the informal (unofficial) market has far exceeded the reported gross domestic product (GDP). International agencies such as the World Bank and the IMF cannot operate effectively without political stability.

EXAM PRACTICE

PAPER 2

7 The charts below show health expenditure as a percentage of the total GDP in Gambia (Figure 4.5) and Luxembourg (Figure 4.6) from 2000 to 2010.

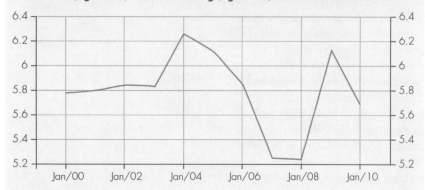

Figure 4.5 Health expenditure (% of GDP) in Gambia

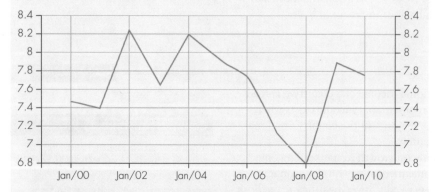

Figure 4.6 Health expenditure (% of GDP) in Luxembourg

With reference to Figure 4.5 and Figure 4.6, explain how health expenditure as a percentage of GDP contributes to an economy's economic development. [4]

8 Using an appropriate diagram, explain how economic growth can lead to economic development. [4]

4.4 The role of international trade

Revised ☐

International trade and economic development

Revised ☐

Trade problems facing LEDCs

Revised ☐

There are potential gains from international trade that can help countries to experience economic development, for example export revenue for domestic producers and increased employment opportunities for workers. However, international trade can cause problems for many LEDCs, thus creating barriers to economic development. Such barriers include the following three factors:

- over-specialisation on a narrow range of products
- price volatility of primary-sector output
- inability of LEDCs to access and compete in international markets.

Over-specialisation on a narrow range of products

- Over-specialisation refers to an individual or country focusing on producing only a small range of products for trade. Thus, over-specialisation limits economic growth and development.
- Food and agricultural exports account for a large proportion of total export earnings for most LEDCs.

Price volatility of primary-sector output

- Price volatility refers to unstable market prices for primary-sector output, such as agricultural production and mining.
- A major drawback of LEDCs specialising in the output of primary-sector exports is that the prices of primary products are highly volatile and often exhibit a downwards trend.
- In many LEDCs, technological progress is relatively slow in primary-sector production, thus limiting the ability of LEDCs to compete on an international scale.
- Supply of primary-sector output tends to be inelastic in supply, so producers cannot respond quickly to changes in the market. Again, this puts LEDCs in an unfavourable position.
- Consequences of a long-term decline in the average price of primary-sector output include a fall in export earnings for LEDCs, a fall in domestic employment and a deteriorating current account on the balance of payments.
- LEDCs are more vulnerable to external shocks such as adverse weather conditions and natural disasters, thus making price predictions highly inaccurate. Such volatility in prices therefore creates uncertainty and obstructs international trade.

Inability to access international markets

- Many LEDCs find it difficult to enter foreign markets, especially when trying to compete with MEDCs. For example, France, the UK and the USA subsidise their domestic agricultural industries, so farmers in LEDCs simply cannot compete.
- LEDCs struggle to access international markets due to the trade protection policies imposed by MEDCs in regional trading blocs. For example, the European Union (EU) imposes a common external tariff on non-member countries such as LEDCs.

Expert tip

The syllabus guide states that students must be able to explain how these factors are barriers to development for LEDCs with reference to specific examples. Make sure you revise the examples given in class or through your own studies.

Long-term changes in the terms of trade *(HL only)*

Revised

The **terms of trade** (TOT) refers to the index of average export prices in relation to the index of average import prices. If average export prices rise relatively to average import prices, the terms of trade have improved as each dollar of export earnings can now buy more imports.

In LEDCs, primary-sector output dominates national incomes and employment. However, primary-sector output tends to receive lower prices than tertiary-sector output in the long term, thus worsening the terms of trade for LEDCs. Therefore, LEDCs that rely on the export of primary-sector output tend to face a deterioration in their TOT over the long term.

A deterioration in the terms of trade means that the country has to sell a greater volume of exports to finance a given amount of imports.

In general, the gains from international trade favour more economically developed countries (MEDCs) due to their better terms of trade and because of the highly unequal distribution of income in LEDCs.

A long-term deterioration in the terms of trade for an LEDC will have several detrimental impacts:

- Mounting debt problems occur as the LEDC struggles to pay for imports from its low export earnings.
- Financing international trade becomes more difficult for the LEDC.
- Rising unemployment due to the deteriorating TOT limits economic growth and therefore employment opportunities.

Ultimately, this leads to falling standards of living for the citizens of the LEDC in the long run.

Trade strategies for economic growth and economic development

Revised

Import substitution

Import substitution is an inward-looking strategy of economic growth and development that encourages domestic production and the purchase of domestic output through protectionist policies such as tariffs and quotas. It is a development strategy often used to protect infant industries from larger foreign producers.

However, there are drawbacks of using import substitution as a growth and development strategy. For example, consumers pay higher prices, so there is a loss of consumer surplus and the use of trade protection is detrimental to economic efficiency.

Export promotion

Export promotion is an outward-looking strategy of economic growth and development through international trade with overseas customers. Countries that adopt an outward development strategy tend to benefit from increased specialisation and a greater choice of goods and services being available.

Export promotion exposes domestic firms to foreign competition, possibly resulting in greater efficiency, higher productivity and relatively lower production costs. Supporters of this trade strategy for economic development advocate international trade, while supporters of import substitution prefer to use trade protection.

Trade liberalisation

Trade liberalisation involves the freeing up of international trade without government interference in the exchange of goods and services across borders, for example the removal of tariffs and quotas. Another way to achieve this is to remove barriers and restrictions to foreign direct investments (FDI). This would enable multinational corporations to operate within the LEDC, thus creating employment opportunities.

The argument for trade liberalisation is based on the notion that free trade and market forces improve the global allocation of resources, thereby improving economic efficiency. In turn, this leads to economic growth and development.

However, negative impacts of trade liberalisation policies include unemployment (caused by privatisation as firms cut costs and achieve efficiency) and social welfare losses due to less government involvement (i.e. cuts in government spending), affecting many people in LEDCs.

The role of the WTO

The World Trade Organization (WTO) is the international body set up to encourage and oversee non-discriminatory and open trade negotiations between its member countries. The WTO has the right to create favourable international trade terms for LEDCs. It also has the right to sanction member countries that violate their trade agreements, thereby helping to promote economic harmony between its members.

By encouraging international trade, the WTO stimulates economic growth and development for the global economy.

Bilateral trade agreements

Bilateral trade agreements are preferential international trade deals between two countries that strive to reduce and/or abolish trade barriers such as tariffs and quotas. Some examples, such as those between Canada and China or the USA and Costa Rica lead to an increase in export earnings for both countries. In addition, this leads to an increase in gross domestic product and more job opportunities in both countries.

A potential disadvantage of bilateral trade agreements is that foreign goods from the partner country could be more appealing to consumers, thus causing problems for domestic firms.

Regional trade agreements

Regional trade agreements are preferential international trade deals that rely on economic cooperation between member states located near to each other, for example the Association of South East Asian Nations (ASEAN) and the North American Free Trade Agreement (NAFTA).

Benefits of regional trade agreements that involve LEDCs include trade creation between the member countries (as a result of economic cooperation) and reduced dependency on MEDCs.

A problem for some countries engaged in regional trade agreements is that they have had to bail out weaker trading partners. For example, France and Germany have supported vulnerable members of the EU such as Portugal, Italy, Greece and Spain during the euro debt crisis.

Diversification

Diversification is an economic growth and development strategy that involves countries broadening their supply of goods and services in export markets. It helps to overcome the problems of over-specialisation (which tends to limit economic growth and development for many LEDCs) and create new employment opportunities.

Diversification can help LEDCs to reduce their vulnerability to falling prices in primary-sector output and declining terms of trade. It can also help LEDCs to reduce their vulnerability to external supply-side shocks such as extreme weather conditions or natural disasters.

However, diversification carries potential disadvantages. For instance, there is a relatively high risk of failure as LEDCs lack expertise and higher costs are incurred due to a broader range of products being manufactured.

EXAM PRACTICE

PAPER 2

9 With the aid of an appropriate diagram, explain how the price volatility of primary products creates a barrier to economic development. **[4]**

EXAM PRACTICE *(HL ONLY)*

PAPER 3

10 Brazil is the world's largest exporter of coffee. However, market reforms in former communist Vietnam have caused a significant increase in the global supply of coffee.

The world's top five coffee exporters (kilograms)

COUNTRY	COFFEE EXPORTS (KG)
Brazil	2550 million
Vietnam	900 million
Ivory Coast	696 million
Indonesia	411 million
Ethiopia	330 million

Suggest how the situation above is likely to affect the terms of trade for coffee exporters. **[4]**

4.5 The role of foreign direct investment (FDI)

Revised ☐

Foreign direct investment and multinational corporations (MNCs)

Revised ☐

The meaning of FDI and MNCs

Revised ☐

Foreign direct investment is the money devoted by MNCs to business operations abroad, for example building production facilities overseas or acquiring (taking over) a domestic firm. It can thus help to improve economic development in LEDCs. For example, China's investment projects in Latin America and sub-Saharan Africa have helped to create jobs and boost economic growth in these regions.

Globalisation and the promotion of freer international trade by the World Trade Organization (WTO) has encouraged a significant increase in foreign direct investment in LEDCs.

More economically developed countries (MEDCs) account for the vast majority of the world's FDI. This is because the largest multinational corporations are from MEDCs. MNCs have production plants and/or service operations in overseas countries – for example, Nike has production facilities in Indonesia. These MNCs have grown by using joint ventures and strategic alliances with firms in LEDCs. This has resulted in a large increase in FDI in LEDCs.

> Keyword definitions
> **Foreign direct investment** (FDI) refers to the long-term capital expenditure of multinational companies in overseas countries, such as Apple's manufacturing plants in China.
>
> **Multinational corporations** (MNCs) are businesses that operate in two or more countries, i.e. they have operations outside of their home country, such as Japan's Toyota, Nissan and Honda, which all have production plants in the UK and USA.

FDI expenditure is highly dependent on changes in the state of the world economy. During economic booms, FDI tends to rise significantly as firms believe that they can increase their profits by expanding overseas.

Reasons why MNCs expand into LEDCs

Revised ☐

Table 4.4 Reasons why MNCs expand into LEDCs

Cheaper production costs	Many MNCs have operations in LEDCs in order to exploit lower costs of production – for example, it is far cheaper for Nike to hire workers in Indonesia, China and Vietnam than in the USA.
Economies of scale	By operating on a larger scale due to a larger customer base, MNCs are able to exploit economies of scale, thereby reducing their unit costs of production. By operating in overseas markets, MNCs are also able to achieve risk-bearing economies.
Access to natural resources	MNCs are keen to expand into LEDCs because many LEDCs are well-endowed in natural resources, which can then be exploited.
Increased sales revenue	Access to fast-growing economies with large populations, such as Indonesia, Nigeria, Bangladesh, Vietnam and Ethiopia, presents enormous opportunities for MNCs.
Avoiding trade barriers	By locating within the LEDC, the multinational corporation is able to avoid trade barriers such as tariffs, quotas and administrative obstacles. For example, the German carmaker Volkswagen has production plants in India, Indonesia and Nigeria.
Logistical reasons	MNCs locate overseas to reduce delivery times to customers in LEDCs and emerging markets. For example, the US power-tool firm Black & Decker has production units in China, so its products sold in East Asia do not have to be exported from the USA.
Financial incentives	In order to attract FDI, the governments of LEDCs often offer MNCs incentives to locate in their country, including tax rebates, grants, subsidies and cheaper rents.

Characteristics of LEDCs that attract FDI

Revised ☐

- Low-cost factor inputs – In many LEDCs, an abundant supply of labour means relatively lower labour costs. In addition, many LEDCs are rich in natural resources – for example, Angola and Sudan are rich in oil supplies. Thus, MNCs are attracted to establish themselves in such countries.
- A regulatory framework that favours profit repatriation – Laws and regulations are usually less strict in LEDCs, thereby allowing MNCs to be exempt from directives such as minimum-wage laws and safety regulations.
- Favourable tax rules – As LEDCs often compete to attract FDI, favourable tax rules are granted to MNCs that locate in their country, such as low rates of corporation tax or delayed tax payments.

Expert tip

Economics is based on the assumption that economic agents (households and firms) act rationally, i.e. in their own best interest. This suggests that MNCs spend money on FDI in order to increase their own revenues and profits, rather than to promote economic development. After all, companies operate to satisfy the financial interests of their shareholders rather than to create social welfare.

Advantages and disadvantages of FDI for LEDCs

Revised ☐

Table 4.5 Advantages and disadvantages of FDI for LEDCs

Advantages	Disadvantages

■ Foreign direct investment is a major source of national income for LEDCs. It is far more stable than financial aid, with long-term benefits for LEDCs. In the long run, FDI in LEDCs helps to shift both the long-run aggregate supply and aggregate demand curves to the right.
■ Higher national income, resulting from FDI, can help LEDCs to close their savings gap. As the level of savings in the LEDC increases, more funds become available for investment in the economy, with long-term benefits to the country.
■ The profits generated from the investments of MNCs in an LEDC contribute to the country's tax revenues.
■ FDI allows the transfer of technology and more efficient work practices from MEDCs to LEDCs.
■ FDI and direct rivalry from MNCs can force domestic producers in the host country to become more efficient and competitive.
■ FDI by a multinational corporation provides many employment opportunities in an LEDC. This has the added benefits of skills transfer from MEDCs to LEDCs, higher consumption expenditure and increased income tax revenue for the government.
■ The presence of MNCs in LEDCs provides domestic households and firms with a wider range of choice. Increased competition can also lead to lower prices in the economy.
■ The (potential) presence of MNCs often encourages governments in LEDCs to invest in infrastructure. MNCs may also help to provide some of the funding for this. Such investments help to benefit the country as a whole.
	■ Although FDI helps to create employment opportunities in LEDCs, MNCs often bring in their own management teams whilst locally hired employees are low-skilled workers. This reduces the benefits of skills transfer to the LEDCs.
	■ The lenient regulatory framework in LEDCs means that MNCs often exploit their position by:
	  ☐ disregarding issues of health and safety at work, for example long working hours and poor working conditions
	  ☐ ignoring the external costs of their activities in LEDCs, for example pollution of the natural environment (land, air and sea) and the depletion of non-renewable resources.
	■ FDI from large MNCs makes domestic rivals less competitive due to the advantages enjoyed by the MNCs, for example economies of scale, technological know-how and tax rebates from the LEDC government. In extreme cases, this can lead to the collapse of domestic firms.
	■ In most cases, the profits generated by MNCs are repatriated to their home country rather than reinvested to further improve the facilities and infrastructure in LEDCs. Thus, critics argue that MNCs exploit and profit from LEDCs without really giving much back.
	■ Some MNCs are criticised for having too much power when negotiating tax breaks and other financial incentives. Many LEDCs have very limited bargaining power as MNCs have the option to redirect their FDI to neighbouring LEDCs that are willing to offer better conditions.
	■ Critics argue that the growing presence and power of MNCs creates a loss in the cultural, political and economic identity of LEDCs in favour of economically developed nations, for example the consumption of fast foods, soft drinks and expensive branded goods.

EXAM PRACTICE

PAPER 2

11 Explain how foreign direct investment (FDI) can help less economically developed countries (LEDCs) to break out of the poverty trap. **[4]**

12 Using an appropriate diagram, explain how FDI can help less economically developed countries (LEDCs) to achieve economic growth. **[4]**

Common mistake

Students often comment that MNCs exploit workers by paying them low wages. Whilst wages paid to workers in LEDCs are comparatively lower than in the MNC's home country, they are usually higher than wages paid by local firms. It would be unreasonable to expect MNCs to pay workers in Nicaragua the same wages as workers in the USA due to the different costs of living in these countries.

4.6 The roles of foreign aid and multilateral development assistance

Revised ☐

Foreign aid

Revised ☐

Foreign aid refers to assistance in the form of goods and services granted to LEDCs for the purpose of economic development. It is concessional and non-commercial, i.e. it is a gift from the donor rather than a loan. Foreign aid makes up for the shortcomings of the free market that fails to provide assistance to LEDCs during times of need, such as emergency relief aid following a natural disaster.

Foreign aid to LEDCs can be granted by governments of donor countries or by non-governmental organisations (NGOs), such as Oxfam. Donations by private individuals are usually made through an NGO.

NGOs operate independently of any form of government, often pursuing aims to improve social wellbeing. Examples of such NGOs include Oxfam and the Bill & Melinda Gates Foundation.

Classifications and types of aid

Official development assistance (ODA) is foreign aid from donor governments, rather than from NGOs.

Humanitarian aid refers to altruistic aid, typically given to save lives and maintain human dignity in response to violence, natural disasters and national emergencies. It consists of food aid, medical aid and emergency relief aid (e.g. aid for reconstruction work).

Development aid is foreign aid aimed at helping recipient countries to achieve their economic development objectives, for example to eradicate extreme poverty, improve education, reduce child mortality and improve the overall standards of living.

Development aid can be provided by individual countries, by NGOs, or by multilateral organisations such as the World Bank and Save the Children.

In general, the priority of development aid from NGOs is to provide foreign aid on a small scale to help LEDCs to achieve development objectives.

Development aid includes the following:

- **Grants** – These comprise non-repayable financial assistance provided by governments, i.e. they do not have to be repaid. Most grants are given to fund specific projects.
- **Concessional long-term loans** – Also known as **soft loans**, these are loans with highly favourable conditions, such as low interest rates and long repayment periods.
- **Project aid** – As the name suggests, this is foreign aid for specific developmental projects, such as financial support for schools (education) or for hospitals and sanitation (healthcare).
- **Programme aid** – This is financial aid given to a specific industry, for example funding of education or the financial sector.

Tied aid is financial assistance granted with conditions attached – usually the need to spend the foreign aid on buying products from the donor country. Bilateral foreign aid is often a feature of tied (conditional) aid.

Tied aid is often criticised as the LEDC's requirement to buy goods and services from the donating country might not be appropriate. It is often perceived as an indirect subsidy for suppliers in the donor country. Hence, tied aid can harm the competitiveness of LEDCs. Nevertheless, a valid reason for (or advantage of) tied aid is that it ensures that financial aid is used for appropriate purposes whilst benefiting the donor country.

> **Expert tip**
>
> Foreign aid can be classified according to the *source* and the *purpose*.

Motivation for giving aid

Table 4.6 Motivation for giving aid

Motives for giving aid	Details
Humanitarian motives	Foreign aid is provided for humanitarian reasons, for example emergency relief to help with natural disasters or wars. It is also given to achieve the UN's Millennium Development Goals (MDGs), such as eradicating famine and improving maternal health.
Economic motives	Donors give ODA because it is in their financial interest to do so as this builds better economic ties with the recipient countries – for example, tied aid provides economic benefits to the donor country.
Political motives	Many European countries such as the UK and France provide ODA to their former colonies. Historically, the USA has provided ODA to support capitalism and free market practices. Japan has given aid to Nicaragua to influence its vote on banning whaling.

Expert tip

The IB Guide specifies that students need to be able to compare and contrast the extent, nature and sources of official development assistance (ODA) for *two* LEDCs. A good start is to read the free UNDP online report on ODA: http://tinyurl.com/lt97ozo

Evaluation of foreign aid

Revised

Advantages of foreign aid

- Without foreign aid, many of the world's poorest countries would struggle to ever get out of the poverty cycle. Thus, there are both humanitarian and economic benefits to providing ODA.
- Foreign aid in the form of ODA and concessionary long-term loans can be used to increase the productive capacity of the LEDC, thus helping it to achieve economic growth.
- Foreign aid can help to reduce or eradicate extreme poverty (one of the UN's Millennium Development Goals).
- As a form of injection into the circular flow of income, foreign aid can help to reduce inequalities and unemployment in the LEDC.

Disadvantages of foreign aid

- Foreign aid in the form of loans imposes interest repayments, so this adds to the financial burden of many LEDCs, especially as debts have to be repaid in foreign currencies.
- LEDCs tend to prefer more favourable terms of international trade to help their economic development than outright foreign aid – for example, food aid and tied aid do little for the long-term prosperity of an LEDC.
- Most economists argue that economic development should be based on promoting free international trade, such as increasing the exports of LEDCs, instead of relying on foreign aid. This is because ODA does not necessarily lead to development, whereas trade does.
- Foreign aid can create economic dependence on donors from MEDCs. This does not help the country to develop in the long run.
- Corrupt governments in LEDCs often misuse foreign aid rather than passing on the funds to local projects that would benefit local industries and communities.
- More often than not, ODA is insufficient to really help LEDCs develop their economies. The aftershock of the global financial crisis of 2008 also led to a decline in donations (as a percentage of the GDP of MEDCs).
- The type of foreign aid given is not always appropriate – for example it might promote capital-intensive projects rather than labour-intensive output, which are better suited for LEDCs. Foreign aid might also involve political interferences rather than direct economic benefits.

Expert tip

'Give a man a fish, and you feed him for a day; show him how to catch fish, and you feed him for a lifetime' (Anne Isabella Thackeray Ritchie,1837–1919). This is a useful quote to remember for the aid versus trade debate regarding economic development.

Expert tip

When evaluating foreign aid, consider the following questions as a framework:

- What are the types of foreign aid being given?
- What are the underlying motives behind giving this aid?
- Is the foreign aid being given for the right reasons?

Multilateral development assistance

Revised

Multilateral development assistance is foreign aid delivered through international institutions such as the World Bank and the International Monetary Fund (IMF).

These multilateral institutions are international organisations made up of member governments around the world. These member states pool resources together, thus enabling large-scale development programmes to be funded.

Multilateral development assistance is generally seen as a less political form of foreign aid than bilateral aid and tied aid as it encourages international cooperation rather than focusing on the financial interests of donor countries.

Multilateral development assistance often takes the form of non-concessionary loans, i.e. lending that incurs interest and repayment periods determined by market forces. However, this differs from commercial bank lending as the loans are specifically for development purposes.

The role of the International Monetary Fund (IMF)

Revised ▢

The International Monetary Fund (IMF) is an international multilateral financial institution set up in 1944 by 29 member countries. Today, there are 188 members of the IMF. Its goal is to oversee the international financial system and to promote global monetary cooperation. Thus, the IMF helps to facilitate sustainable economic growth and development.

The IMF fulfils its role by assessing the economic policies of all member states in order to stabilise exchange rates and making short-term non-concessional loans to countries that experience difficulties making their international payments.

Traditionally, most of the lending from the IMF went to LEDCs. However, the global financial crisis of 2008 saw a significant amount of lending to MEDCs with huge balance of payments problems, such as Portugal, Italy, Ireland and Greece.

The governance of the IMF is often criticised because the wealthier member states have a greater share of the voting rights. Thus, the welfare of LEDCs and their development priorities are often overlooked.

The role of the World Bank

Revised ▢

The World Bank is the international organisation that lends money to LEDCs for economic development projects and structural change. The majority of loans are for physical capital projects, for example irrigation systems, road networks, schools, hospitals and transportation links.

The World Bank was set up in 1944 (at the same time as the IMF) to provide foreign development assistance (concessionary and non-concessionary lending) to low- and middle-income countries to reduce poverty and improve standards of living. It is made up of two international financial institutions:

- **The International Bank for Reconstruction and Development (IBRD)** – The IBRD provides loans to middle-income countries (not LEDCs), so the funds are not technically classified as foreign aid. Most of the lending from the World Bank is made by the IBRD.
- **The International Development Association (IDA)** – Member countries of the IDA offer concessionary, interest-free loans of up to 30 years to low-income countries in order to reduce poverty.

The World Bank is the largest and most familiar development bank in the world. It made around $30 billion in development loans and assistance in 2013. It has been criticised for offering most of its lending to middle-income countries rather than to LEDCs that face conditions of extreme poverty, especially as its requirements for eligibility of funding disqualify many poor and heavily indebted countries.

Common mistake

Many students tend to think of the World Bank as a single institution, but it comprises the IBRD and the IDA.

EXAM PRACTICE *(HL ONLY)*

PAPER 3

13 In 1970, the world's wealthiest countries agreed to donate 0.7% of their annual gross national income (GNI) as official development assistance (ODA). Although the USA is often the largest donor in monetary terms, it ranks amongst the smallest when measured against the 0.7% target.

Figure 4.7 ODA from the USA at constant prices (US$ billion)

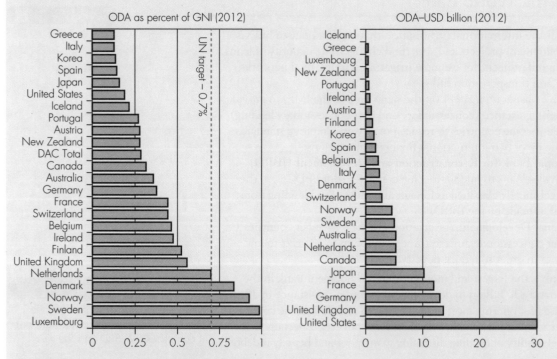

Figure 4.8 ODA from selected OECD countries

a Define the terms 'gross national income (GNI)' and 'official development assistance (ODA)'. [4]

b Using the information above, Figures 4.7 and 4.8, and your knowledge of economics, evaluate the effectiveness of foreign aid in contributing to economic development. [8]

4.7 The role of international debt

Foreign debt

The meaning of foreign debt

Internal debt is the money owed by a country to domestic lenders, such as private banks, because the government has a budget deficit (government expenditure exceeds government revenues). By contrast, **external debt** is money owed to foreign creditors (lenders).

Creditors are the financial institutions that lend money to others. Foreign creditors include commercial banks, foreign governments and international financial institutions such as the World Bank and the IMF.

Debts can be incurred by private individuals, firms and/or the government. Foreign debts are often incurred by countries with weak institutions (including the domestic monetary system) and poor infrastructure, forcing them to borrow from foreign creditors to develop their economies.

Foreign debt is a potentially serious matter for many LEDCs because the burden of interest payments and strict loan terms have often resulted in huge opportunity costs, for example cutting expenditure on education and healthcare in order to repay these loans.

It is not uncommon for LEDCs to be heavily indebted because relatively high interest rates and/or domestic inflation reduce the value of their currency (foreign debts have to be repaid in foreign currencies). This makes their debt financing increasingly unsustainable.

The problems of foreign debt can be traced back to the global oil crisis of 1973 when oil prices increased by 500% due to the Arab–Israeli War (or the Yom Kippur War). This created a huge surplus of profit for exporters of oil, deposited in banks, with the money being lent to LEDCs.

The subsequent oil crisis of 1979 caused a worldwide recession, with LEDCs unable to export enough of their commodities to pay off their debts. Many LEDCs defaulted on their loans.

Foreign debt can cause both economic and social instability. For example, the global financial crisis caused huge problems, even for MEDCs – unemployment reached 28% in both Spain and Greece. Ultimately, high levels of foreign debts can make LEDCs even poorer.

> **Keyword definition**
> **Foreign debt** (or **external debt**) refers to loans of a country that need to be repaid to overseas lenders such as the World Bank and the IMF.

> **Common mistake**
> Not all debt is detrimental to the wellbeing of LEDCs. This depends on the level of affordability of the debt. Borrowing money to fund structural changes and economic development can be beneficial to LEDCs – it is when the foreign debt is unaffordable that problems arise.

Heavily indebted countries

Some countries have become so heavily indebted that they have had to reschedule their debt repayments to banks and other lenders. **Debt rescheduling** means lengthening the time it takes to repay the loans, often leading to further borrowing and escalating debts.

HIPCs are also highly vulnerable to external shocks that are beyond their control, such as natural disasters and oil crises (which cause inflation). These shocks add to their soaring debts.

Some HIPCs suffer from **debt overhang**, i.e. existing debts are so unaffordable that they find it extremely difficult to borrow more money. Debts incurred by some HIPCs exceed government revenue from taxpayers, thus causing a **debt trap**, i.e. they are unable to ever repay their debts.

In extreme cases, the failure of HIPCs to repay foreign debts has caused **perpetual debts** to occur, i.e. taking out subsequent loans to service (pay for) existing debts. This reduces their financial status, thus making future foreign investment in these countries less attractive.

In many cases, LEDCs incur huge debts because loans and financial aid are misused by corrupt leaders, for example to finance military spending and weapons.

> **Keyword definition**
> A **heavily indebted poor country (HIPC)** is a low-income nation with a huge outstanding debt, making it eligible for special financial assistance from the IMF and the World Bank.

The mounting debt burden faced by HIPCs has led to international pressures for creditors to cancel the debts (known as **debt forgiveness**) in an attempt to restart or improve the economic development of HIPCs. However, this could cause some HIPCs to become complacent (or reckless) as they are protected from their irresponsible behaviour, so may continue to be careless in the future.

Instead, **conditional assistance** can be given to HIPCs, i.e. debt relief granted on the condition that HIPCs meet a range of targets for structural changes, such as poverty-reduction programmes. Debt relief includes both partial and complete debt forgiveness for HIPCs.

The rescheduling of debt and conditional assistance are mainly facilitated by international financial institutions such as the IMF and the World Bank. Both these organisations have key roles in resolving the international debt problems of LEDCs and HIPCs.

The **International Monetary Fund** (IMF) acts as an international lender of last resort to countries with urgent or major balance of payments problems. If a country is expected to default on its loans, the IMF can intervene, using conditional assistance.

The **World Bank** is an international finance organisation concerned with lending money on a long-term basis to LEDCs to assist in their economic development.

International debt and the balance of payments

Revised

The servicing of international debts can cause balance of payments problems for the indebted country.

Many LEDCs have a high **debt service ratio** (the ratio of foreign debt, including interest repayments, to its export earnings). This means that they need to generate more export earnings to fund their foreign debts. A low debt service ratio suggests a healthier financial position.

HIPCs import far less than their populations need from MEDCs as there is a long-term decline in the real value of their own exports and their currencies. Some HIPCs spend more money on debt financing than they spend on education or healthcare.

There is less of an incentive for direct investment in highly indebted countries. This has a negative impact on the financial account of the balance of payments of such countries.

Portfolio investment in highly indebted countries is also likely to fall, again having a negative impact on the financial account. For example, investor confidence in Iceland fell dramatically following the nation's debt crisis and collapse of banks during the global financial crisis.

> **Expert tip**
>
> HL students should consider the nature of deteriorating **terms of trade** faced by most LEDCs, i.e. a fall in the index of average export prices to average import prices. This creates further problems for LEDCs as each unit of exports is worth less than before in funding their import expenditure.

EXAM PRACTICE (HL ONLY)

PAPER 3

14 With reference to the table below, explain why excessive foreign debt creates a problem for the economic development of a country. **[4]**

COUNTRY	DEBT-TO-GDP RATIO (%)
Zimbabwe	150.9
Lebanon	139.5
Bhutan	89.4
Guyana	63.3

4.8 The balance between markets and intervention

Strengths and weaknesses of market-orientated policies

Market-orientated policies

Market-orientated policies focus on increasing the productive capacity of the economy by improving healthcare, education and infrastructure to achieve economic development. They also focus on improving the supply-side of the economy by using the price mechanism (e.g. floating exchange rates rather than fixed or managed exchange rate systems) and liberalised capital flows between countries (the free movement of foreign exchange).

Supporters of market-orientated policies argue that market forces allocate resources efficiently, thus enhancing economic development. Such policies also create incentives to invest in the economy. Examples of market-orientated policies include:

- **Deregulation** – This refers to the reduction or removal of rules and regulations in a particular industry, therefore creating a greater degree of competition and encouraging market forces to allocate resources.
- **Trade liberalisation** – This refers to policies that encourage free trade, including the free movement of capital flows, by removing barriers to international trade. The IMF believes that trade liberalisation promotes economic growth, development and poverty reduction.
- **Privatisation** – This is the process of transferring ownership of public-sector assets to private-sector ownership. Private-sector firms, driven by financial motives, are argued to be more economically efficient than bureaucrats running public-sector organisations.
- **Labour market reforms** – These are policies that remove inefficiencies in the labour market, thereby creating greater flexibility and productivity, for example reducing the power of labour unions, cutting unemployment benefits and abolishing minimum wages.
- **Tax reforms** – Lower rates of income tax and corporation tax create incentives to work and to supply, i.e. tax reforms can motivate people to seek employment opportunities and firms give greater incentives for firms to raise output, thus achieving growth and development.

> **Keyword definition**
> **Market-orientated policies** are dynamic, outward-looking, macroeconomic policies used to stimulate economic growth and development via market forces, for example using anti-monopoly regulation to encourage competition and efficiency.

Strengths of market-orientated policies

- Efficiency – The key benefit of market-orientated development policies, such as trade deregulation and privatisation, is that resources are allocated more efficiently than through government intervention in economic activity.
- Competitiveness – Labour market reforms, for example, create incentives to work. These policies therefore help to improve labour market flexibility and productivity, resulting in a more internationally competitive labour force.
- Economic growth – The profit motive in free markets encourages people to work hard and firms to take entrepreneurial risks, such as expenditure on investment and innovation. Thus, market-orientated policies have a positive impact on economic growth.
- Benefits of free trade – Free trade policies can lead to many benefits, such as increased consumer choice, lower prices and improved quality. They also enable firms to sell to more customers, beyond the borders of the country. This inevitably contributes to growth and development.

- Investment opportunities – The liberalisation of trade and capital flows reduces barriers to international trade and exchange. This is an important factor in attracting foreign direct investment (FDI), i.e. the capital expenditure of multinational corporations in overseas economies.

Weaknesses of market-orientated policies

- Market failure – The inability of any market-orientated policy to deal with market failure is its main weakness – for example, negative production and consumption externalities are not dealt with. LEDCs also lack sufficient provision of merit goods such as education and healthcare.
- The development of a dual economy – This occurs when two distinct economic sectors exist within a country, with different levels of development. It is common in LEDCs with a low-income sector catering for local demand and another for export-driven international markets.
- Income inequalities – The advantages of economic development do not automatically trickle down to benefit the poorer members of society, so government intervention is required to tackle the problems of income inequalities. Tax reforms can also cause income inequalities.

Strengths and weaknesses of interventionist policies

Interventionist-orientated policies

Interventionist policies are used to correct market deficiencies, such as providing adequate housing to ensure a minimum social safety net for all members of society. This is highly unlikely to occur in the absence of government intervention.

The provision of **merit goods** (such as education and healthcare) and **public goods** (such as flood control systems and street lighting) help to improve the economic development for the majority of people in society.

Government intervention is also required to provide appropriate infrastructure, such as roads, ports, airports and telecommunications networks. Proper infrastructure is needed to encourage foreign direct investment (FDI) to support economic development.

Interventionist-orientated policies are used to protect the welfare of workers, for example by establishing health and safety at work legislation and by setting minimum wages. They can also be used to protect the welfare of consumers, for example anti-monopoly legislation.

> **Keyword definition**
> **Interventionist-orientated policies** refer to the use of government involvement to stimulate or regulate economic growth and development.

Strengths of interventionist policies

- Provision of infrastructure – Without government intervention, there would be a lack of infrastructure (the physical structures required for the effective operation of society), for example roads, railways and telecommunications networks.
- Investment in human capital – The private sector is unlikely to provide sufficient investment in human capital through education and training, especially in LEDCs. Thus interventionist policies are required to encourage more provision of such merit goods.
- Provision of a stable macroeconomic economy – Development requires government intervention to provide a safe and stable economic environment to protect the interest of the economy by interventionist demand and supply-side policies.

■ Provision of a **social safety net** – Interventionist policies through direct government provision and a social welfare system ensure that all members of society have access to basic necessities, thus preventing absolute poverty in the economy.

Interventionist policies can be used to tackle inequalities, which hinder the development and prosperity of LEDCs. For example, cultural and historical contexts in many countries mean that women are not given the same opportunities as men. Thus, intervention is necessary.

Intervention is also required when a country faces a major emergency or disaster, such as a civil war. Without intervention, the productive capacity of the country will decline along with a fall in FDI and standards of living.

Weaknesses of interventionist policies

Revised ☐

■ Excessive **bureaucracy** – This refers to administrative systems, structures and regulations. There is over-regulation in many LEDCs, which leads to economic inefficiencies rather than economic growth and development.
■ **Poor planning** – Political instability and conflict, common in many LEDCs, can cause major delays in production, thus limiting opportunities for economic development. The lack of market signals (forces of demand and supply) means that the planning is often unrealistic.
■ **Corruption** – Dishonest governments that misuse sources of finance reduce the effectiveness of policies intended to promote economic development. Corruption reduces trust between individuals, firms and governments, thus acting as a deterrent to FDI.

> **Common mistake**
>
> Students often claim that eradicating corruption is a prerequisite to economic development. It is unlikely that corruption can be eradicated (it exists in economically developed countries too), but development occurs when corruption is reduced.

Market with government intervention

Revised ☐

Good governance refers to the moral conduct of public affairs and the management of public resources. It can be seen as the opposite of corruption, so is important for the development process of an economy. Good governance applies to anyone in a position of responsibility with decision-making power, including government officials, lawmakers, the military, scientific researchers and religious leaders.

Good governance requires the following:
■ transparency in government policies and government affairs
■ determined effort to limit corrupt practices, such as enforced fines and sanctions
■ provision of a welfare safety net for citizens who suffer from ill health and/or unemployment
■ accountable and law-abiding policies.

Due to the advantages of interventionist-orientated policies and market-orientated policies, a **complementary approach** may be the best way to achieve economic development, i.e. a balanced use of both market-orientated development policies and government intervention.

Evidence suggests that neither extremes work in the real world, for example the collapse of communism due to its bureaucratic inefficiencies in the latter part of the twentieth century and the need for government intervention following the global financial meltdown of 2008.

Are you ready?

Use this checklist to record progress as you revise. Tick each box when you have:

- revised and understood a topic
- tested yourself using the **Exam practice** questions and gone online to check your answers.

Section 1 Microeconomics	Revised	Tested	Exam ready
Competitive markets: demand and supply			
Markets and demand	☐	☐	☐
Supply	☐	☐	☐
Market equilibrium	☐	☐	☐
The role of the price mechanism	☐	☐	☐
Market efficiency	☐	☐	☐
Elasticity			
Price elasticity of demand (PED)	☐	☐	☐
Cross price elasticity of demand (XED)	☐	☐	☐
Income elasticity of demand (YED)	☐	☐	☐
Price elasticity of supply (PES)	☐	☐	☐
Government intervention			
Indirect taxes	☐	☐	☐
Subsidies	☐	☐	☐
Price controls	☐	☐	☐
Market failure			
The meaning of market failure	☐	☐	☐
Types of market failure	☐	☐	☐

Theory of the firm and market structures *(HL only)*	Revised	Tested	Exam ready
Production and costs	☐	☐	☐
Revenues	☐	☐	☐
Profit	☐	☐	☐
Goals of firms	☐	☐	☐
Perfect competition	☐	☐	☐
Monopoly	☐	☐	☐
Monopolistic competition	☐	☐	☐
Oligopoly	☐	☐	☐
Price discrimination	☐	☐	☐

Section 2 Macroeconomics

The level of overall economic activity

	Revised	Tested	Exam ready
Economic activity	☐	☐	☐
The business cycle	☐	☐	☐

Aggregate demand and aggregate supply

	Revised	Tested	Exam ready
Aggregate demand (AD)	☐	☐	☐
Aggregate supply (AS)	☐	☐	☐
Equilibrium	☐	☐	☐
The Keynesian multiplier *(HL only)*	☐	☐	☐

Macroeconomic objectives

	Revised	Tested	Exam ready
Low unemployment	☐	☐	☐
Low and stable rate of inflation	☐	☐	☐
Economic growth	☐	☐	☐
Equity in the distribution of income	☐	☐	☐

Fiscal policy	Revised	Tested	Exam ready
The government budget	☐	☐	☐
The role of fiscal policy	☐	☐	☐
Monetary policy			
Interest rates	☐	☐	☐
The role of monetary policy and short-term demand management	☐	☐	☐
Supply-side policies			
The role of supply-side policies	☐	☐	☐
Interventionist supply-side policies	☐	☐	☐
Market-based supply-side policies	☐	☐	☐
Evaluation of supply-side policies	☐	☐	☐

Section 3 International economics

International trade	Revised	Tested	Exam ready
Free trade	☐	☐	☐
Restrictions on free trade: trade protection	☐	☐	☐
Exchange rates			
Freely floating exchange rates	☐	☐	☐
Government intervention	☐	☐	☐
The balance of payments			
The structure of the balance of payments	☐	☐	☐
Current account deficits	☐	☐	☐
Current account surpluses	☐	☐	☐

	Revised	Tested	Exam ready
Economic integration			
Forms of economic integration	☐	☐	☐
The terms of trade *(HL only)*			
The meaning of the terms of trade *(HL only)*	☐	☐	☐
Causes of changes in the terms of trade *(HL only)*	☐	☐	☐
Consequences of changes in the terms of trade *(HL only)*	☐	☐	☐
Section 4 Development economics			
Economic development			
The nature of economic growth and economic development	☐	☐	☐
Measuring development			
Measurement methods	☐	☐	☐
The role of domestic factors			
Domestic factors and economic development	☐	☐	☐
The role of international trade			
International trade and economic development	☐	☐	☐
The role of foreign direct investment (FDI)			
Foreign direct investment and multinational corporations (MNCs)	☐	☐	☐
The roles of foreign aid and multilateral development assistance			
Foreign aid	☐	☐	☐
Multilateral development assistance	☐	☐	☐

The role of international debt	Revised	Tested	Exam ready
Foreign debt	☐	☐	☐
The balance between markets and intervention			
Strengths and weaknesses of market-oriented policies	☐	☐	☐
Strengths and weaknesses of interventionist policies	☐	☐	☐

My study and revision notes

Glossary

Ad valorem tax imposes a percentage tax on the value of a good or service. Examples include property taxes, tariffs (taxes on imports) and sales taxes.

Aggregate demand is the total value of all goods and services demanded in the economy, per time period.

Allocative efficiency happens when resources are distributed so that consumers and producers get the maximum possible benefit; thus no one can be made better off without making someone else worse off.

Asymmetric information exists when one economic agent (buyer or seller) in an economic transaction has more information than the other in a certain market – for example, life assurance policies, stock market products, pension fund schemes, second-hand cars and works of art.

Bilateral trade agreement is a contractual trade arrangement between two countries, such as closer economic partnership agreements (CEPAs).

Business cycle describes the fluctuations in economic activity in a country over time. These fluctuations create a long-term trend of growth in the economy.

Cap-and-trade schemes (CATS) are government-regulated emissions trading schemes using a market-based approach. The regulator sets a limit (the cap) on the total amount of emissions allowed in an industry and firms are issued emissions permits.

Circular flow of income model is a macroeconomic tool used to explain how economic activity and national income are determined.

Complements are products that are jointly demanded, such as cinema movies and popcorn or pencils and erasers.

Contraction see *Movements*

Cost–push inflation is triggered by higher costs of production thus shifting aggregate supply to the left and forcing up average prices.

Cross price elasticity of demand (XED) measures the degree of responsiveness of demand for one product following a change in the price of another product.

Consumer surplus refers to the benefits to buyers who are able to purchase a product for less than they are willing to do so.

Current account deficit exists when the sum of the outflows from the current account exceeds the inflows into the account – for example, net import expenditure on goods and services is greater than net export earnings.

Deflationary gap (also known as a **recessionary gap**) exists when the real national output equilibrium is below the full employment level of output.

Demand–pull inflation is inflation triggered by higher levels of aggregate demand in the economy, which drives up the general price level.

Diminishing returns occur in the short run when a variable factor input (such as labour) is successively added to a fixed factor (such as capital), which eventually reduces the marginal and hence total output.

Disposable income is earnings after taxes have been accounted for, i.e. the actual take-home income that workers are able to spend.

Economic costs are the explicit and implicit costs of all resources used by a firm in the production process.

Economic growth is the increase in the level of economic activity, i.e. the annual percentage growth in national output.

Economic profit occurs when total revenue exceeds total economic costs. It is profit that is over and above normal profit. A firm might choose to continue.

Expansion see *Movements*

Expenditure reducing policies are designed to cut a current account deficit by lowering disposable income to limit aggregate demand and import expenditure in particular.

Expenditure switching policies are intended to encourage households and firms to buy domestically produced goods and services rather than imported alternatives by raising the relative price of imports or reducing the relative price of exports.

Explicit costs are the identifiable and therefore accountable costs related to the output of a product. Examples include wages, raw material costs, utility bills and rent.

External costs (also known as **negative externalities**) are costs incurred by a third party in an economic transaction for which no compensation is paid.

Green GDP is a measure of GDP that accounts for environmental destruction from economic activity by deducting the environmental costs associated with the output of goods and services.

Gross domestic product (GDP) is the value of all final output of goods and services produced by firms within the country, per year.

Gross national product (GNP) is the value of all final output of goods and services produced by a country's citizens, both domestically and abroad.

Human Development Index (HDI) is a composite indicator (of life expectancy, educational attainment and income) used as an alternative to real GDP or GNI per capita as a measure of economic development.

Implicit costs are the opportunity costs of the output, i.e. the income from the best alternative that is foregone.

Income elasticity of demand (YED) measures the degree of responsiveness of demand following a change in income.

Indirect tax is a government levy on the sale of certain goods and services. It includes specific taxes and *ad valorem* taxes.

Inferior goods have a negative relationship between income and quantity demanded, i.e. customers switch to a superior (luxury) product as their income rises (e.g. canned food products versus fresh food products).

Interest rates can refer to the price of borrowing money or the return from saving money at financial institutions such as banks.

International trade is the exchange of goods and services beyond national borders. It involves the sale of exports (goods and services sold to overseas buyers) and imports (foreign goods and services bought by domestic households and firms).

Keynesian multiplier is a model that shows that any increase in the value of injections results in an even greater increase in the value of national income. It also shows that any increase in the value of withdrawals leads to a greater fall in the value of national output.

Labour force consists of the employed, the self-employed and the unemployed, i.e. all those in work and all those actively seeking employment.

Long run is the period of time when all factors of production are variable, so all costs of production are variable.

Luxury goods are superior goods and services as their demand is highly income elastic, i.e. an increase in income leads to a proportionally greater increase in the demand for luxuries.

Marginal private benefit (MPB) is the additional value enjoyed by households and firms from the consumption or production (output) of an extra unit of a particular good or service.

Marginal private cost (MPC) is the additional cost of production for firms or the extra charge paid by customers for the output or consumption of an extra unit of a good or service.

Marginal propensity to consume (MPC) measures the proportion of each extra dollar of household income that is spent by consumers, i.e. $MPC = \dfrac{\Delta C}{\Delta Y}$.

An increase in the MPC will tend to increase the value of the multiplier.

Marginal propensity to import (MPM) measures the proportion of each extra dollar of household income that is spent on imports, i.e. $MPM = \dfrac{\Delta M}{\Delta Y}$.

Marginal propensity to save (MPS) measures the proportion of each extra dollar of income that is saved by households, i.e. $\dfrac{\Delta S}{\Delta Y}$.

Marginal propensity to tax (MPT) measures the proportion of each extra dollar of household income that is levied by the government, i.e. $\dfrac{\Delta T}{\Delta Y}$.

Marginal social benefit (MSB) is the added benefit to society from the production or consumption of an extra unit of output, i.e. the sum of MPC and marginal external costs.

Marginal social cost (MSC) is the extra cost of an economic transaction to society, i.e. the sum of MPB and marginal external benefits.

Market equilibrium occurs when the quantity demanded for a product is equal to the quantity supplied of the product, i.e. there are no shortages or surpluses.

Market failure exists when the price mechanism (the market forces of demand and supply) allocates scarce resources in an inefficient way, i.e. there is either over-provision or under-provision of certain goods and services.

Merit goods are products that create positive externalities (spillover effects) when they are produced or consumed. Hence, the social benefits from the production and consumption of merit goods are greater than the private benefits.

Micro-credit schemes are loans of small amounts to individuals on low incomes in LEDCs for self-employment projects that generate income, so they can care for themselves and their families.

Movements are caused by price fluctuations along an existing demand curve. A rise in price results in a *contraction* in quantity demanded, whereas a fall in price causes an *expansion* in quantity demanded.

Multilateral trade agreement is a legally binding trade deal between more than two countries, for example in a free trade area. Such trade agreements are made within the guidelines of the World Trade Organization (WTO).

Natural monopoly exists when the industry can only sustain one supplier, to avoid wasteful competition and to maximise economies of scale by having a single provider.

Normal goods are products that customers tend to buy more of as their income level increases. They comprise necessities (such as food) and luxuries (such as cars).

Normal profit is the minimum revenue needed to keep a firm in business. Hence, it is also referred to as **zero economic profit** and occurs at the point where a firm breaks even by covering both economic and implicit costs from its sales revenue.

Poverty trap (or poverty cycle) is a vicious cycle of poverty causing greater poverty. Low-income earners spend most, if not all, of their income on meeting their essential needs, so they have insufficient funds to invest in their future and are trapped in poverty.

Price elasticity of supply (PES) measures the degree of responsiveness of quantity supplied of a product following a change in its price along a given supply curve.

Private benefits are the benefits of production and consumption enjoyed by a firm, individual or government.

Private costs of production and consumption are the actual costs incurred by a firm, individual or government.

Producer surplus is the difference between the price that firms actually receive and the price they were willing and able to supply at.

Revenue is the money received from the sale of a firm's output.

Short run is the period of time when at least one factor of production, such as land or capital, is fixed in the production process.

Social benefits are the true (or full) benefits of consumption or production, i.e. the sum of private benefits and external benefits.

Social costs are the true (or full) costs of consumption or production, i.e. the sum of private costs and external costs.

Specific tax, also known as a **per unit tax**, imposes a fixed amount of tax on each product. Examples include taxes on cigarettes, air passenger tax and electronic road pricing and road tolls.

Subsidy is financial assistance from the government to encourage output (such as the sale of exports), to reduce the price of certain merit goods (such as education, training and healthcare), or to keep down the cost of living (such as food prices).

Substitutes are products that can be used instead of each other, such as Coca-Cola or Pepsi and tea or coffee.

Supply is the *willingness* and *ability* of firms to provide a good or service at given price levels, per time period.

Trade creation occurs when economic integration shifts, trade deals away from higher-cost producers from outside the trading bloc to lower-cost producers within the trading bloc, due to the removal of trade barriers.

Trade diversion occurs when economic integration shifts trade deals away from lower-cost producers outside the trading bloc to higher-cost producers within the trading bloc due to the trade agreements of the customs union.

Unemployment occurs when people are willing and able to work and actively seeking employment but are unable to find work.